Mastering Java Persistence

From Basics to Expert Proficiency

Contents

Introduction

Java Persistence is a critical aspect of modern Java development, enabling applications to interact with databases in a structured manner. This book, "Mastering Java Persistence: From Basics to Expert Proficiency," is dedicated to equipping you with the knowledge and tools needed to effectively utilize Java Persistence in your projects. This book encompasses a comprehensive range of topics, each selected to provide a deep understanding of the principles and practices of Java Persistence.

The importance of Object-Relational Mapping (ORM) cannot be overstated. ORM frameworks facilitate the translation of data between incompatible systems, specifically between the object-oriented world of Java and the relational world of databases. Java Persistence API (JPA) is a powerful ORM standard, providing a uniform interface for interacting with relational databases. Mastery of JPA is essential for any developer involved in large-scale enterprise applications or any application requiring persistent data storage.

Our journey begins with an introduction to Java Persistence, setting the stage for what follows. We will start by understanding the key concepts in JPA, such as entities, primary keys, and the EntityManager. This foundational knowledge is crucial as it forms the basis of more advanced topics covered later in the book.

Following this, we delve into the practical aspects of getting started with JPA. This includes setting up your development environment, configuring data sources, and creating your first entity classes. By guiding you through these initial steps, we aim to provide you with a clear and practical understanding of how to begin using JPA in your applications.

Once the basics are in place, we will explore entity mapping in detail. This coverage spans from basic property mappings to more advanced relationships and inheritance strategies. Understanding these mappings is essential for accurately representing your application's data model in the database.

Advanced entity mappings further enhance your ability to model complex data structures and relationships. Topics such as composite primary keys, bidirectional relationships, entity graphs, and concurrency control are discussed in depth. This advanced knowledge allows you to optimize your data model and interactions for both performance and correctness.

Querying is another critical aspect of using JPA effectively. This book covers the Java Persistence Query Language (JPQL) and the Criteria API, offering you the tools needed to perform both simple and complex queries against your data. The ability to create dynamic and parameterized queries is crucial for building flexible and responsive applications.

Spring Data JPA is introduced to extend the capabilities of JPA, simplifying the data access layer of your applications. This includes an overview of Spring Data JPA and its integration with Spring Boot, creating powerful and manageable data repositories. Building upon this, we will discuss CRUD (Create, Read, Update, Delete) operations, which are fundamental to any application that interacts with a database.

Building RESTful web services is a common requirement in modern applications. This book covers how to leverage Spring Data to expose data repositories as RESTful services, enabling interaction with your data through standard web protocols. This chapter provides a thorough understanding of how to build, customize, and secure your RESTful endpoints.

Performance tuning and best practices form an essential part of mastering Java Persistence. Efficient fetching strategies, caching, batch processing, and query optimization are discussed to help you build performant applications. Best practices for entity design, mapping, and query formulation ensure that your applications are both efficient and maintainable.

Finally, testing and debugging are integral to the development process. This book provides detailed guidance on setting up a test environment, writing effective test cases, and debugging common issues in JPA applications. This ensures that you can confidently develop robust and reliable applications.

In summary, "Mastering Java Persistence: From Basics to Expert Proficiency" is designed to be a complete guide to Java Persistence. Each chapter builds upon the previous ones, providing you with a structured and comprehensive understanding of JPA and its related technologies. By the end of this book, you will have gained the skills and knowledge necessary to effectively implement and manage Java Persistence in your applications.

Chapter 1

Introduction to Java Persistence

This chapter provides a foundational understanding of Java Persistence, emphasizing its importance and the role of Object-Relational Mapping (ORM). It introduces the Java Persistence API (JPA), explaining key concepts like entities, primary keys, and the EntityManager. The chapter also discusses the architecture of a JPA application and offers a brief overview of Hibernate as an implementation of JPA. Additionally, the advantages and disadvantages of using JPA are examined, followed by practical guidance on setting up a development environment and creating a basic JPA application. Common tools and frameworks used in JPA development are also highlighted.

1.1 What is Java Persistence?

Java Persistence involves the storing, retrieving, and managing of Java objects in a relational database in a way that encourages structure and reuse while bringing efficient data interaction capabilities to Java applications. Leveraging persistence mechanisms ensures that data remains available across multiple invocations of an application, providing continuity and a reliable way to maintain data long-term.

At its core, Java Persistence abstracts the complex interactions that typically take place between object-oriented programming models in Java and relational database systems. Since relational databases are not natively designed to store Java objects, persistence frameworks use Object-Relational Mapping (ORM) to bridge this gap, thereby addressing the object-relational impedance mismatch.

An ideal Java persistence mechanism supports the following key features:

- **Object-Relational Mapping (ORM):** A technique that maps Java objects to database tables, enabling developers to manipulate database records using Java objects.
- **Transaction Management:** Ensuring that multiple database operations either complete fully or leave the database in a consistent state.
- **Querying:** Providing a standardized way to create queries on the database that can, in many frameworks, utilize object-oriented principles.
- **Caching:** Minimizing the time it takes to retrieve frequently accessed data by storing data temporarily in memory.

To solidify your understanding, let us examine an example scenario where Java persistence plays a crucial role. Consider an e-commerce application where various entities such as customers, orders, and products need persistent storage. Directly managing these entities through JDBC would require a significant amount of boilerplate code and manual mapping logic. By incorporating Java Persistence mechanisms, this process is streamlined, reducing code complexity and improving maintainability.

For instance, to illustrate how entities are typically managed, consider a 'Product' entity in Java:

```
import javax.persistence.Entity;
import javax.persistence.Id;
import javax.persistence.GeneratedValue;

@Entity
public class Product {
    @Id
    @GeneratedValue
    private Long id;
    private String name;
    private double price;

    // Constructors, getters, and setters omitted for brevity
```

```
}
```

In this snippet:

- The '@Entity' annotation specifies that this class is an entity and is mapped to a database table.
- The '@Id' annotation denotes the primary key of the entity.
- The '@GeneratedValue' annotation provides a specification for the primary key generation strategy.

By marking the 'Product' class with these annotations, the Java Persistence provider determines how to persist instances of 'Product' in the database without the need for explicit SQL statements.

Understanding and implementing Java Persistence is more than just employing a set of annotations. It demands comprehension of the persistence context, entity lifecycle, and the underlying persistence mechanisms provided by frameworks like JPA (Java Persistence API), Hibernate, and others. Typically, the core components associated with Java Persistence include:

- **Entities:** These are lightweight Java classes annotated to map to database tables.
- **EntityManager:** An API used to interact with the persistence context, facilitating CRUD (Create, Read, Update, Delete) operations on entities.
- **Persistence Unit:** A set of all entity classes that are managed by an EntityManager in an application.

The abstraction and simplification provided by Java Persistence facilitate a consistent approach to managing relational data, which significantly enhances a developer's productivity and focuses on addressing business logic rather than lower-level data-handling details.

One practical example of storing and retrieving an entity using the EntityManager might look like this:

```
EntityManagerFactory emf = Persistence.createEntityManagerFactory("my-persistence-
    unit");
EntityManager em = emf.createEntityManager();

// Create a new product
```

```
em.getTransaction().begin();
Product newProduct = new Product();
newProduct.setName("Laptop");
newProduct.setPrice(999.99);
em.persist(newProduct);
em.getTransaction().commit();

// Retrieve a product by ID
Product foundProduct = em.find(Product.class, newProduct.getId());
System.out.println("Retrieved Product: " + foundProduct.getName());

em.close();
emf.close();
```

This example highlights key EntityManager methods such as 'persist' for storing a new entity and 'find' for retrieving an entity based on its primary key. The code demonstrates the initiation and committing of transactions, which are essential for ensuring data integrity and consistency.

Through these illustrations and discussions, it is clear that Java Persistence serves as a vital aspect of any Java-based application that requires robust data management capabilities, efficiently bridging the gap between the object-oriented paradigm of Java applications and the relational paradigm of databases.

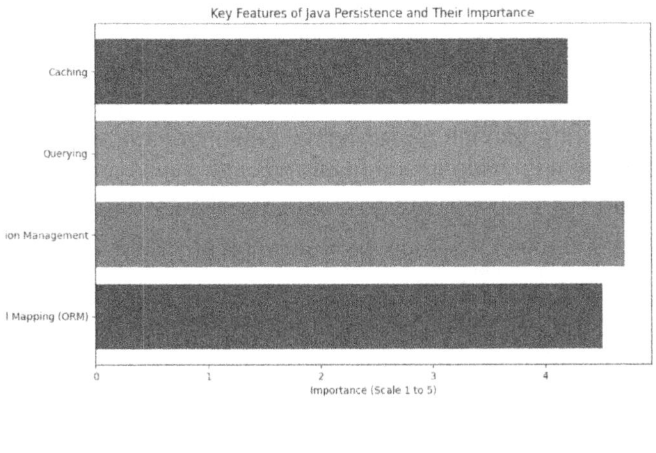

1.2 Importance of Object-Relational Mapping (ORM)

Object-Relational Mapping (ORM) serves as a pivotal technique in bridging the gap between object-oriented programming languages and relational database systems. The significance of ORM arises primarily from its ability to automate the tedious and error-prone process of persisting object data to database tables without requiring explicit SQL code for CRUD (Create, Read, Update, Delete) operations.

At its core, ORM provides a mapping between the program's domain model and the relational database schema. This linkage is crucial for several reasons:

- **Separation of Concerns:** By using ORM, developers can maintain a clear separation between business logic and database interaction. This modularity enhances code maintainability and readability.
- **Productivity:** ORM frameworks generate much of the boilerplate code required for database operations, allowing developers to focus more on business logic rather than database handling.
- **Abstraction and Fewer Errors:** ORM reduces the likelihood of errors by abstracting database access code. This abstraction layer also means developers do not need to be experts in SQL to perform data operations.
- **Portability:** With ORM, applications become less dependent on specific database vendors. The mapping layer can handle database-specific details, facilitating easier switching between different database systems.
- **Object-Oriented Querying:** ORM frameworks facilitate querying databases using object-oriented paradigms. This can make queries more intuitive for developers familiar with object-oriented programming languages.

To illustrate, consider the challenge of mapping a simple 'User' object to a relational database table manually. The 'User' object may look as follows in Java:

```
public class User {
    private Long id;
```

```
    private String username;
    private String email;

    // Getters and setters
    public Long getId() { return id; }
    public void setId(Long id) { this.id = id; }
    public String getUsername() { return username; }
    public void setUsername(String username) { this.username = username; }
    public String getEmail() { return email; }
    public void setEmail(String email) { this.email = email; }
}
```

Storing this 'User' object in a relational database without ORM would necessitate explicit SQL code:

```
-- SQL to create the users table
CREATE TABLE users (
    id BIGINT AUTO_INCREMENT PRIMARY KEY,
    username VARCHAR(255) NOT NULL,
    email VARCHAR(255) NOT NULL
);

-- SQL to insert a user
INSERT INTO users (username, email) VALUES ('john_doe', 'john@example.com');
```

With ORM, the developer solely annotates the class and lets the framework handle the SQL generation and execution. For example, using JPA, the 'User' entity can be annotated as follows:

```
import javax.persistence.*;

@Entity
@Table(name = "users")
public class User {
    @Id
    @GeneratedValue(strategy = GenerationType.IDENTITY)
    private Long id;

    @Column(nullable = false, unique = true)
    private String username;

    @Column(nullable = false, unique = true)
    private String email;

    // Getters and setters remain unchanged
}
```

By associating the class with the 'users' table through the '@Entity' and '@Table' annotations, and defining primary key generation via '@Id' and '@GeneratedValue', the ORM framework can automatically generate appropriate SQL statements during runtime. The developer can then leverage the 'EntityManager' to interact with the database:

```
EntityManager em = entityManagerFactory.createEntityManager();
em.getTransaction().begin();
```

```
User user = new User();
user.setUsername("john_doe");
user.setEmail("john@example.com");

em.persist(user);
em.getTransaction().commit();
em.close();
```

This level of abstraction is instrumental in improving developer productivity and reducing the error rate. Moreover, since ORM frameworks such as Hibernate support lazy loading, caching, and fetching strategies, they further enhance application performance and scalability.

Therefore, the role of ORM in modern application development extends beyond simplicity and convenience. It introduces an essential layer that aligns object-oriented programming with relational database management, ensuring efficient, maintainable, and scalable codebases.

1.3 Overview of Java Persistence API (JPA)

Java Persistence API (JPA) is a Java specification for accessing, persisting, and managing data between Java objects and a relational database. JPA serves as a bridge that allows developers to map Java objects directly to database tables, thereby eliminating the need for writing extensive SQL queries. By providing a standard approach for ORM, JPA ensures that developers can focus on the business logic rather than database interactions.

The core of JPA consists of a set of annotations and interfaces that manage the mapping between Java objects and relational databases. These annotations and interfaces collectively facilitate the automation of ORM tasks, such as CRUD operations (Create, Read, Update, Delete).

Annotations: JPA introduces several annotations that simplify the configuration of mappings. The most commonly used annotations include:

- **@Entity**: This annotation specifies that the class is an entity and is mapped to a database table.
- **@Table**: This annotation is used to specify the table in the database with which the entity is mapped.
- **@Id**: It denotes the primary key of the entity.

- **@GeneratedValue**: This annotation provides for the specification of generation strategies for the values of primary keys.
- **@Column**: It specifies the details of the column to which a field or property will be mapped.
- **@OneToMany**, **@ManyToOne**, **@ManyToMany**, **@OneToOne**: These annotations define the relationships between two entities.

```
@Entity
@Table(name="Student")
public class Student {
    @Id
    @GeneratedValue(strategy = GenerationType.IDENTITY)
    private Long id;

    @Column(name = "first_name")
    private String firstName;

    @Column(name = "last_name")
    private String lastName;

    // Standard getters and setters
}
```

Interfaces: To interact with the database, JPA provides several key interfaces:

- **EntityManager**: This is the primary interface used to interact with the persistence context. It provides methods for managing the lifecycle of entities, creating queries, and other operations.
- **EntityTransaction**: This interface is used to manage transactions in a resource-local environment.
- **Query**: It is used to perform queries on entities.
- **TypedQuery**: It extends the Query interface to allow for type-safe queries.
- **Persistence**: This is a bootstrap class used to obtain an EntityManagerFactory, which is then used to create EntityManager instances.

```
EntityManagerFactory emf = Persistence.createEntityManagerFactory("StudentPU");
EntityManager em = emf.createEntityManager();

em.getTransaction().begin();
Student student = new Student();
student.setFirstName("John");
```

```
student.setLastName("Doe");
em.persist(student);
em.getTransaction().commit();

em.close();
emf.close();
```

EntityManager Lifecycle: An **EntityManager** instance is associated with a persistence context. There are two types of persistence contexts:

- **Transaction-scoped persistence context**: The persistence context is bound to a transaction. When the transaction ends, the persistence context is closed, and all entities managed by it are detached.
- **Extended persistence context**: The persistence context can span across multiple transactions. It is typically used in stateful environments such as in stateful session beans.

The typical lifecycle of an EntityManager includes the following states:

- **New**: An instance just created and not yet associated with any persistence context.
- **Managed**: An instance that is currently associated with a persistence context.
- **Detached**: An instance that is no longer associated with the persistence context.
- **Removed**: An instance that is scheduled for removal from the database upon transaction completion.

```
EntityManager em = emf.createEntityManager();

em.getTransaction().begin();
Student student = em.find(Student.class, 1L); // Entity is now in managed state

em.remove(student); // Entity is scheduled for removal
em.getTransaction().commit(); // Entity is removed from the database

em.close();
```

JPA's provision of these annotations and interfaces greatly abstracts the complexities involved in database interactions. Through the reduction of boilerplate code and support for database-agnostic development, it enhances productivity and maintains flexibility. JPA's role in managing the object-relational impedance mismatch is crucial for modern enterprise applications, enabling developers to focus more on business logic while ensuring efficient and consistent data access patterns.

1.4 Key Concepts in JPA: Entity, Primary Key, and EntityManager

The Java Persistence API (JPA) revolves around several fundamental concepts that form the backbone of its functionality. Understanding these concepts is crucial for proficient utilization of JPA in Java development. This section explores three of these essential constructs: Entity, Primary Key, and EntityManager.

An **Entity** in JPA represents a table in a relational database. An entity is a lightweight, persistent domain object that typically corresponds to a single row in a table. To declare a class as an entity, it must be annotated with the @Entity annotation. Here is an example of a simple entity class:

```
import javax.persistence.Entity;
import javax.persistence.Id;

@Entity
public class Person {
    @Id
    private Long id;
    private String name;
    private int age;
```

```
    // Constructors, getters, and setters
    public Person() {}

    public Person(Long id, String name, int age) {
        this.id = id;
        this.name = name;
        this.age = age;
    }

    public Long getId() {
        return id;
    }

    public void setId(Long id) {
        this.id = id;
    }

    public String getName() {
        return name;
    }

    public void setName(String name) {
        this.name = name;
    }

    public int getAge() {
        return age;
    }

    public void setAge(int age) {
        this.age = age;
    }
}
```

The **Primary Key** uniquely identifies an entity. It is marked with the @Id annotation in the entity class. The type of the primary key can be any type supported by the database, such as Long, Integer, String, etc. JPA also allows primary keys to be generated automatically using the @GeneratedValue annotation combined with various strategies like AUTO, IDENTITY, SEQUENCE, and TABLE. Here is an example demonstrating auto-generated primary keys:

```
import javax.persistence.Entity;
import javax.persistence.Id;
import javax.persistence.GeneratedValue;
import javax.persistence.GenerationType;

@Entity
public class Product {
    @Id
    @GeneratedValue(strategy = GenerationType.AUTO)
    private Long id;
    private String name;
    private double price;

    // Constructors, getters, and setters
    public Product() {}

    public Product(String name, double price) {
```

```
        this.name = name;
        this.price = price;
    }

    public Long getId() {
        return id;
    }

    public void setId(Long id) {
        this.id = id;
    }

    public String getName() {
        return name;
    }

    public void setName(String name) {
        this.name = name;
    }

    public double getPrice() {
        return price;
    }

    public void setPrice(double price) {
        this.price = price;
    }
}
```

The **EntityManager** is the primary interface used for interacting with the persistence context. It is responsible for managing entities, including operations such as insert, update, delete, and query. The EntityManager is created from an EntityManagerFactory, which is configured with persistence unit settings. Below is an example of how to use the EntityManager to persist an entity:

```
import javax.persistence.EntityManager;
import javax.persistence.EntityManagerFactory;
import javax.persistence.Persistence;

public class JPAExample {
    public static void main(String[] args) {
        EntityManagerFactory emf = Persistence.createEntityManagerFactory("example-
            unit");
        EntityManager em = emf.createEntityManager();

        em.getTransaction().begin();

        Product product = new Product("Laptop", 1500.00);
        em.persist(product);

        em.getTransaction().commit();

        em.close();
        emf.close();
    }
}
```

When working with entities, the EntityManager handles various operations such as:

- persist(entity): To save a new entity to the database.
- merge(entity): To update an existing entity or save it if it does not exist.
- remove(entity): To delete an entity from the database.
- find(entityClass, primaryKey): To retrieve an entity by its primary key.
- createQuery(queryString): To execute JPQL (Java Persistence Query Language) queries.

Each of these operations corresponds to specific database actions that facilitate the manipulation and query of data. The EntityTransaction interface is used to manage transactions, encapsulating the lifecycle of a unit of work and maintaining atomicity and isolation. Firmer control over transactions ensures data consistency and integrity.

Here is an extended example that includes finding an entity and updating it:

```
import javax.persistence.EntityManager;
import javax.persistence.EntityManagerFactory;
import javax.persistence.Persistence;

public class JPAExtendedExample {
    public static void main(String[] args) {
        EntityManagerFactory emf = Persistence.createEntityManagerFactory("example-
            unit");
        EntityManager em = emf.createEntityManager();

        em.getTransaction().begin();

        // Creating and persisting new entity
        Product product = new Product("Smartphone", 800.00);
        em.persist(product);

        em.getTransaction().commit();

        // Finding and updating the existing entity
        em.getTransaction().begin();
        Product existingProduct = em.find(Product.class, product.getId());
        if (existingProduct != null) {
            existingProduct.setPrice(750.00);
            em.merge(existingProduct);
        }

        em.getTransaction().commit();

        em.close();
```

```
        emf.close();
    }
}
```

Mastering the use of entities, primary keys, and the EntityManager is pivotal in leveraging JPA's capabilities to build robust, scalable, and maintainable Java applications with efficient data persistence and retrieval.

1.5 Architecture of a JPA Application

A comprehensive understanding of the architecture of a Java Persistence API (JPA) application is essential for any developer aiming to harness the full potential of JPA for effective data management. The architecture of a JPA application consists of several key components that work together cohesively to facilitate object-relational mapping, database operations, and transaction management.

At the core of a JPA application are the mappings between Java objects (entities) and relational database tables. These mappings are defined through annotations or XML descriptors and are managed by the JPA provider, such as Hibernate.

Entity Classes

Entity classes are Plain Old Java Objects (POJOs) that represent the data stored in a database table. Each entity corresponds to a table, and its fields represent columns in the table. Entities are annotated using JPA annotations, which define the mapping between the class fields and database columns.

```
import javax.persistence.Entity;
import javax.persistence.Id;

@Entity
public class Person {
    @Id
    private Long id;
    private String name;
    private String email;

    // Getters and setters omitted for brevity
}
```

In the example above, the Person class is annotated with @Entity, indicating that it is a JPA entity. The @Id annotation marks the id field as the primary key of the entity.

Persistence Context and EntityManager

The EntityManager is the primary interface for interacting with the persistence context. It is responsible for managing the lifecycle of entities, including CRUD (Create, Read, Update, Delete) operations and queries. The persistence context is akin to a cache where entity instances are managed, ensuring that there is only one instance of each entity per persistence context.

```
import javax.persistence.EntityManager;
import javax.persistence.EntityManagerFactory;
import javax.persistence.Persistence;

public class PersonService {
    private EntityManagerFactory emf =
        Persistence.createEntityManagerFactory("my-persistence-unit");

    public void savePerson(Person person) {
        EntityManager em = emf.createEntityManager();
        em.getTransaction().begin();
        em.persist(person);
        em.getTransaction().commit();
        em.close();
    }
}
```

In this example, the savePerson method uses the EntityManager to begin a transaction, persist the Person entity, commit the transaction, and then close the EntityManager. This demonstrates a basic persistence operation in a JPA application.

Persistence Unit

A persistence unit defines a set of entity classes and their respective configurations. It is specified in the persistence.xml file, which is part of the META-INF directory. The persistence unit configuration specifies details such as the JPA provider, database connection properties, and JPA-specific settings.

```
<?xml version="1.0" encoding="UTF-8" ?>
<persistence xmlns="http://java.sun.com/xml/ns/persistence"
    xs xmlns:xsi="http://www.w3.org/2001/XMLSchema-instance"
    xsi:schemaLocation="http://java.sun.com/xml/ns/persistence
    http://java.sun.com/xml/ns/persistence/persistence_2_0.xsd"
    version="2.0">

    <persistence-unit name="my-persistence-unit">
        <provider>org.hibernate.jpa.HibernatePersistenceProvider</provider>
        <class>com.example.Person</class>
        <properties>
            <property name="javax.persistence.jdbc.url" value="jdbc:h2:mem:test"/>
            <property name="javax.persistence.jdbc.user" value="sa"/>
            <property name="javax.persistence.jdbc.password" value=""/>
            <property name="javax.persistence.jdbc.driver" value="org.h2.Driver"/>
        </properties>
```

```
    </persistence-unit>
</persistence>
```

The persistence.xml file shown above defines a persistence unit named my-persistence-unit, specifying the Hibernate JPA provider and relevant properties for database connection.

Entity Transactions

Transactions in JPA are managed using the EntityTransaction interface, which ensures consistency and atomicity of database operations. Each transaction starts with begin() and ends with either commit() or rollback().

```
public void updatePersonEmail(Long personId, String newEmail) {
    EntityManager em = emf.createEntityManager();
    EntityTransaction tx = em.getTransaction();

    try {
        tx.begin();
        Person person = em.find(Person.class, personId);
        if (person != null) {
            person.setEmail(newEmail);
        }
        tx.commit();
    } catch (Exception e) {
        if (tx.isActive()) {
            tx.rollback();
        }
        throw e;
    } finally {
        em.close();
    }
}
```

The updatePersonEmail method demonstrates transaction management with proper error handling to perform operations on the Person entity.

JPQL and Criteria API

JPA defines the Java Persistence Query Language (JPQL), which is similar to SQL but operates on entity objects rather than tables. Additionally, the Criteria API provides a programmatic way to construct queries.

```
public List<Person> findPeopleByName(String name) {
    EntityManager em = emf.createEntityManager();
    TypedQuery<Person> query = em.createQuery(
        "SELECT p FROM Person p WHERE p.name = :name", Person.class);
    query.setParameter("name", name);
    return query.getResultList();
}
```

The findPeopleByName method uses a JPQL query to retrieve Person entities based on their name.

```
public List<Person> findPeopleByEmailDomain(String domain) {
    EntityManager em = emf.createEntityManager();
    CriteriaBuilder cb = em.getCriteriaBuilder();
    CriteriaQuery<Person> cq = cb.createQuery(Person.class);
    Root<Person> person = cq.from(Person.class);

    cq.select(person)
      .where(cb.like(person.get("email"), "%" + domain));

    TypedQuery<Person> query = em.createQuery(cq);
    return query.getResultList();
}
```

In findPeopleByEmailDomain, the Criteria API is used to construct a query that finds persons whose email contains the specified domain.

Caching

JPA supports two levels of caching: first-level and second-level. The first-level cache is the persistence context cache, ensuring efficient management of entity instances within the same transaction scope. The second-level cache is shared across multiple transactions and sessions, improving performance by reducing database access for frequently used entities.

The described architecture components provide a robust framework for building scalable, maintainable, and efficient JPA applications. Proficiency in these components is essential for leveraging the full power of JPA in enterprise applications.

1.6 Introduction to Hibernate

Hibernate is one of the most widely used implementations of the Java Persistence API (JPA). It is an object-relational mapping (ORM) library for Java, which abstracts the object storage in relational databases. This section delves into what Hibernate is, its architecture, features, and how it fits within the JPA framework.

Hibernate bridges the gap between object-oriented programming models and relational databases. It allows developers to work with data in the form of Java objects, providing a more intuitive and flexible approach to database interactions. Hibernate automatically maps Java classes to database tables, simplifying the tedious and error-prone process of interacting with databases through low-level JDBC (Java

Database Connectivity) code.

The architecture of Hibernate includes several critical components:

- **SessionFactory**: This is a factory for creating Session instances, which are the primary interface for interacting with the database. The SessionFactory is immutable and thread-safe, typically created once at application startup.
- **Session**: This is a single-threaded, short-lived object that represents a conversation between the application and the database. It wraps a JDBC java.sql.Connection and is responsible for executing CRUD (Create, Read, Update, Delete) operations.
- **Transaction**: This API allows for atomic units of work. It abstracts away the underlying transaction management specifics and ensures consistent data handling.
- **Query**: Interfaces for querying the database. These queries can be written in HQL (Hibernate Query Language) or JPQL (Java Persistence Query Language).
- **Criteria**: An API for creating queries in an object-oriented manner.

The Hibernate architecture can be depicted as follows:

```
+--------------------+
|   Configuration    |
+--------------------+
         |
         v
+--------------------+
|   SessionFactory   |
+--------------------+
         |
         v
+---------------------+
|       Session       |
+---------------------+
  |        |        |
  v        v        v
CRUD     Query   Transaction
```

Configuration: Hibernate's configuration is typically done through an XML configuration file named hibernate.cfg.xml or through Java-based configuration. This configuration defines database connectivity properties, session factory settings, and mapping details.

Below is an example of a basic hibernate.cfg.xml:

```
<hibernate-configuration>
    <session-factory>
        <property name="hibernate.dialect">org.hibernate.dialect.MySQLDialect</
            property>
        <property name="hibernate.connection.driver_class">com.mysql.cj.jdbc.Driver
            </property>
        <property name="hibernate.connection.url">jdbc:mysql://localhost:3306/
            yourdatabase</property>
        <property name="hibernate.connection.username">yourusername</property>
        <property name="hibernate.connection.password">yourpassword</property>
        <property name="hibernate.hbm2ddl.auto">update</property>

        <mapping class="com.yourpackage.YourEntityClass"/>
    </session-factory>
</hibernate-configuration>
```

SessionFactory: Once the configuration is set, the SessionFactory is created. This object is thread-safe and intended to be instantiated once. During application initialization, the Configuration object is used to build the SessionFactory.

Example of building a SessionFactory in Java:

```
Configuration configuration = new Configuration().configure();
SessionFactory sessionFactory = configuration.buildSessionFactory();
```

Sessions and Transactions: Sessions are created from the SessionFactory. Each Session represents a single unit of work, which can span multiple transactions. The session interface includes methods for saving, updating, deleting, and querying objects.

Here is an example of using a session to persist an object:

```
Session session = sessionFactory.openSession();
Transaction transaction = session.beginTransaction();
YourEntityClass entity = new YourEntityClass();
entity.setProperty("value");
session.save(entity);
transaction.commit();
session.close();
```

Query and Criteria API: Hibernate provides several ways to execute queries against the database. The HQL and JPQL are object-oriented query languages similar to SQL but operate on the on the entity bean types, while the Criteria API allows for programmatic creation of queries.

Example of a query using HQL:

```
Session session = sessionFactory.openSession();
Query query = session.createQuery("from YourEntityClass where property = :value");
query.setParameter("value", "someValue");
List results = query.list();
session.close();
```

Example of a query using Criteria API:

```
Session session = sessionFactory.openSession();
CriteriaBuilder builder = session.getCriteriaBuilder();
CriteriaQuery<YourEntityClass> criteria = builder.createQuery(YourEntityClass.class)
    ;
Root<YourEntityClass> root = criteria.from(YourEntityClass.class);
criteria.select(root).where(builder.equal(root.get("property"), "someValue"));
Query<YourEntityClass> query = session.createQuery(criteria);
List<YourEntityClass> results = query.getResultList();
session.close();
```

Hibernate also supports caching to improve performance. Caching can be managed at both the session level and the query level. Shutting down the session factory when the application is terminating ensures that all resources are released properly.

```
sessionFactory.close();
```

Hibernate is a pivotal technology within the Java ecosystem due to its comprehensive features, robustness, and flexibility in handling ORM tasks. While the configuration and initial coding can seem intensive, the long-term benefits of using Hibernate for large-scale enterprise applications include maintainability, scalability, and productivity.

1.7 Advantages and Disadvantages of Using JPA

Java Persistence API (JPA) offers developers extensive features for simplifying database operations in Java applications. However, understanding both its strengths and limitations is crucial for making informed decisions on whether to adopt JPA for a project. Here, we explore the advantages and disadvantages of using JPA in detail.

Advantages of Using JPA:

- **Abstraction and Simplification:** JPA abstracts the complexity of database interactions, allowing developers to focus more on business logic rather than SQL queries. This simplification is achieved through its use of annotations and high-level API calls, which reduces boilerplate code and minimizes the chances of SQL injection vulnerabilities.

- **Portability:** JPA is an integral part of Java EE and Jakarta EE specifications, making it portable across different relational database management systems (RDBMSs). Applications built using JPA can switch databases with minimal changes to the codebase, thus offering flexibility and helping future-proof the application against changing database vendors.

- **Manageability and Understandability:** Entities in JPA are POJOs (Plain Old Java Objects), which makes it easier for developers to understand and manage data models. Using POJOs ensures that data access code is clean and consistent with the domain model, promoting better code readability and maintainability.

- **Declarative Transactions:** JPA supports declarative transaction management, allowing developers to control transaction boundaries using annotations rather than explicit code. This feature ensures a more straightforward configuration and maintenance of transactional behavior within the application.

- **Caching:** JPA implementations often include built-in caching mechanisms (e.g., first-level and second-level caching in Hibernate), which can drastically improve the performance of applications by reducing the load on the database.

- **Optimistic Locking:** JPA provides support for optimistic locking, which helps in handling concurrent access to entities. This feature prevents issues such as lost updates when multiple transactions are trying to modify the same entity simultaneously.

- **Query Flexibility:** JPA offers robust querying capabilities through JPQL (Java Persistence Query Language) and the Criteria API. JPQL allows for writing database-agnostic queries, while the Criteria API provides a type-safe approach to constructing queries dynamically.

Disadvantages of Using JPA:

- **Performance Overhead:** The abstraction layer introduced by JPA can sometimes cause performance overhead due to additional processing required for mapping objects to database tables. This overhead can become significant for applications with high transaction throughput or complex queries.

- **Learning Curve:** Despite its simplicity in abstracting database interactions, JPA has a steep learning curve for developers unfamiliar with ORM concepts. Mastery of JPA requires understanding various annotations, mappings, lifecycle states of entities, and performance tuning techniques.

- **Complexity in Advanced Mappings:** While JPA simplifies straightforward entity relationships, it can introduce complexity when dealing with advanced mappings such as inheritance (single-table, joined-table, table-per-class) and many-to-many relationships. Improper configuration of these mappings can lead to inefficient queries and increased development effort.

- **Limited Control Over SQL:** JPA generates SQL statements behind the scenes, which provides convenience but can limit the developer's control over specific SQL optimizations and tuning. There are scenarios where hand-tuned SQL queries might be more efficient than JPA-generated queries.

- **Bulk Operations Limitations:** JPA is not very well-suited for batch processing or bulk updates/delete operations. Although some JPA implementations provide extensions for bulk operations, they often bypass the JPA lifecycle and caching mechanisms, leading to potential discrepancies and requiring careful handling.

- **Lazy Loading Pitfalls:** JPA supports lazy loading for assoc query n, it can lead to unexpected *LazyInitializationException* errors or "N + 1 select" issues, where an excessive number of database queries are executed due to improper lazy loading configurations.

- **Vendor Lock-In:** Although JPA is a specification, different JPA providers (e.g., Hibernate, EclipseLink) may implement features in slightly different ways or offer proprietary extensions. This can lead to vendor lock-in, making it challenging to switch JPA implementations without significant code changes.

Understanding these advantages and disadvantages equips developers with the knowledge to leverage JPA effectively while being mindful of potential pitfalls, thus making informed decisions based on specific application requirements.

1.8 Setting Up Your Development Environment for JPA

To effectively utilize Java Persistence API (JPA) in your applications, establishing a robust development environment is imperative. This setup ensures a seamless workflow, aiding in the efficient management of database operations through JPA. Below is a step-by-step guide to setting up your environment, encompassing the installation and configuration of necessary tools and libraries.

Prerequisites:

- JDK 8 or higher
- Integrated Development Environment (IDE) like IntelliJ IDEA, Eclipse, or NetBeans
- Build tool such as Maven or Gradle
- A relational database (e.g., MySQL, PostgreSQL, or H2 for testing purposes)

1. Installing the JDK:

Ensure that JDK 8 or higher is installed on your system. You can download the JDK from the official Oracle website or adopt the OpenJDK distribution. Ensure the correct installation by checking the Java version through the terminal or command prompt:

```
$ java -version
```

Once installed, set the JAVA_HOME environment variable to the JDK installation path.

2. Configuring the Integrated Development Environment (IDE):

Select an IDE of your choice. IntelliJ IDEA is widely used and well-suited for JPA.

Installing IntelliJ IDEA:

- Visit the JetBrains website and download the Community or Ultimate version.
- Follow the installation instructions specific to your operating system.

Setting Up Eclipse:

- Download Eclipse IDE for Java Developers from the official Eclipse website.
- Install and launch Eclipse, then configure it to use the installed JDK.

3. Integrating Build Tools:

Build tools like Maven and Gradle manage dependencies and streamline project builds.

Using Maven:

- Install Maven by downloading it from the Apache Maven website.
- Check the installation by running:

```
$ mvn -v
```

- In IntelliJ IDEA or Eclipse, you can create a new Maven project by selecting File → New → Project → Maven.

Example of a Maven pom.xml file:

```
<project xmlns="http://maven.apache.org/POM/4.0.0"
        xmlns:xsi="http://www.w3.org/2001/XMLSchema-instance"
        xsi:schemaLocation="http://maven.apache.org/POM/4.0.0 http://maven.
            apache.org/xsd/maven-4.0.0.xsd">
   <modelVersion>4.0.0</modelVersion>
   <groupId>com.example</groupId>
   <artifactId>jpa-example</artifactId>
   <version>1.0-SNAPSHOT</version>

   <dependencies>
      <dependency>
         <groupId>javax.persistence</groupId>
         <artifactId>javax.persistence-api</artifactId>
         <version>2.2</version>
      </dependency>
      <dependency>
         <groupId>org.hibernate</groupId>
         <artifactId>hibernate-core</artifactId>
         <version>5.4.32.Final</version>
      </dependency>
      <dependency>
         <groupId>com.h2database</groupId>
         <artifactId>h2</artifactId>
         <version>1.4.200</version>
      </dependency>
   </dependencies>

   <build>
```

```
        <plugins>
            <plugin>
                <groupId>org.apache.maven.plugins</groupId>
                <artifactId>maven-compiler-plugin</artifactId>
                <version>3.8.1</version>
                <configuration>
                    <source>11</source>
                    <target>11</target>
                </configuration>
            </plugin>
        </plugins>
    </build>
</project>
```

Using Gradle:

- Install Gradle by downloading it from the Gradle website.
- Verify the installation by running:

```
$ gradle -v
```

- In IntelliJ IDEA or Eclipse, you can create a new Gradle project by selecting File → New → Project → Gradle.

Example of a Gradle build.gradle **file:**

```
plugins {
    id 'java'
}

group 'com.example'
version '1.0-SNAPSHOT'

sourceCompatibility = '11'

repositories {
    mavenCentral()
}

dependencies {
    implementation 'javax.persistence:javax.persistence-api:2.2'
    implementation 'org.hibernate:hibernate-core:5.4.32.Final'
    implementation 'com.h2database:h2:1.4.200'
    testImplementation 'junit:junit:4.12'
}

test {
    useJUnitPlatform()
}
```

4. Configuring the Database:

For the purposes of initial setup and testing, using an in-memory database like H2 can be advantageous.

Example H2 Configuration:

- Add the H2 dependency to your pom.xml (Maven) or build.gradle (Gradle).
- Configure persistence.xml in src/main/resources/META-INF/persistence.xml:

```
<persistence xmlns="http://java.sun.com/xml/ns/persistence"
            xmlns:xsi="http://www.w3.org/2001/XMLSchema-instance"
            xsi:schemaLocation="http://java.sun.com/xml/ns/persistence
                                http://java.sun.com/xml/ns/persistence/
                                    persistence_2_0.xsd"
            version="2.0">
    <persistence-unit name="jpa-example" transaction-type="
        RESOURCE_LOCAL">
        <provider>org.hibernate.jpa.HibernatePersistenceProvider</provider>
        <class>com.example.entity.MyEntity</class>
        <properties>
            <property name="javax.persistence.jdbc.driver" value="org.h2.
                Driver"/>
            <property name="javax.persistence.jdbc.url" value="jdbc:h2:mem:
                testdb"/>
            <property name="javax.persistence.jdbc.user" value="sa"/>
            <property name="javax.persistence.jdbc.password" value=""/>
            <property name="hibernate.dialect" value="org.hibernate.dialect.
                H2Dialect"/>
            <property name="hibernate.hbm2ddl.auto" value="update"/>
        </properties>
    </persistence-unit>
</persistence>
```

5. Creating Your First JPA Entity:

Once the environment is set, you can create a simple JPA entity to verify the setup.

Example Java Entity Class:

```
package com.example.entity;

import javax.persistence.Entity;
import javax.persistence.GeneratedValue;
import javax.persistence.GenerationType;
import javax.persistence.Id;

@Entity
public class MyEntity {
    @Id
    @GeneratedValue(strategy = GenerationType.IDENTITY)
    private Long id;
    private String name;

    // Getters and Setters
    public Long getId() {
        return id;
    }

    public void setId(Long id) {
        this.id = id;
    }
```

```
    public String getName() {
        return name;
    }

    public void setName(String name) {
        this.name = name;
    }
}
```

Build and run your project to ensure everything is correctly configured. If there are no exceptions or errors, your JPA development environment is successfully set up. Further steps include creating a repository for data access operations and running more complex queries.

1.9 Hello World with JPA: Your First JPA Application

Creating your first JPA application involves several crucial steps that transform theoretical knowledge into practical implementation. This section delineates each step in detail to aid in the successful creation of a "Hello World" application using JPA.

Begin by ensuring your development environment is set up correctly. Refer to the previous section on setting up your development environment for JPA to verify you have a working installation of JDK, an Integrated Development Environment (IDE) like IntelliJ IDEA, and a relational database such as MySQL or H2.

Step 1: Project Setup

Create a new Maven project in your chosen IDE. Maven, a powerful project management tool, simplifies the process of managing dependencies and building the project. The project's directory structure should follow the Maven standard layout:

```
/src
  /main
    /java
  /resources
  /test
    /java
```

Add the required dependencies in the pom.xml file. Ensure you include the dependencies for JPA API, Hibernate, and the H2 database for simplicity.

```
<dependencies>
```

```
    <!-- JPA API -->
    <dependency>
        <groupId>javax.persistence</groupId>
        <artifactId>javax.persistence-api</artifactId>
        <version>2.2</version>
    </dependency>
    <!-- Hibernate ORM -->
    <dependency>
        <groupId>org.hibernate</groupId>
        <artifactId>hibernate-core</artifactId>
        <version>5.4.32.Final</version>
    </dependency>
    <!-- H2 Database -->
    <dependency>
        <groupId>com.h2database</groupId>
        <artifactId>h2</artifactId>
        <version>1.4.200</version>
    </dependency>
</dependencies>
```

Step 2: Configuration

Create a configuration file named persistence.xml under src/main/resources/META-INF. This file configures the JPA behavior and defines the connection properties.

```
<persistence xmlns="http://xmlns.jcp.org/xml/ns/persistence"
             version="2.2">
    <persistence-unit name="HelloWorldPU">
        <provider>org.hibernate.jpa.HibernatePersistenceProvider</provider>
        <class>com.example.jpa.HelloWorld</class>
        <properties>
            <property name="javax.persistence.jdbc.driver" value="org.h2.Driver"/>
            <property name="javax.persistence.jdbc.url" value="jdbc:h2:mem:testdb"
                />
            <property name="javax.persistence.jdbc.user" value="sa"/>
            <property name="javax.persistence.jdbc.password" value=""/>
            <property name="hibernate.dialect" value="org.hibernate.dialect.H2Dialect
                "/>
            <property name="hibernate.hbm2ddl.auto" value="update"/>
            <property name="hibernate.show_sql" value="true"/>
        </properties>
    </persistence-unit>
</persistence>
```

Step 3: Creating the Entity

Define the entity class that represents the application's data model. In this example, create a class named HelloWorld in the package com.example.jpa.

```
package com.example.jpa;

import javax.persistence.Entity;
import javax.persistence.GeneratedValue;
import javax.persistence.GenerationType;
import javax.persistence.Id;
```

```
@Entity
public class HelloWorld {

    @Id
    @GeneratedValue(strategy = GenerationType.IDENTITY)
    private Long id;
    private String message;

    // Constructors, getters, and setters

    public HelloWorld() {
    }

    public HelloWorld(String message) {
        this.message = message;
    }

    public Long getId() {
        return id;
    }

    public void setId(Long id) {
        this.id = id;
    }

    public String getMessage() {
        return message;
    }

    public void setMessage(String message) {
        this.message = message;
    }
}
```

Step 4: EntityManager Setup and Basic Operations

Create a class to handle the persistence operations using EntityManager. This class will contain the code to insert and retrieve HelloWorld messages.

```
package com.example.jpa;

import javax.persistence.EntityManager;
import javax.persistence.EntityManagerFactory;
import javax.persistence.Persistence;

public class HelloWorldApp {

    public static void main(String[] args) {

        EntityManagerFactory emf = Persistence.createEntityManagerFactory("
            HelloWorldPU");
        EntityManager em = emf.createEntityManager();

        // Create and persist an entity
        em.getTransaction().begin();
        HelloWorld hello = new HelloWorld("Hello World with JPA");
        em.persist(hello);
        em.getTransaction().commit();
```

```
        // Retrieve the entity
        HelloWorld retrievedHello = em.find(HelloWorld.class, hello.getId());
        System.out.println("Retrieved Message: " + retrievedHello.getMessage());

        em.close();
        emf.close();
    }
}
```

Step 5: Running the Application

Compile and run the application. The output generated should reflect the stored message as shown below:

```
Hibernate: create table HelloWorld (id bigint not null auto_increment,
    message varchar(255), primary key (id))
Hibernate: insert into HelloWorld (message) values (?)
Hibernate: select helloworld0_.id, helloworld0_.message as message2_0_
    from HelloWorld helloworld0_ where helloworld0_.id=?
Retrieved Message: Hello World with JPA
```

This exercise covers the essential flow from setting up the project to executing basic CRUD (Create, Read, Update, Delete) operations using JPA. Experiment by adding more entities, refining configurations, and extending the application to solidify your understanding of Java Persistence API.

1.10 Common JPA Tools and Frameworks

In Java Persistence, various tools and frameworks exist to facilitate the development and maintenance of JPA applications. These tools provide a range of functionalities that enhance productivity, streamline development processes, and ensure robust and efficient data management. This section delves into some of the most common JPA tools and frameworks, detailing their features, advantages, and common use cases.

Hibernate

Hibernate is one of the most widely used ORM frameworks in the Java ecosystem. It provides a comprehensive and mature implementation of the Java Persistence API (JPA). Hibernate simplifies database interactions by mapping Java objects to database tables, allowing developers to focus on business logic rather than database intricacies.

- **Features**
    - Automatic table generation.

  - Transparent persistence without explicit JDBC.
  - HQL (Hibernate Query Language) for writing database queries.
  - Caching mechanisms to enhance performance.
  - Lazy and eager data fetching strategies.

- **Advantages**
  - Large community and extensive documentation.
  - Proven performance and reliability.
  - Rich support for complex mappings and relationships.
  - Integrates well with Spring, another widely used Java framework.

- **Common Use Cases**
  - Enterprise applications requiring robust ORM capabilities.
  - Systems where performance and scalability are crucial.
  - Projects that demand extensive database interaction and complex queries.

EclipseLink

EclipseLink is another powerful JPA implementation offering various features for effective persistence management. As the reference implementation for JPA, EclipseLink is known for its comprehensive support and standard compliance.

- **Features**
  - Out-of-the-box support for various databases.
  - Advanced caching mechanisms, including distributed caching.
  - Support for multiple persistence units and dynamic weaving.
  - Support for NoSQL databases.
  - SQL query generation monitoring tools.

- **Advantages**
  - Strong compliance with JPA specifications.

  - Enhanced performance through advanced caching and batch processing.
  - Versatile and extensible for various database architectures.
  - Good integration with Oracle tools and databases.

- **Common Use Cases**
  - Enterprise applications needing a standardized JPA implementation.
  - Projects involving combinations of SQL and NoSQL databases.
  - Applications requiring enhanced ORM features and monitoring capabilities.

OpenJPA

OpenJPA is an Apache project offering another robust JPA implementation. It aims to provide a high-performance and scalable persistence solution for Java applications.

- **Features**
  - Tight integration with various database platforms.
  - Support for entity lifecycle listeners and callback methods.
  - Advanced ORM features with flexible mapping options.
  - Pluggable architecture to customize persistence behavior.
  - Extensive logging and diagnostic capabilities.
- **Advantages**
  - High degree of customization and flexibility.
  - Performance optimization features.
  - Comprehensive documentation and support from the Apache community.
- **Common Use Cases**
  - Large-scale applications requiring finely tuned performance.
  - Projects needing custom ORM behavior and lifecycle management.

- Systems requiring detailed logging and monitoring of database interactions.

Spring Data JPA

Spring Data JPA is a part of the broader Spring Data project and provides an abstraction layer on top of JPA. It simplifies JPA-based data access layers by reducing boilerplate code.

- **Features**
  - Repository abstraction for CRUD operations.
  - Query derivation mechanisms from method names.
  - Easy integration with Spring Boot.
  - Support for pagination and sorting.
  - Custom query support using @Query annotation.
- **Advantages**
  - Reduces boilerplate code, increasing developer productivity.
  - Seamless integration with other Spring ecosystem projects.
  - Strong community support and documentation.
  - Simplifies database layer unit testing.
- **Common Use Cases**
  - Applications within the Spring ecosystem.
  - Projects requiring rapid development and frequent data layer modifications.
  - Systems where CRUD operations dominate the business logic.

Datanucleus

Datanucleus is a versatile data management framework supporting JPA among other persistence APIs. It is designed to be extensible and adaptable to various backend data stores.

- **Features**
  - Support for both relational and non-relational databases.

  - Flexibility with different persistent APIs beyond JPA.
  - Advanced query capabilities including JDOQL and JPQL.
  - Lifecycle management and versioning support.
  - High-level API to abstract underlying data store complexities.

- **Advantages**
  - Broad support for multiple data store types including NoSQL.
  - Cross-database compatibility enhancing project portability.
  - Comprehensive mapping options catering to diverse data models.

- **Common Use Cases**
  - Applications requiring multi-database support.
  - Projects leveraging non-relational data stores.
  - Systems needing high flexibility in data store interactions.

In utilizing these tools and frameworks, developers can enhance the efficiency and maintainability of their JPA-based applications. The choice of tool or framework depends heavily on the specific requirements of the project, including performance needs, database types, and desired levels of abstraction and flexibility. By carefully selecting and configuring these tools, developers can leverage their powerful features to build robust, scalable, and maintainable persistence layers.

Chapter 2

Getting Started with JPA

This chapter introduces the steps necessary to begin using Java Persistence API (JPA) in your projects. It starts with setting up the development environment and configuring persistence units via the persistence.xml file. The chapter then guides you through configuring a data source, creating entity classes, and performing basic persistence operations such as saving, retrieving, updating, and deleting entities. Additionally, it covers the role of the EntityManager and EntityTransaction, discusses JPA properties and settings, and emphasizes the use of JPA annotations.

2.1 Setting Up Your JPA Development Environment

To begin working with the Java Persistence API (JPA), it is essential to set up a suitable development environment. This section provides a detailed, step-by-step guide to configuring your environment, ensuring all necessary components are correctly installed and configured for a smooth development experience.

1. Install Java Development Kit (JDK)

JPA is a specification that is part of the Java Standard Edition (Java SE), and as such, requires the Java Development Kit (JDK). Ensure you have JDK 8 or higher installed. Verify the installation by running the following command in your terminal:

```
java -version
```

The output should indicate the installed JDK version:

```
java version "11.0.2" 2019-01-15 LTS
Java(TM) SE Runtime Environment 18.9 (build 11.0.2+9-LTS)
Java HotSpot(TM) 64-Bit Server VM 18.9 (build 11.0.2+9-LTS, mixed mode)
```

2. Install an Integrated Development Environment (IDE)

An IDE enhances productivity by providing tools for code editing, debugging, and running your applications. Popular choices include IntelliJ IDEA, Eclipse, and NetBeans. Download and install your preferred IDE from their respective websites.

3. Install Apache Maven

Maven is a powerful tool for managing a project's build, reporting, and documentation. It is frequently used to manage dependencies and to build JPA projects. Install Maven by following the instructions on the official [Maven website](https://maven.apache.org/install.html).

Verify Maven installation by running:

```
mvn -version
```

The command should output the Maven version and Java version:

```
Apache Maven 3.6.3 (Red Hat 3.6.3-5)
Maven home: /usr/share/maven
Java version: 11.0.2, vendor: Oracle Corporation, runtime: /usr/lib/jvm/java-11-openjdk
Default locale: en_US, platform encoding: UTF-8
OS name: "linux", version: "5.3.0-46-generic", arch: "amd64", family: "unix"
```

4. Add JPA Dependencies in Maven Project

Create a new Maven project in your IDE. Open the pom.xml file and include the JPA dependency. For this example, we will use Hibernate as the JPA provider. Add the following dependencies:

```
<dependencies>
    <dependency>
        <groupId>org.hibernate</groupId>
        <artifactId>hibernate-core</artifactId>
        <version>5.4.30.Final</version>
    </dependency>
    <dependency>
        <groupId>javax.persistence</groupId>
        <artifactId>javax.persistence-api</artifactId>
        <version>2.2</version>
    </dependency>
    <dependency>
        <groupId>com.h2database</groupId>
        <artifactId>h2</artifactId>
        <version>1.4.200</version>
    </dependency>
```

```
</dependencies>
```

The dependencies include:

- **hibernate-core**: Implements the JPA specification.
- **javax.persistence-api**: Defines the API for JPA.
- **h2**: An in-memory database useful for testing purposes.

5. Configure persistence.xml File

Create a directory structure src/main/resources/META-INF and within this directory, create a file named persistence.xml. This file configures the persistence unit and database connection settings. Populate persistence.xml with the following content:

```
<?xml version="1.0" encoding="UTF-8"?>
<persistence xmlns="http://xmlns.jcp.org/xml/ns/persistence" version="2.2">
    <persistence-unit name="examplePU" transaction-type="RESOURCE_LOCAL">
        <provider>org.hibernate.jpa.HibernatePersistenceProvider</provider>
        <class>com.example.entity.YourEntity</class>
        <properties>
            <property name="javax.persistence.jdbc.driver" value="org.h2.Driver"/>
            <property name="javax.persistence.jdbc.url" value="jdbc:h2:mem:test;
                DB_CLOSE_DELAY=-1"/>
            <property name="javax.persistence.jdbc.user" value="sa"/>
            <property name="javax.persistence.jdbc.password" value=""/>
            <property name="hibernate.dialect" value="org.hibernate.dialect.H2Dialect
                "/>
            <property name="hibernate.hbm2ddl.auto" value="update"/>
            <property name="hibernate.show_sql" value="true"/>
        </properties>
    </persistence-unit>
</persistence>
```

Key elements in the persistence.xml:

- persistence-unit name="examplePU": Defines the name of the persistence unit.
- provider: Specifies the JPA provider (e.g., Hibernate).
- class: Includes entity class references.
- property tags: Configure database connection parameters and Hibernate-specific settings.

6. Database Configuration

Embedded databases like H2 are useful for development and testing. The configuration above sets an in-memory H2 database. For production use, you must configure a production-ready database like MySQL, PostgreSQL, etc., by adjusting the database-specific properties in persistence.xml.

7. Create Entity Classes

Create your first entity class to ensure everything is set up correctly. Create a package com.example.entity and within it, create a class YourEntity.java:

```
package com.example.entity;

import javax.persistence.Entity;
import javax.persistence.Id;

@Entity
public class YourEntity {

    @Id
    private Long id;
    private String name;

    // Getters and Setters
    public Long getId() {
        return id;
    }

    public void setId(Long id) {
        this.id = id;
    }

    public String getName() {
        return name;
    }

    public void setName(String name) {
        this.name = name;
    }
}
```

8. Run and Test

Finally, create a test class to persist an instance of YourEntity. Create a class TestJPA.java:

```
package com.example;

import javax.persistence.EntityManager;
import javax.persistence.EntityManagerFactory;
import javax.persistence.Persistence;
import com.example.entity.YourEntity;

public class TestJPA {
    public static void main(String[] args) {
        EntityManagerFactory emf = Persistence.createEntityManagerFactory("
                examplePU");
```

```
        EntityManager em = emf.createEntityManager();

        em.getTransaction().begin();

        YourEntity entity = new YourEntity();
        entity.setId(1L);
        entity.setName("Sample Name");

        em.persist(entity);

        em.getTransaction().commit();
        em.close();
        emf.close();
    }
}
```

Run the TestJPA class to verify the setup. The console should display SQL statements, indicating successful persistence of the entity.

This setup ensures a functional environment for developing JPA applications, integrating essential tools and components for effective persistence operations.

2.2 Understanding Persistence Units and Persistence.xml

A persistence unit in JPA is a fundamental concept that plays a critical role in the configuration and management of your database interactions. It essentially defines the set of all entity classes that are managed by the EntityManager in an application. Additionally, it enables configuration of the various settings that control how your application interacts with the database.

At the core of defining a persistence unit is the *persistence.xml* file. This is an XML configuration file located in the META-INF directory of your application's classpath. The *persistence.xml* file houses the necessary metadata required for bootstrapping JPA and connecting to the underlying database.

The structure of *persistence.xml* is dictated by the JPA specification, and it typically includes elements such as *persistence*, *persistence-unit*, *properties*, and more. Below is a detailed example of a *persistence.xml* file:

```
<?xml version="1.0" encoding="UTF-8"?>
<persistence xmlns="http://xmlns.jcp.org/xml/ns/persistence" version="2.2">
    <persistence-unit name="myPersistenceUnit">
        <class>com.example.MyEntity</class>
```

```
    <properties>
        <property name="jakarta.persistence.jdbc.url" value="jdbc:mysql://
            localhost:3306/mydb"/>
        <property name="jakarta.persistence.jdbc.user" value="username"/>
        <property name="jakarta.persistence.jdbc.password" value="password"/>
        <property name="jakarta.persistence.jdbc.driver" value="com.mysql.cj.jdbc.
            Driver"/>
    </properties>
  </persistence-unit>
</persistence>
```

The <persistence> element is the root element and can contain one or more <persistence-unit> elements. Each <persistence-unit> defines a separate persistence unit.

- name attribute of <persistence-unit>: This is a required attribute that uniquely identifies the persistence unit. It is referenced in your application code to acquire an EntityManagerFactory for the specific persistence unit.
- <class> element: It specifies the fully qualified class names of the entity classes included in the persistence unit. Each entity class represents a table in the database.
- <properties> element: This element allows you to define various properties related to database connectivity, caching, and more. These properties are specific to the JPA provider you are using (like Hibernate, EclipseLink, etc.).

Essential Properties

Several key properties are commonly included within the <properties> element:

- jakarta.persistence.jdbc.url - Specifies the JDBC URL for the database.
- jakarta.persistence.jdbc.user - Defines the username for database access.
- jakarta.persistence.jdbc.password - Sets the password for database access.
- jakarta.persistence.jdbc.driver - Indicates the fully qualified name of the JDBC driver class.

Customizing the Persistence Context

The <properties> section allows more customization options beyond basic connection settings. Here are some additional properties that can be useful:

```
<property name="hibernate.dialect" value="org.hibernate.dialect.MySQL8Dialect"/>
<property name="hibernate.show_sql" value="true"/>
<property name="hibernate.format_sql" value="true"/>
<property name="hibernate.hbm2ddl.auto" value="update"/>
```

- hibernate.dialect: Specifies the SQL dialect that Hibernate will use to communicate with the database. The dialect defines how SQL queries should be generated by the ORM.
- hibernate.show_sql: If set to true, Hibernate will log all SQL queries generated to the console, which can be helpful for debugging.
- hibernate.format_sql: When set to true, this property formats the SQL queries for better readability in logs.
- hibernate.hbm2ddl.auto: This property manages the database schema. For instance, update will update an existing schema, and create-drop will create a fresh schema at startup and drop it at shutdown.

Integration with Application Code

Once the *persistence.xml* file is configured, it needs to be integrated with your application. The EntityManager is the primary JPA interface required for interacting with the persistence context.

To obtain an EntityManager instance, you must first create an EntityManagerFactory by referring to the persistence unit name defined in the *persistence.xml*. This can be done as follows:

```
EntityManagerFactory emf = Persistence.createEntityManagerFactory("
    myPersistenceUnit");
EntityManager em = emf.createEntityManager();
```

This configuration ensures that the entity manager is aware of the persistence context defined by your persistence unit. All subsequent operations, such as persisting, retrieving, updating, and deleting entities, are facilitated through this EntityManager instance.

```
2022-04-12 10:30:45 INFO  Hibernate: HHH000204: Processing PersistenceUnitInfo [name: myPersistenceUnit ...]
2022-04-12 10:30:45 INFO  Hibernate: HHH000412: Hibernate Core {5.4.0.Final}
2022-04-12 10:30:45 INFO  Hibernate: HHH000206: hibernate.properties not found
2022-04-12 10:30:45 INFO  Hibernate: HHH000021: Bytecode provider name : javassist
2022-04-12 10:30:46 INFO  Hibernate: HHH000400: Using dialect: org.hibernate.dialect.MySQL8Dialect
```

The provided code snippets and examples demonstrate the essence of configuring and utilizing persistence units within a JPA application. Proper understanding and setup of the *persistence.xml* ensure efficient management of your application's data layer, adhering to the principles and specifications outlined by JPA. This forms the foundation upon which robust, scalable, and maintainable JPA applications are built.

2.3 Configuring a Data Source

Configuring a data source is a crucial step in setting up your Java Persistence API (JPA) environment. A data source, in essence, establishes the connection between your application and the underlying database. This section delves into the methodologies, best practices, and specific configuration details required to successfully set up a data source in your JPA project.

The configuration of a data source can be accomplished primarily via two methods: configuration through the persistence.xml file and programmatic configuration.

Configuration via persistence.xml: The persistence.xml file is a configuration file that defines the persistence units deployed in your application. Each persistence unit can specify a data source, among other settings like JPA properties and classes. Here is a basic example of how to configure a data source within the persistence.xml file:

```
<?xml version="1.0" encoding="UTF-8"?>
<persistence xmlns="http://xmlns.jcp.org/xml/ns/persistence"
          xmlns:xsi="http://www.w3.org/2001/XMLSchema-instance"
          xsi:schemaLocation="http://xmlns.jcp.org/xml/ns/persistence
          http://xmlns.jcp.org/xml/ns/persistence/persistence_2_1.xsd"
          version="2.1">

   <persistence-unit name="myPersistenceUnit" transaction-type="
       RESOURCE_LOCAL">
      <provider>org.hibernate.jpa.HibernatePersistenceProvider</provider>
      <class>com.example.MyEntity</class>
      <properties>
         <property name="javax.persistence.jdbc.url" value="jdbc:mysql://localhost
             :3306/mydatabase"/>
         <property name="javax.persistence.jdbc.user" value="root"/>
         <property name="javax.persistence.jdbc.password" value="password"/>
         <property name="javax.persistence.jdbc.driver" value="com.mysql.jdbc.
             Driver"/>
         <property name="hibernate.dialect" value="org.hibernate.dialect.
             MySQL5Dialect"/>
      </properties>
   </persistence-unit>
</persistence>
```

The above XML snippet demonstrates a typical configuration wherein the database URL, username, password, and driver are specified within the properties element of the persistence unit. Each property is essential for establishing the connection to the database.

Property Explanation:

- javax.persistence.jdbc.url: The JDBC URL pointing to your database instance. Make sure to use the correct protocol and port.

- javax.persistence.jdbc.user: The username for database authentication.

- javax.persistence.jdbc.password: The corresponding password for the specified user.

- javax.persistence.jdbc.driver: The fully qualified name of the JDBC driver class.

- hibernate.dialect: Hibernate-specific property used to specify the SQL dialect of the database. Proper specification of the dialect allows Hibernate to generate optimized SQL statements.

Programmatic Configuration: For more dynamic scenarios, configuring the data source programmatically is often more useful. This can be done within your application setup code, typically when configuring the EntityManagerFactory. Here is an example using Hibernate:

```
import org.hibernate.cfg.Configuration;
import javax.persistence.EntityManagerFactory;
import javax.persistence.Persistence;

public class DataSourceConfig {

    public EntityManagerFactory configureProgrammatically() {
        Configuration config = new Configuration();

        config.setProperty("hibernate.connection.url", "jdbc:mysql://localhost:3306/
            mydatabase");
        config.setProperty("hibernate.connection.username", "root");
        config.setProperty("hibernate.connection.password", "password");
        config.setProperty("hibernate.connection.driver_class", "com.mysql.jdbc.Driver"
            );
        config.setProperty("hibernate.dialect", "org.hibernate.dialect.MySQL5Dialect");

        return Persistence.createEntityManagerFactory("myPersistenceUnit", config.
            getProperties());
    }
}
```

In this approach, the configuration properties are set programmatically through Hibernate's Configuration class before creating an instance of EntityManagerFactory. This allows for more flexibility as the properties can be dynamically determined or altered at runtime.

Integration with Application Servers: In enterprise applications that run within an application server like WildFly, WebLogic, or Glassfish, data sources are often configured at the server level. This allows for centralized database configurations and pooling mechanisms. This is coupled with JNDI (Java Naming and Directory Interface) lookups.

Here is an example excerpt to demonstrate how you might reference a previously configured data source via JNDI in persistence.xml:

```
<persistence-unit name="jndiPersistenceUnit" transaction-type="JTA">
    <jta-data-source>java:/MyJndiDataSource</jta-data-source>
    <class>com.example.MyEntity</class>
</persistence-unit>
```

- jta-data-source: This element defines the JNDI name of the data source, which must be pre-configured on the application server.

When using JNDI, pooling, and transaction management can leverage the capabilities provided by the server, often resulting in better performance and resource management.

Properly configuring a data source ensures that your JPA setup can reliably connect and interact with the underlying database. This step lays the foundation for any subsequent operations and significantly influences the overall robustness and performance of the application.

2.4 Creating Your First Entity Class

In Java Persistence API (JPA), an entity is a lightweight, persistent domain object that typically represents a table in a relational database. Each instance of an entity corresponds to a row in that table. Entities are one of the fundamental building blocks of JPA that allow for object-relational mapping (ORM). This section will guide you through the process of creating your first entity class in JPA.

To create an entity class, follow these steps:

- Define a simple plain old Java object (POJO) class.

- Annotate the class with JPA annotations to map it to a database table.
- Define fields in the class that correspond to columns in the table.
- Annotate these fields to specify the primary key and any other constraints or mappings.

Consider that we aim to create an entity class representing a User in our application. This User will have a unique identifier (ID), a username, an email address, and a password.

```
import javax.persistence.Entity;
import javax.persistence.Id;
import javax.persistence.GeneratedValue;
import javax.persistence.GenerationType;
import javax.persistence.Column;

@Entity
public class User {

    @Id
    @GeneratedValue(strategy = GenerationType.IDENTITY)
    private Long id;

    @Column(nullable = false, unique = true)
    private String username;

    @Column(nullable = false)
    private String email;

    @Column(nullable = false)
    private String password;

    // Getters and Setters
    public Long getId() {
        return id;
    }

    public void setId(Long id) {
        this.id = id;
    }

    public String getUsername() {
        return username;
    }

    public void setUsername(String username) {
        this.username = username;
    }

    public String getEmail() {
        return email;
    }

    public void setEmail(String email) {
        this.email = email;
    }
```

```
    public String getPassword() {
        return password;
    }

    public void setPassword(String password) {
        this.password = password;
    }
}
```

Steps Explained

- **Class Definition and @Entity Annotation**:

  The first step is to define a standard Java class and annotate it with @Entity. The @Entity annotation specifies that the class is an entity and is mapped to a database table.

```
import javax.persistence.Entity;

@Entity
public class User {
    // Class content
}
```

- **Primary Key with @Id and @GeneratedValue**:

  Every entity must have a primary key, which uniquely identifies each instance of the entity. Use the @Id annotation to denote the primary key field. Additionally, JPA provides several strategies for primary key generation. In this example, we use GenerationType.IDENTITY to let the database handle the primary key generation.

```
@Id
@GeneratedValue(strategy = GenerationType.IDENTITY)
private Long id;
```

- **Column Mapping with @Column**:

  The @Column annotation is used to specify the mapped column details. In our example, the username field is annotated with @Column(nullable = false, unique = true), indicating that the username must be unique and cannot be null. The email and password fields are similarly annotated, ensuring that these fields cannot be null.

```
@Column(nullable = false, unique = true)
private String username;

@Column(nullable = false)
private String email;
```

```
@Column(nullable = false)
private String password;
```

- **Getters and Setters**:

  Encapsulation is a fundamental concept in Java, and each field in the entity should be private. Provide public getter and setter methods for each field to allow access and modification.

```
public Long getId() {
    return id;
}

public void setId(Long id) {
    this.id = id;
}

public String getUsername() {
    return username;
}

public void setUsername(String username) {
    this.username = username;
}

public String getEmail() {
    return email;
}

public void setEmail(String email) {
    this.email = email;
}

public String getPassword() {
    return password;
}

public void setPassword(String password) {
    this.password = password;
}
```

Persistence Context and Lifecycle

Once the entity class is defined, it can be managed by the persistence context. Entities in JPA follow a lifecycle that includes states such as new, managed, detached, and removed. Understanding the lifecycle is critical for effectively working with JPA and performing operations like persisting, merging, and removing entities.

Executing the persistence operations involves utilizing the EntityManager, which will be discussed in detail in a later section. For now, ensure your entity is properly defined and ready for these operations.

2.5 Persisting Entities to the Database

Persisting entities to the database is a fundamental operation in JPA, enabling the interaction between your Java application and a relational database. The process involves creating an instance of an entity, managing its lifecycle through the EntityManager, and synchronizing it with the database.

To persist an entity, it must first be managed by an EntityManager. The EntityManager acts as an interface for performing CRUD (Create, Read, Update, Delete) operations on the database.

Consider the following entity class defined previously in the chapter:

```
@Entity
public class Book {
    @Id
    @GeneratedValue(strategy = GenerationType.AUTO)
    private Long id;

    private String title;
    private String author;

    // Constructors, getters, setters
    public Book() {}

    public Book(String title, String author) {
        this.title = title;
        this.author = author;
    }

    // Getter and Setter methods
}
```

To persist an instance of the Book entity to the database, follow these basic steps:

1. Obtain an instance of EntityManager from the EntityManagerFactory. 2. Begin a transaction using EntityTransaction. 3. Use the EntityManager's persist method to make the entity managed and persistent. 4. Commit the transaction to synchronize the state with the database. 5. Close the EntityManager.

Here is a practical example demonstrating these steps:

```
import javax.persistence.EntityManager;
import javax.persistence.EntityManagerFactory;
import javax.persistence.EntityTransaction;
import javax.persistence.Persistence;

public class PersistBook {
    public static void main(String[] args) {
        EntityManagerFactory emf = Persistence.createEntityManagerFactory("example-
                unit");
```

```
        EntityManager em = emf.createEntityManager();

        // Begin the transaction
        EntityTransaction et = em.getTransaction();
        et.begin();

        // Create and persist a new Book entity
        Book book = new Book("Effective Java", "Joshua Bloch");
        em.persist(book);

        // Commit the transaction
        et.commit();

        // Close the EntityManager
        em.close();
        emf.close();
    }
}
```

Upon executing the above code, a new record will be inserted into the corresponding table of the database. Below is a typical output one might observe in the database:

```
ID | TITLE          | AUTHOR
----------------------------------------
1  | Effective Java| Joshua Bloch
```

It is essential to understand the entity states in JPA: new, managed, detached, and removed. When an entity instance is created using new, it is in the new state. Invoking persist on an EntityManager transitions the entity to the managed state, meaning any changes to the entity state will be synchronized with the database once the transaction is committed. Here's a detailed look at these key states:

- **New (Transient):** The entity instance is newly created and has not yet been associated with an EntityManager.
- **Managed (Persistent):** After invoking persist, the entity is under the management of an EntityManager. Any changes to the entity are tracked and synchronized with the database upon transaction commit.
- **Detached:** When an EntityManager is closed or the entity is explicitly detached, it enters the detached state. The entity and its context are no longer synchronized.
- **Removed:** The entity is marked for deletion and will be deleted from the database upon transaction commit.

The following code snippet shows how to detach an entity:

```
Book book = em.find(Book.class, 1L);
em.detach(book);
// changes to 'book' will no longer affect the database
```

Working with transactions is critical. JPA requires an active transaction for any operation that modifies the database (persist, remove, merge). The EntityTransaction's methods begin, commit, and rollback manage these transactions. Transactions enable the grouping of operations, ensuring consistency and integrity of data by either fully applying all changes on commit or discarding them on rollback:

```
EntityTransaction et = em.getTransaction();
et.begin();

try {
    Book book = new Book("Java Concurrency in Practice", "Brian Goetz");
    em.persist(book);

    // Simulate an error
    if (true) {
        throw new RuntimeException("Simulated error");
    }

    et.commit(); // This won't be reached if an exception is thrown
} catch (Exception e) {
    et.rollback(); // Roll back transaction if an error occurs
    e.printStackTrace();
}
```

Effective use of transactions is crucial for data integrity, especially in real-world applications where multiple operations depend on each other contextually.

The process shown provides clarity on how JPA makes persistent data management intuitive and robust, ensuring entities are not only effectively synchronized with the underlying database but also maintain data consistency and integrity across your Java applications.

2.6 Retrieving Entities from the Database

Once you have persisted entities into your database, the next essential step is to retrieve them effectively. This section focuses on leveraging the Java Persistence API (JPA) to query and retrieve entities using various approaches. We will explore basic entity retrieval, JPQL (Java Persistence Query Language), and the Criteria API. Understanding these retrieval mechanisms is crucial for building robust data access layers in your Java applications.

To begin with, you must have a working EntityManager instance. The EntityManager is the primary interface used for interacting with the persistence context and managing entity instances. Below is an example of how you can obtain an EntityManager instance in a typical JPA setup:

```
EntityManagerFactory emf = Persistence.createEntityManagerFactory("my-persistence-
    unit");
EntityManager em = emf.createEntityManager();
```

Basic Retrieval Using find: The EntityManager provides a method find to retrieve an entity using its primary key. Let's assume you have an entity class Employee defined as follows:

```
@Entity
public class Employee {
    @Id
    @GeneratedValue(strategy = GenerationType.IDENTITY)
    private Long id;

    private String name;
    private String department;

    // Getters and setters
}
```

To retrieve an Employee entity by its primary key:

```
Employee employee = em.find(Employee.class, 1L); // Retrieves the Employee entity
    with id 1
```

The find method returns the entity instance if it exists in the database, or null if no entity is found with the specified primary key.

Retrieval Using JPQL Queries: Java Persistence Query Language (JPQL) is an SQL-like query language used for querying entity objects. It operates on the entity object model rather than directly on database tables. Below are examples of using JPQL to retrieve entities.

Retrieving All Entities:

```
String jpql = "SELECT e FROM Employee e";
TypedQuery<Employee> query = em.createQuery(jpql, Employee.class);
List<Employee> employees = query.getResultList();
```

This query selects all Employee entities from the database.

Retrieving Entities with Conditions:

```
String jpql = "SELECT e FROM Employee e WHERE e.department = :dept";
TypedQuery<Employee> query = em.createQuery(jpql, Employee.class);
query.setParameter("dept", "Engineering");
List<Employee> employees = query.getResultList();
```

This query retrieves all Employee entities that belong to the "Engineering" department.

Retrieval Using Named Queries: Named queries are defined using the @NamedQuery annotation. Named queries provide a way to define queries once and use them across the application. Here's how you can define and use a named query to retrieve all Employee entities:

```
@Entity
@NamedQuery(name = "Employee.findAll", query = "SELECT e FROM Employee e")
public class Employee {
    // Class definition
}
```

To execute the named query:

```
TypedQuery<Employee> query = em.createNamedQuery("Employee.findAll",
        Employee.class);
List<Employee> employees = query.getResultList();
```

Retrieval Using Criteria API: The Criteria API is a type-safe way to generate dynamic queries in JPA. It allows developers to build queries programmatically using the JPA Criteria classes. Below is an example of using the Criteria API to retrieve all Employee entities.

```
CriteriaBuilder cb = em.getCriteriaBuilder();
CriteriaQuery<Employee> cq = cb.createQuery(Employee.class);
Root<Employee> employee = cq.from(Employee.class);
cq.select(employee);

TypedQuery<Employee> query = em.createQuery(cq);
List<Employee> employees = query.getResultList();
```

In this example, we first obtain a CriteriaBuilder from the EntityManager, then create a CriteriaQuery object for the Employee class. The Root object represents the entity in the query. We then specify the select clause and execute the query to retrieve the result list.

Handling Query Results: When executing queries, it is crucial to handle the possibility of no results or multiple results. The TypedQuery interface offers methods such as getSingleResult() and getResultList() for this purpose. Below are examples of handling single result and no result scenarios:

```
try {
    Employee employee = query.getSingleResult();
    // Process the employee
} catch (NoResultException e) {
    // Handle case where no employee is found
} catch (NonUniqueResultException e) {
    // Handle case where more than one result is found
}
```

In this code snippet, getSingleResult() retrieves a single entity from the query result. If there is no result, a NoResultException is thrown, and if more than one result is found, a NonUniqueResultException is thrown.

```
Employee{id=1, name='John Doe', department='Engineering'}
Employee{id=2, name='Jane Doe', department='HR'}
```

Mastering these retrieval techniques ensures efficient data access and manipulation in JPA-based applications.

2.7 Updating and Deleting Entities

In this section, we delve into the mechanisms involved in updating and deleting entities within JPA. Both operations are crucial for maintaining the integrity and accuracy of your database. Understanding these processes requires a solid grasp of the EntityManager and the EntityTransaction, as introduced in prior sections.

Updating Entities

Updating an entity in JPA involves modifying an entity instance's state and ensuring these changes are synchronized with the database. The essential steps include retrieving the entity, updating its fields, and then committing the transaction.

First, fetch the entity from the database using the find or getReference method of the EntityManager. For instance, assume we have an entity class Employee:

```
EntityManager em = entityManagerFactory.createEntityManager();
EntityTransaction transaction = em.getTransaction();
transaction.begin();

Employee employee = em.find(Employee.class, 1001);
employee.setFirstName("John");
employee.setLastName("Doe");
```

The find method retrieves the entity with the specified primary key, and once the entity is managed, any changes made to its fields will be tracked by the persistence context and propagated to the database upon committing the transaction.

After modifying the entity, commit the transaction to save the changes:

```
transaction.commit();
em.close();
```

JPA tracks changes to managed entities automatically, so there is no need to explicitly update the entity. The entity is updated when the transaction is committed.

Deleting Entities

Deleting an entity requires making the entity managed, if it is not already, and then invoking the remove method of the EntityManager. To delete an entity, follow these steps:

1. Retrieve the entity. 2. Begin a transaction. 3. Call the remove method with the entity. 4. Commit the transaction.

Consider the Employee example:

```
EntityManager em = entityManagerFactory.createEntityManager();
EntityTransaction transaction = em.getTransaction();
transaction.begin();

Employee employee = em.find(Employee.class, 1001);
if (employee != null) {
    em.remove(employee);
}

transaction.commit();
em.close();
```

It is essential to check if the entity exists before attempting to remove it. The deletion will propagate to the database upon committing the transaction.

Cascade Type Considerations

When dealing with entities that have relationships (e.g., one-to-many or many-to-one), it is vital to understand the cascading options provided by JPA. Cascade operations can automatically apply entity state changes to associated entities, reducing boilerplate code.

For example, if Employee has a one-to-many relationship with Address, configured with CascadeType.REMOVE:

```
@Entity
public class Employee {
    // Other fields and methods...

    @OneToMany(cascade = CascadeType.REMOVE, mappedBy = "employee")
    private List<Address> addresses;
}
```

When removing an Employee, the associated Address entities are also removed automatically:

```
Employee employee = em.find(Employee.class, 1001);
if (employee != null) {
    em.remove(employee);
```

```
}
```

This simplifies the deletion process when dealing with related entities.

Operational Considerations

It is crucial to handle potential exceptions that can arise during update and delete operations, such as EntityNotFoundException, OptimisticLockException, or database constraint violations. Proper transaction management ensures data integrity and consistency.

Here's an example with exception handling:

```
try {
    transaction.begin();

    // Operations: find, update, or remove entities
    transaction.commit();
} catch (Exception ex) {
    if (transaction.isActive()) {
        transaction.rollback();
    }
    throw new RuntimeException("Error during transaction", ex);
} finally {
    em.close();
}
```

By incorporating these best practices, you ensure reliable and efficient persistence management in your JPA applications, maintaining data integrity and consistency across operations.

2.8 Introduction to EntityManager and EntityTransaction

The EntityManager interface is a primary component of JPA, playing a pivotal role in interacting with the persistence context. It manages the lifecycle of entities and facilitates CRUD (Create, Read, Update, Delete) operations. In conjunction with EntityTransaction, it ensures that these operations are within the bounds of atomic transactions, adhering to the ACID (Atomicity, Consistency, Isolation, Durability) principles. Understanding how to effectively use EntityManager and EntityTransaction is crucial for working with JPA.

EntityManager

EntityManager is an interface provided by JPA, which acts as an intermediary between the application and the persistence layer. When an entity instance becomes managed via the EntityManager, any changes to it are automatically synchronized with the database in a transactional context. Below is a simple example illustrating the use of EntityManager to persist an entity:

```
EntityManagerFactory emf = Persistence.createEntityManagerFactory("my-persistence-
    unit");
EntityManager em = emf.createEntityManager();

em.getTransaction().begin();
MyEntity entity = new MyEntity();
entity.setName("Sample Entity");
em.persist(entity);
em.getTransaction().commit();

em.close();
emf.close();
```

In this example:

- EntityManagerFactory is used to create EntityManager instances. It should be created once and reused to create multiple EntityManager instances.
- A transaction is begun using em.getTransaction().begin().
- The persist method is used to make an entity instance managed and persistent.
- The transaction is committed using em.getTransaction().commit().
- The EntityManager and EntityManagerFactory are closed to release resources.

EntityTransaction

EntityTransaction interface provides control over transactions in the context of an EntityManager. When working outside a container, i.e., in Java SE applications, it is vital to programmatically control transaction boundaries. The following methods are essential for using EntityTransaction:

- begin(): Starts a new transaction.
- commit(): Commits the transaction, making all changes permanent.
- rollback(): Rolls back the transaction, undoing all changes.

- setRollbackOnly(): Marks the current transaction so that the only possible outcome is a rollback.
- isActive(): Checks if the transaction is currently active.

Consider a scenario where an application needs to handle exceptions and ensure consistency:

```
EntityManagerFactory emf = Persistence.createEntityManagerFactory("my-persistence-
    unit");
EntityManager em = emf.createEntityManager();
EntityTransaction tx = em.getTransaction();

try {
    tx.begin();
    MyEntity entity = em.find(MyEntity.class, 1L);
    entity.setName("Updated Entity");
    em.merge(entity);
    tx.commit();
} catch (Exception e) {
    if (tx.isActive()) {
        tx.rollback();
    }
    e.printStackTrace();
} finally {
    em.close();
    emf.close();
}
```

In this advanced use case:

- EntityTransaction is explicitly retrieved from the EntityManager.
- Within a try block, the transaction is begun, an entity is retrieved and updated, and the transaction is committed.
- If any exception occurs, a rollback is performed to maintain consistency.
- Finally, the EntityManager and EntityManagerFactory are closed to release resources.

Proper exception handling ensures that resources are appropriately released and application state remains consistent.

Persistence Context

The persistence context is a set of entity instances that are managed by the EntityManager. Changes to these entities are tracked and can be automatically synchronized with the database. The lifecycle of entities within the persistence context may vary based on whether it is a transaction-scoped or extended context. Transaction-scoped persistence context is the default in JPA and is tied to the lifecycle of a single transaction, whereas an extended persistence context can span multiple transactions.

Consider the following operation sequence:

```
EntityManager em = emf.createEntityManager();
em.getTransaction().begin();
MyEntity entity = em.find(MyEntity.class, 1L); // Managed, entity is in persistence
    context
entity.setName("Another Update");
em.getTransaction().commit(); // Changes are flushed to the database
em.close();
```

Here:

- The entity is retrieved within a transactional context.
- The entity's state is modified.
- On transaction commit, EntityManager automatically synchronizes the changes with the database.

Mastering the EntityManager and EntityTransaction interfaces is essential for effective interaction with the persistence layer in JPA. They enable the developer to manage entity states and ensure data integrity through transactional operations, significantly enhancing the robustness of the application.

2.9 Configuring JPA Properties and Settings

Configuring JPA properties and settings is an essential step in optimizing and customizing the behavior of the Java Persistence API (JPA) in your application. These configurations can profoundly affect the performance, usability, and functionality of your persistence layer. This section delves into the common and advanced configurations you can apply in JPA, typically through the persistence.xml file and programmatically within your application code.

```
<persistence xmlns="http://xmlns.jcp.org/xml/ns/persistence"
        xmlns:xsi="http://www.w3.org/2001/XMLSchema-instance"
        xsi:schemaLocation="http://xmlns.jcp.org/xml/ns/persistence
                   http://xmlns.jcp.org/xml/ns/persistence/persistence_2_2
                   .xsd"
        version="2.2">
```

```
    <persistence-unit name="myPersistenceUnit" transaction-type="
        RESOURCE_LOCAL">
        <provider>org.hibernate.jpa.HibernatePersistenceProvider</provider>
        <class>com.example.MyEntity</class>

        <properties>
            <property name="javax.persistence.jdbc.url" value="jdbc:h2:mem:testdb"
                />
            <property name="javax.persistence.jdbc.user" value="sa"/>
            <property name="javax.persistence.jdbc.password" value=""/>
            <property name="javax.persistence.jdbc.driver" value="org.h2.Driver"/>
            <property name="hibernate.dialect" value="org.hibernate.dialect.H2Dialect
                "/>
            <property name="hibernate.hbm2ddl.auto" value="update"/>
        </properties>
    </persistence-unit>

</persistence>
```

The persistence.xml file is the cornerstone of JPA configuration. It defines one or more persistence units, each containing relevant properties. In the example above, the myPersistenceUnit persistence unit uses Hibernate as the JPA provider and includes fundamental settings for the database URL, user credentials, driver class, dialect, and schema generation strategy.

Common JPA Properties

- javax.persistence.jdbc.url: Specifies the database JDBC URL.
- javax.persistence.jdbc.user: Defines the database user.
- javax.persistence.jdbc.password: Sets the database password.
- javax.persistence.jdbc.driver: Indicates the JDBC driver class name.

Hibernate-Specific Properties

- hibernate.dialect: Determines the SQL dialect for specific databases.
- hibernate.hbm2ddl.auto: Controls schema generation:
  - validate: Validate the schema, do not make changes to the database.
  - update: Update the schema.
  - create: Create the schema, destroying any previous data.

- create-drop: Create the schema on startup and drop it on shutdown.

Additional JPA Properties

- javax.persistence.schema-generation.database.action: Controls database schema generation, similar to hibernate.hbm2ddl.auto.
- javax.persistence.schema-generation.scripts.action: Specifies the action (e.g., none, create, drop) for generating scripts.
- javax.persistence.schema-generation.scripts.create-target: Determines the target file for schema creation scripts.
- javax.persistence.schema-generation.scripts.drop-target: Specifies the target file for schema drop scripts.
- javax.persistence.cache.storeMode: Configures the store mode for second-level cache.
- javax.persistence.cache.retrieveMode: Configulates the retrieval mode for the second-level cache.

Application-Level Configuration

While most configurations are defined within persistence.xml, some properties can be programmatically configured at runtime. Typically, this is done when creating an EntityManagerFactory.

```
Map<String, Object> properties = new HashMap<>();
properties.put("javax.persistence.jdbc.url", "jdbc:h2:mem:testdb");
properties.put("javax.persistence.jdbc.user", "sa");
properties.put("javax.persistence.jdbc.password", "");
properties.put("javax.persistence.jdbc.driver", "org.h2.Driver");
properties.put("hibernate.dialect", "org.hibernate.dialect.H2Dialect");

EntityManagerFactory emf = Persistence.createEntityManagerFactory("
    myPersistenceUnit", properties);
EntityManager em = emf.createEntityManager();
```

This approach is useful for dynamically setting properties based on the environment (development, testing, production) without modifying the persistence.xml file.

JPA Logging

Understanding and debugging JPA's behavior often requires detailed logs. The amount and detail of the logs can be controlled using the following properties:

- hibernate.show_sql: If set to true, Hibernate will output the SQL queries to the console.
- hibernate.format_sql: If true, the SQL output is formatted.
- hibernate.use_sql_comments: Adds comments to the SQL output to indicate the source entity and operations.
- javax.persistence.query.timeout: Sets the query timeout duration in milliseconds.

```
<property name="hibernate.show_sql" value="true"/>
<property name="hibernate.format_sql" value="true"/>
<property name="hibernate.use_sql_comments" value="true"/>
```

Connection Pooling

Efficient use of database connections is critical for application performance. JPA providers often integrate with connection pooling mechanisms. For instance, Hibernate integrates with the HikariCP connection pool.

```
<property name="javax.persistence.jdbc.url" value="jdbc:h2:mem:testdb"/>
<property name="javax.persistence.jdbc.user" value="sa"/>
<property name="javax.persistence.jdbc.password" value=""/>
<property name="javax.persistence.jdbc.driver" value="org.h2.Driver"/>
<property name="hibernate.hikari.minimumIdle" value="5"/>
<property name="hibernate.hikari.maximumPoolSize" value="20"/>
<property name="hibernate.hikari.idleTimeout" value="30000"/>
```

Key properties include the minimum and maximum pool size and the connection idle timeout, allowing fine-grained control over connection management.

These configurations streamline and enhance the efficiency and reliability of JPA operations within varying deployment contexts. Careful adjustment of these settings can lead to significant improvements in both performance and development productivity.

2.10 Using JPA Annotations

JPA annotations play a crucial role in mapping Java objects to database tables. These annotations provide a way to define how Java objects are stored, retrieved, updated, and deleted in the database. It allows for easy configuration of your entity classes without relying on XML descriptors. This section delves into the essential JPA annotations and their uses.

The @Entity annotation designates a class as an entity and maps it to a database table. For example:

```
@Entity
public class Student {
    @Id
    private Long id;
    private String name;
    private int age;
    // getters and setters
}
```

In this example, the Student class is annotated with @Entity, signaling that it should be mapped to a database table. The @Id annotation marks the id field as the primary key. By default, the class name becomes the table name, and the field names become the column names, but these defaults can be overridden.

The @Table annotation customizes the table name and other table attributes. The following code specifies a different table name:

```
@Entity
@Table(name = "TBL_STUDENT")
public class Student {
    @Id
    private Long id;
    private String name;
    private int age;
    // getters and setters
}
```

The @Column annotation provides finer control over the column mappings. For instance, to specify a different column name for the name attribute, use the annotation as shown:

```
@Entity
@Table(name = "TBL_STUDENT")
public class Student {
    @Id
    @GeneratedValue(strategy = GenerationType.IDENTITY)
    private Long id;

    @Column(name = "FULL_NAME", nullable = false)
    private String name;

    @Column(name = "AGE", columnDefinition = "INTEGER default 0")
    private int age;
    // getters and setters
}
```

Here, the name field is mapped to the FULL_NAME column, and the

AGE field is mapped to the AGE column with a default value specified in the database. The nullable attribute ensures that the name column cannot be null.

The @GeneratedValue annotation specifies that the primary key is automatically generated. In the example, the GenerationType.IDENTITY strategy is used, which relies on the database's identity column feature to generate values automatically.

Unidirectional and bidirectional relationships between entities are defined using @OneToMany, @ManyToOne, @OneToOne, and @ManyToMany annotations. The following is an example of a unidirectional one-to-many relationship:

```
@Entity
public class Department {
    @Id
    private Long id;
    private String name;

    @OneToMany
    @JoinColumn(name = "DEPARTMENT_ID") // Join column in the Employee
        table
    private List<Employee> employees = new ArrayList<>();
    // getters and setters
}
```

In this example, the Department entity contains a list of Employee entities, and the foreign key DEPARTMENT_ID is specified in the Employee table using the @JoinColumn annotation.

For a bidirectional one-to-many relationship, the @ManyToOne annotation is used on the Employee side:

```
@Entity
public class Employee {
    @Id
    private Long id;
    private String name;

    @ManyToOne
    @JoinColumn(name = "DEPARTMENT_ID")
    private Department department;
    // getters and setters
}
```

This results in a bidirectional mapping wherein the Department entity is aware of its employees, and each Employee entity is aware of its Department.

To establish many-to-many relationships, the @ManyToMany annotation is employed, often with a join table that maps entity relationships:

```
@Entity
public class Student {
    @Id
    private Long id;
    private String name;

    @ManyToMany
    @JoinTable(
        name = "STUDENT_COURSE",
        joinColumns = @JoinColumn(name = "STUDENT_ID"),
        inverseJoinColumns = @JoinColumn(name = "COURSE_ID")
    )
    private List<Course> courses = new ArrayList<>();
    // getters and setters
}
```

```
@Entity
public class Course {
    @Id
    private Long id;
    private String title;

    @ManyToMany(mappedBy = "courses")
    private List<Student> students = new ArrayList<>();
    // getters and setters
}
```

The @JoinTable annotation specifies the STUDENT_COURSE join table, mapping the Student entity's ID to the Course entity's ID. The mappedBy attribute in the Course class indicates that the students field in Course is the inverse side of the relation, which is mapped by the courses field in Student.

The @Embedded and @Embeddable annotations allow entity composition, where an entity can include the fields of another class as its attributes:

```
@Embeddable
public class Address {
    private String street;
    private String city;
    private String state;
    private String zipCode;
    // getters and setters
}
```

```
@Entity
public class Employee {
    @Id
    private Long id;
    private String name;

    @Embedded
    private Address address;
    // getters and setters
}
```

In this example, the Address class is annotated with @Embeddable, making it embeddable in other entities. The Employee entity includes Address as a component.

These JPA annotations provide the foundation for mapping Java objects to relational database tables, facilitating effective data persistence and retrieval operations. By combining these annotations, you can precisely control the entity configurations, relationships, and database behaviors essential for robust Java applications.

Chapter 3

Entity Mapping Basics

This chapter covers the fundamental concepts of entity mapping in JPA, starting with mapping basic properties using annotations like @Column and @Basic. It explains how to map primary keys with @Id and @GeneratedValue, as well as embedded and transient properties with @Embedded and @Transient. The chapter also delves into mapping relationships between entities, including @OneToOne, @OneToMany, @ManyToOne, and @ManyToMany associations. Furthermore, it discusses inheritance strategies for entities and customization of column and table names to align with database schemas.

3.1 Understanding Entity Mapping in JPA

Java Persistence API (JPA) provides a standardized approach for Object-Relational Mapping (ORM). It allows developers to work with relational data in Java applications using domain objects, abstracting away most of the underlying database interactions. At the core of JPA lie entities, which are lightweight, persistent domain objects that represent tables in a relational database. Understanding entity mapping in JPA involves grasping how Java classes map to database tables, columns, and relationships.

An entity in JPA is defined with the @Entity annotation. This annotation is used at the class level and marks the class as a JPA entity. For example:

```
import javax.persistence.Entity;
import javax.persistence.Table;

@Entity
@Table(name = "students")
public class Student {
    // Class fields and methods
}
```

In the above example, the @Entity annotation tells JPA that the Student class is an entity. The @Table annotation can also be used to specify the table name in the database that this entity maps to. If the @Table annotation is omitted, JPA assumes the table name matches the class name.

Individual fields within the entity class are mapped to columns in the table. By default, JPA maps each field to a column with the same name as the field. Fields can be explicitly mapped using the @Column annotation.

```
import javax.persistence.Column;
import javax.persistence.Id;

@Entity
@Table(name = "students")
public class Student {

    @Id
    @Column(name = "student_id")
    private Long id;

    @Column(name = "first_name")
    private String firstName;

    @Column(name = "last_name")
    private String lastName;

    // Getters and setters
}
```

In this example, the student_id column in the students table is mapped to the id field in the Student entity, first_name to firstName, and last_name to lastName.

Fields in an entity class can be categorized by their persistence strategies. The basic properties of an entity are typically annotated with @Basic, indicating that they are to be persisted in the database. However, this annotation is optional for most cases since it is implicitly understood. The @Basic annotation is more relevant when dealing with fetch strategies or optional persistent fields.

Mapping primary keys is essential in JPA, as each entity must have a unique identifier. The @Id annotation marks a field as the primary key. Primary key values can be automatically generated using the @GeneratedValue annotation.

```
import javax.persistence.GeneratedValue;
import javax.persistence.GenerationType;

@Entity
@Table(name = "students")
public class Student {

    @Id
    @GeneratedValue(strategy = GenerationType.IDENTITY)
    @Column(name = "student_id")
    private Long id;

    // Other fields and methods
}
```

In this case, the student_id column is set as the primary key, with values automatically generated by the database (using the IDENTITY generation strategy).

Entities can embed other objects using the @Embedded annotation. This allows the entity to include multiple related fields as components without creating separate entities for each one.

```
import javax.persistence.Embedded;

@Entity
@Table(name = "students")
public class Student {

    @Id
    @GeneratedValue(strategy = GenerationType.IDENTITY)
    @Column(name = "student_id")
    private Long id;

    private String firstName;
    private String lastName;

    @Embedded
    private Address address;

    // Getters and setters
}
```

Here, the Address class is a non-entity class that contains address-related fields. The @Embedded annotation indicates that the attributes of the Address object are mapped to the students table as if they were direct fields of the Student entity.

The @Transient annotation is applied to fields that should not be persisted. Such fields are ignored by the persistence provider and have no corresponding column in the database table.

```
import javax.persistence.Transient;

@Entity
@Table(name = "students")
public class Student {

    @Id
    @GeneratedValue(strategy = GenerationType.IDENTITY)
    @Column(name = "student_id")
    private Long id;

    private String firstName;
    private String lastName;

    @Transient
    private int age;

    // Getters and setters
}
```

In the example above, the age field is marked with the @Transient annotation, indicating that this field will not be persisted in the database. The students table will not have a column for age.

Understanding how to accurately map entities to database tables allows developers to seamlessly transition between working with domain models in Java and relational data in a database. This mapping forms the foundation of JPA and influences many advanced concepts and operations within the JPA framework.

3.2 Mapping Basic Properties: @Column and @Basic

In Java Persistence API (JPA), mapping entity properties to database columns is essential for defining how an entity's attributes are persisted to the underlying database tables. The @Column and @Basic annotations are fundamental tools for this task.

The @Column annotation is used to specify the mapped column for a persistent property or field. By default, if @Column is not specified, the field will be mapped to a column with the same name as the field. However, @Column provides significant flexibility and various customization options.

Consider the following example:

```
@Entity
public class Person {
    @Id
```

```
    @GeneratedValue(strategy = GenerationType.IDENTITY)
    private Long id;

    @Column(name = "first_name")
    private String firstName;

    @Column(name = "last_name", nullable = false)
    private String lastName;

    @Column(name = "birth_date", updatable = false)
    private LocalDate birthDate;
}
```

In this example, the Person entity has three attributes: firstName, lastName, and birthDate. Each attribute is annotated with @Column to specify the corresponding column names in the database.

The name attribute of @Column specifies the name of the column in the database. In this example, name = "first_name" maps the firstName field to the first_name column in the database. If @Column is omitted, the default column name would be the same as the field name, so the firstName field would map to a column named firstName.

Other useful attributes of the @Column annotation include:

- **nullable**: Defines whether the column can accept null values. The default is true. If set to false, attempting to persist a null value in this column will result in an exception. For example:

  ```
  @Column(name = "last_name", nullable = false)
  private String lastName;
  ```

  In this case, the last_name column must have a value; it cannot be null.

- **updatable**: Indicates whether the column is updatable. The default is true. If set to false, the column value will not be included in SQL UPDATE statements. For example:

  ```
  @Column(name = "birth_date", updatable = false)
  private LocalDate birthDate;
  ```

  Here, birth_date will not be updated after the initial insert.

- **length**: Sets the column length for a String property. The length attribute is particularly relevant for VARCHAR columns in the database.

- **unique**: Ensures that all values in the column are unique. This attribute is useful for columns that require unique values, such as usernames or email addresses. For example:

```
@Column(name = "email", unique = true)
private String email;
```

With this configuration, the email column will reject duplicate entries within the table.

The @Basic annotation is used for explicit marking of attributes as basic mappings. By default, persistent fields without any other specific mapping annotations are treated as Basic. The @Basic annotation can be used to control optionality.

In the absence of @Basic, fields are implicitly considered as basic mappings. However, @Basic provides the optional attribute which determines if a field is optional. The default value is true.

Here is an example illustrating the use of @Basic:

```
@Entity
public class Employee {
    @Id
    @GeneratedValue(strategy = GenerationType.IDENTITY)
    private Long id;

    @Basic(optional = false)
    private String name;

    @Basic(fetch = FetchType.LAZY)
    private String profilePicture;
}
```

In this example, the name field is marked with optional = false, indicating that it is a mandatory field and cannot be null. The profilePicture field uses FetchType.LAZY, allowing the data to be fetched lazily when accessed.

The fetch attribute of @Basic can be FetchType.LAZY or FetchType.EAGER, defining whether the data should be eagerly fetched or lazily fetched. The default fetch type for basic attributes is FetchType.EAGER.

- **FetchType.EAGER**: The data is fetched immediately and is ready when the entity is loaded.
- **FetchType.LAZY**: The data is fetched on-demand when accessed.

Understanding how to use @Column and @Basic effectively allows for fine-grained control over the mapping between Java entity attributes and database columns, enhancing the ability to design a robust and flexible persistence layer.

3.3 Mapping Primary Keys: @Id and @GeneratedValue

In Java Persistence API (JPA), the primary key is a crucial aspect of entity mapping. It uniquely identifies each entity instance within a database table. Properly mapping primary keys is essential for ensuring data integrity and facilitating efficient querying. This section addresses the use of @Id and @GeneratedValue annotations to define and manage primary keys in JPA.

The @Id annotation is used to explicitly specify the primary key field or property in an entity. This annotation must be placed on a single field or getter method within the entity class. Consider the following example:

```
@Entity
public class User {
    @Id
    private Long id;

    private String username;
    private String password;

    // Getters and setters
}
```

In the User entity above, the id field is annotated with @Id, indicating that it is the primary key of the entity. Every User instance will have a unique id.

While the @Id annotation marks a field as a primary key, the @GeneratedValue annotation allows JPA to automatically generate the primary key value when a new entity instance is persisted. The @GeneratedValue annotation typically works in conjunction with @Id. It supports several strategies for primary key generation:

- **AUTO**: JPA provider selects an appropriate generation strategy.
- **IDENTITY**: Primary key values are generated by the database incrementally.
- **SEQUENCE**: Primary key values are generated based on a database sequence.

- **TABLE**: Primary key values are generated based on a table that holds the key values.

By default, if no strategy is specified, GenerationType.AUTO is used. Below is an example demonstrating @GeneratedValue with the AUTO strategy:

```
@Entity
public class Product {
    @Id
    @GeneratedValue(strategy = GenerationType.AUTO)
    private Long id;

    private String name;
    private Double price;

    // Getters and setters
}
```

In this example, the id field of the Product entity is annotated with both @Id and @GeneratedValue, and the strategy is set to AUTO. The JPA provider determines the best strategy to generate the primary key.

Using the IDENTITY strategy, where the database is responsible for primary key generation, the annotation is modified as follows:

```
@Entity
public class Order {
    @Id
    @GeneratedValue(strategy = GenerationType.IDENTITY)
    private Long id;

    private String description;

    // Getters and setters
}
```

In this instance, the id field of the Order entity uses GenerationType.IDENTITY, so the database auto-increments the primary key value.

The SEQUENCE strategy relies on a sequence object in the database. This approach is common in databases that support sequences, such as PostgreSQL and Oracle. Here is an example:

```
@Entity
@SequenceGenerator(name = "order_seq", sequenceName = "order_sequence",
     allocationSize = 1)
public class Invoice {
    @Id
    @GeneratedValue(strategy = GenerationType.SEQUENCE, generator = "order_seq
        ")
    private Long id;

    private BigDecimal amount;
```

```
    // Getters and setters
}
```

In this case, the Invoice entity's primary key is generated using the order_sequence defined in the database. The @SequenceGenerator annotation specifies the sequence name and additional parameters like allocationSize, which can improve performance by preallocating sequence values.

The TABLE strategy uses a table to maintain and generate primary keys. This strategy can be used with databases that do not support sequences. Below is a corresponding example:

```
@Entity
@TableGenerator(name = "product_table_gen", table = "key_generator",
      pkColumnName = "gen_name", valueColumnName = "gen_value",
      pkColumnValue = "product_id", allocationSize = 1)
public class Category {
    @Id
    @GeneratedValue(strategy = GenerationType.TABLE, generator = "
         product_table_gen")
    private Long id;

    private String categoryName;

    // Getters and setters
}
```

The Category entity in the above example uses the TABLE strategy. It defines a @TableGenerator for primary key generation based on the key_generator table. The primary key values are stored in and retrieved from this table.

Executing the defined entity classes with appropriate persistence code will achieve automatic primary key generation. For instance, executing the following code snippet to persist a Product entity:

```
public class ProductService {
    @PersistenceContext
    private EntityManager em;

    public void saveProduct(Product product) {
        em.persist(product);
    }
}
```

Upon persisting a Product instance, the id field is automatically assigned a value:

```
Product{id=1, name="Laptop", price=1200.00}
```

Proper understanding and usage of @Id and @GeneratedValue annotations ensure efficient primary key management in JPA entities. This section covered various strategies and examples for defining and generating primary keys, which are fundamental for entity uniqueness in a relational database context.

3.4 Mapping Embedded and Transient Properties: @Embedded and @Transient

Mapping embedded and transient properties in JPA allows for the finer control and organization of entity fields, facilitating efficient data modeling. The @Embedded and @Transient annotations serve distinct purposes: the former for embedding objects within other objects and the latter for excluding fields from persistence.

The @Embedded Annotation

The @Embedded annotation is used to include an embeddable class within an entity. An embeddable class allows us to encapsulate reusable groups of fields, promoting organized and modular entity design. The embeddable class is annotated with @Embeddable.

@Embeddable classes do not have a defined primary key; instead, they rely on the owning entity's primary key. In the context of database design, the properties of an embedded object are flattened and integrated into the entity's table.

Consider an example where we have an Address class that we want to reuse across multiple entities:

```
import javax.persistence.Embeddable;

@Embeddable
public class Address {
    private String street;
    private String city;
    private String state;
    private String zipCode;

    // Getters and Setters
}
```

We can embed the Address class in an Employee entity as follows:

```
import javax.persistence.Entity;
import javax.persistence.GeneratedValue;
import javax.persistence.GenerationType;
import javax.persistence.Id;
import javax.persistence.Embedded;
```

```
@Entity
public class Employee {
    @Id
    @GeneratedValue(strategy = GenerationType.IDENTITY)
    private Long id;

    private String name;

    @Embedded
    private Address address;

    // Getters and Setters
}
```

When the Employee entity is mapped to the database, the fields of the Address object will be included in the Employee table. The resulting table will appear as follows:

```
+----+------+---------+-------+-----+---------+
| id | name | street  | city  | state | zipCode |
+----+------+---------+-------+-----+---------+
```

Nested Embeddables

It is also possible to nest embeddables within other embeddables, thereby creating complex, hierarchical structures. Consider a further refinement where an Address contains a nested embeddable class ZipCode:

```
@Embeddable
public class ZipCode {
    private String primaryCode;
    private String secondaryCode;

    // Getters and Setters
}

@Embeddable
public class Address {
    private String street;
    private String city;
    private String state;

    @Embedded
    private ZipCode zipCode;

    // Getters and Setters
}
```

The corresponding Employee class remains unchanged, but the table structure in the database will encapsulate the nested embeddable fields:

```
+----+------+---------+-------+------+------------+--------------+
| id | name | street  | city  | state| primaryCode| secondaryCode|
+----+------+---------+-------+------+------------+--------------+
```

The @Transient Annotation

In contrast, the @Transient annotation marks a field as non-persistent. This means the field will not be saved to the database or retrieved by JPA. This is useful for fields used specifically for business logic or temporary data that does not need to be stored persistently.

Consider an example where an Employee class contains a calculated fullName field:

```
@Entity
public class Employee {
    @Id
    @GeneratedValue(strategy = GenerationType.IDENTITY)
    private Long id;

    private String firstName;
    private String lastName;

    @Transient
    private String fullName;

    // Getters and Setters

    public String getFullName() {
        return firstName + " " + lastName;
    }
}
```

In this scenario, the field fullName is marked as transient and will not be mapped to any column in the database table:

```
+----+-----------+----------+
| id | firstName | lastName |
+----+-----------+----------+
```

By implementing @Transient, we ensure that fullName is computed at runtime and not stored redundantly in the database.

Usage and Best Practices

When using @Embedded, ensure that the embeddable class is strictly a grouping of related fields and does not contain business logic or behavior, adhering to the spirit of data modeling. Meanwhile, apply @Transient judiciously for fields that are temporary or computed, ensuring clarity and efficiency in data handling.

Combining these annotations effectively allows the creation of well-structured, robust, and maintainable JPA entity models, which align with established database normalization principles while accommodating complex, real-world data relationships.

3.5 Mapping Relationships: @OneToOne

The @OneToOne annotation in Java Persistence API (JPA) is utilized to specify a one-to-one relationship between two entity classes. In a one-to-one relationship, each instance of the first entity matches exactly one instance of the second entity and vice versa. This type of relationship is common in real-world data models, such as between users and their profiles, employees and their workstations, or even between persons and their driver's licenses.

To create a one-to-one mapping, use the @OneToOne annotation on a field or property in the owning entity class. The owning side of the relationship is the side that contains the foreign key reference in the database schema.

Here is a detailed example of how to map a one-to-one relationship.

Consider two classes, Person and Passport. Each Person has a unique Passport, and each Passport is associated with exactly one Person.

The entities can be defined as follows:

```
// Person.java
@Entity
public class Person {

    @Id
    @GeneratedValue(strategy = GenerationType.IDENTITY)
    private Long id;

    @Column(name = "name")
    private String name;

    @OneToOne(cascade = CascadeType.ALL)
    @JoinColumn(name = "passport_id", referencedColumnName = "id")
    private Passport passport;

    // Getters and Setters
}

// Passport.java
@Entity
public class Passport {

    @Id
    @GeneratedValue(strategy = GenerationType.IDENTITY)
    private Long id;

    @Column(name = "passport_number")
    private String passportNumber;

    @OneToOne(mappedBy = "passport")
    private Person person;

    // Getters and Setters
```

```
}
```

This code example illustrates how to configure a one-to-one relationship:

1. **Entity Declaration**: Both Person and Passport are annotated with @Entity to specify they are entity classes.

2. **Primary Key Definition**: The primary key for each entity is annotated with @Id. The @GeneratedValue annotation indicates that the primary key values are automatically generated.

3. **Mapping of Basic Properties**: Properties like name and passportNumber are simply mapped using the @Column annotation.

4. **Defining the One-to-One Relationship**: - In the Person entity, the @OneToOne annotation is used on the passport field. This marks the field as participating in a one-to-one relationship. - The @JoinColumn annotation is used to specify the foreign key column in the Person table that references the primary key of the Passport table. In this case, the foreign key is passport_id, and its referenced column is id. - The cascade attribute in @OneToOne can be set to CascadeType.ALL to cascade all operations from the Person entity to the Passport entity. This ensures that persistence operations (like persist, merge, remove, etc.) on Person are also applied to Passport. - In the Passport entity, the mappedBy attribute indicates that the relationship is bidirectional, with the person property serving as the inverse side of the association.

Executing a test scenario to persist these entities into the database can be illustrated as follows:

```
// Test.java
public class Test {
    public static void main(String[] args) {
        EntityManagerFactory factory = Persistence.createEntityManagerFactory("
            example-unit");
        EntityManager em = factory.createEntityManager();

        em.getTransaction().begin();

        // Creating a new Person and associated Passport
        Person person = new Person();
        person.setName("John Doe");

        Passport passport = new Passport();
        passport.setPassportNumber("A12345678");

        person.setPassport(passport);
        passport.setPerson(person);

        // Persist the person entity
        em.persist(person);
```

```
        em.getTransaction().commit();

        em.close();
        factory.close();
    }
}
```

Output in the database can be displayed using a SQL query to verify the results of the persistence operation:

```
SELECT * FROM Person;
+----+------+------------+
| id | name | passport_id|
+----+------+------------+
| 1  | John | 1          |
+----+------+------------+

SELECT * FROM Passport;
+----+----------------+
| id | passport_number|
+----+----------------+
| 1  | A12345678      |
+----+----------------+
```

In this example, the Test.java class creates an instance of Person and Passport, sets their properties, and associates them with one another. The em.persist(person) line calls persist on the Person object, which in turn cascades the persist operation to the associated Passport object because of the CascadeType.ALL specification.

In the database, the Person table will have a foreign key column passport_id that references the id column of the Passport table, validating the one-to-one relationship.

Ensuring referential integrity and managing the bidirectional relationship appropriately are crucial in maintaining the seamless functioning of the one-to-one mapping in a JPA context.

3.6 Mapping Relationships: @OneToMany

The @OneToMany annotation is used to define a one-to-many relationship between two entities in Java Persistence API (JPA). This relationship signifies that a single instance of an entity (the "one" side) can be associated with multiple instances of another entity (the "many" side). Understanding the proper use of @OneToMany is essential for effective data modeling and efficient database interaction.

A typical one-to-many relationship example is that of a Customer and Order entities. A single Customer can place multiple Orders. In such a scenario, the @OneToMany annotation is placed on the Customer class, indicating that one customer can have many orders associated with them. Let's explore the steps and details involved in mapping this relationship.

Defining the Entity Classes

We start by defining the Customer and Order entity classes. These classes will include the necessary JPA annotations to represent the relationship between them.

```
@Entity
public class Customer {
    @Id
    @GeneratedValue(strategy = GenerationType.IDENTITY)
    private Long id;

    private String name;

    @OneToMany(mappedBy = "customer", cascade = CascadeType.ALL,
        orphanRemoval = true)
    private List<Order> orders = new ArrayList<>();

    // Getters and Setters
}
```

```
@Entity
public class Order {
    @Id
    @GeneratedValue(strategy = GenerationType.IDENTITY)
    private Long id;

    private String product;

    private Double price;

    @ManyToOne
    @JoinColumn(name = "customer_id")
    private Customer customer;

    // Getters and Setters
}
```

Understanding the Annotations

In the Customer entity, the @OneToMany annotation is used on the orders field. Several attributes of the @OneToMany annotation control the behavior of the relationship:

- mappedBy: This attribute specifies the field in the Order entity that owns the relationship. In this case, it is "customer".
- cascade: This attribute specifies the cascading operations that should be applied to the relationship. Using CascadeType.ALL

ensures that all persistence operations (persist, merge, remove, etc.) propagate to the Order entities.

- orphanRemoval: Setting this attribute to true means that if an Order is removed from the orders list in Customer, it will also be removed from the database.

In the Order entity, the @ManyToOne annotation is placed on the customer field to indicate that many orders can be associated with a single customer. The @JoinColumn annotation specifies the foreign key column (customer_id) that will be used to join the Order table with the Customer table.

Bidirectional Relationships

The @OneToMany annotation combined with @ManyToOne sets up a bidirectional relationship. This setup allows navigation from Customer to Order and vice versa. However, keeping both sides of the relationship synchronized requires additional logic in the entity classes.

```
public void addOrder(Order order) {
    orders.add(order);
    order.setCustomer(this);
}

public void removeOrder(Order order) {
    orders.remove(order);
    order.setCustomer(null);
}
```

The addOrder method ensures that when a new Order is added to the orders list, the Customer reference in Order is updated appropriately. Similarly, the removeOrder method handles removal and cleans up the relationship on the Order side.

Example Usage

Let's see an example of using these entities in a typical service class.

```
public class CustomerService {
    @PersistenceContext
    private EntityManager entityManager;

    @Transactional
    public void createCustomerWithOrders() {
        Customer customer = new Customer();
        customer.setName("John Doe");

        Order order1 = new Order();
        order1.setProduct("Laptop");
        order1.setPrice(1200.00);

        Order order2 = new Order();
```

```
        order2.setProduct("Smartphone");
        order2.setPrice(800.00);

        customer.addOrder(order1);
        customer.addOrder(order2);

        entityManager.persist(customer);
    }

    @Transactional
    public void removeOrderFromCustomer(Long customerId, Long orderId) {
        Customer customer = entityManager.find(Customer.class, customerId);
        Order order = entityManager.find(Order.class, orderId);

        if (customer != null && order != null) {
            customer.removeOrder(order);
        }
    }
}
```

In the createCustomerWithOrders method, a new Customer is created along with two Orders. The orders are added to the customer, ensuring the bidirectional relationship is correctly established, and then the customer is persisted. The removeOrderFromCustomer method demonstrates how to remove an Order from a Customer while maintaining the relationship integrity.

Database Schema

By using the annotations as described, JPA will generate a relational database schema automatically. The schema will include two tables, Customer and Order, with a foreign key constraint from the Order table to the Customer table.

```
CREATE TABLE Customer (
    id BIGINT NOT NULL AUTO_INCREMENT,
    name VARCHAR(255),
    PRIMARY KEY (id)
);

CREATE TABLE Order (
    id BIGINT NOT NULL AUTO_INCREMENT,
    product VARCHAR(255),
    price DOUBLE,
    customer_id BIGINT,
    PRIMARY KEY (id),
    FOREIGN KEY (customer_id) REFERENCES Customer(id)
);
```

This schema reflects the one-to-many relationship defined in the JPA entities, ensuring data integrity and enforcing the necessary constraints at the database level.

By understanding and properly using the @OneToMany annotation, developers can model and manage complex relationships between entities effectively, ensuring both simplicity and optimal performance in their JPA applications.

3.7 Mapping Relationships: @ManyToOne

In JPA (Java Persistence API), the @ManyToOne annotation is used to define a many-to-one association between two entities. This is one of the most common relationships in database modeling. In this type of association, multiple instances of an entity (the "many" side) reference a single instance of another entity (the "one" side). This section delves into the mechanics of using the @ManyToOne annotation to map such relationships in JPA.

Basic Usage of @ManyToOne

Let us consider two entities, Order and Customer. Each Order is associated with one Customer, but each Customer can be associated with multiple Orders. To model this relationship, the Order entity will have a field representing the Customer it is associated with, annotated with @ManyToOne:

```
@Entity
public class Order {
    @Id
    @GeneratedValue(strategy = GenerationType.IDENTITY)
    private Long id;

    @ManyToOne
    @JoinColumn(name = "customer_id")
    private Customer customer;

    // other fields, getters, setters, etc.
}
```

In this example, the Order entity contains a Customer field annotated with @ManyToOne. The @JoinColumn annotation specifies the foreign key column (customer_id) in the Order table that will be used to establish the relationship. By default, if @JoinColumn is omitted, JPA uses the default naming conventions to determine the foreign key column name based on the name of the relationship field.

Fetching Strategies

The @ManyToOne annotation supports different fetching strategies defined by the fetch attribute. The available options are FetchType.EAGER and FetchType.LAZY.

- FetchType.EAGER: This strategy indicates that the related entity should be fetched immediately along with the source entity. This is the default fetching strategy for @ManyToOne associations.

```
@ManyToOne(fetch = FetchType.EAGER)
@JoinColumn(name = "customer_id")
private Customer customer;
```

- FetchType.LAZY: This strategy indicates that the related entity should be fetched on demand, i.e., when it is accessed for the first time.

```
@ManyToOne(fetch = FetchType.LAZY)
@JoinColumn(name = "customer_id")
private Customer customer;
```

Choosing the appropriate fetching strategy can significantly impact performance, especially in applications dealing with large datasets or complex relationships.

Cascade Operations

Cascade operations can be defined on the @ManyToOne association using the cascade attribute. The cascading options determine how operations performed on the source entity propagate to the associated entities. Common cascade types include:

- CascadeType.PERSIST: Propagates the persist operation to the associated entity.
- CascadeType.MERGE: Propagates the merge operation to the associated entity.
- CascadeType.REMOVE: Propagates the remove operation to the associated entity.
- CascadeType.REFRESH: Propagates the refresh operation to the associated entity.
- CascadeType.DETACH: Propagates the detach operation to the associated entity.
- CascadeType.ALL: Propagates all operations to the associated entity.

Example:

```
@ManyToOne(cascade = CascadeType.ALL)
@JoinColumn(name = "customer_id")
private Customer customer;
```

Using cascade types can simplify entity management by automatically applying state changes across associated entities, ensuring data consistency and integrity.

Bidirectional Relationships

Often, @ManyToOne relationships are bidirectional, meaning the related entity also references the source entity. Continuing with the Order and Customer example, we can add a bidirectional relationship to the Customer entity:

```
@Entity
public class Customer {
    @Id
    @GeneratedValue(strategy = GenerationType.IDENTITY)
    private Long id;

    @OneToMany(mappedBy = "customer", cascade = CascadeType.ALL)
    private List<Order> orders = new ArrayList<>();

    // other fields, getters, setters, etc.
}
```

In this example, the Customer entity uses the @OneToMany annotation to represent the other side of the relationship. The mappedBy attribute specifies the field in the Order entity that owns the relationship. This setup ensures proper bidirectional relationship mapping in JPA.

Example of Persisting Data

To persist entities with @ManyToOne relationships, follow these steps:

```
// Create a new customer
Customer customer = new Customer();
customer.setName("John Doe");

// Create a new order
Order order = new Order();
order.setOrderDate(LocalDateTime.now());
order.setCustomer(customer);

// Persist the customer (this will also persist the order due to cascading)
entityManager.getTransaction().begin();
entityManager.persist(customer);
entityManager.getTransaction().commit();
```

In this example, persisting the Customer entity will also persist the associated Order entity due to the CascadeType.PERSIST cascade operation specified on the Order entity.

The @ManyToOne annotation is a powerful tool for modeling many-to-one relationships in JPA. Proper usage can result in more maintainable and efficient data access layers, enabling seamless interaction with relational databases.

3.8 Mapping Relationships: @ManyToMany

The @ManyToMany annotation is utilized to define many-to-many relationships between entities in JPA. In a many-to-many association, each instance of Entity A can be associated with multiple instances of Entity B, and each instance of Entity B can also be associated with multiple instances of Entity A. This type of relationship is typically represented by an additional table, often referred to as a join table, which contains foreign keys referencing the primary keys of the associated entities.

To illustrate the @ManyToMany mapping, consider the scenario where we have two entities, Student and Course. A student can be enrolled in multiple courses, and a course can have multiple students enrolled in it. This situation is a canonical example of a many-to-many relationship.

Defining the @ManyToMany Relationship

Firstly, let's define the Student and Course entities with the necessary attributes and mappings. We will start with the Student entity:

```
@Entity
public class Student {
    @Id
    @GeneratedValue(strategy = GenerationType.IDENTITY)
    private Long id;

    @Column(nullable = false)
    private String name;

    @ManyToMany
    @JoinTable(
        name = "student_course",
        joinColumns = @JoinColumn(name = "student_id"),
        inverseJoinColumns = @JoinColumn(name = "course_id")
    )
    private Set<Course> courses = new HashSet<>();

    // Getters and setters
}
```

The @ManyToMany annotation is placed on the courses field. The @JoinTable annotation specifies the details of the join table. In this case, the join table is named student_course. The @JoinColumn annotation defines the foreign key columns in the join table that reference the primary keys of the Student and Course entities.

Next, let's define the Course entity:

```
@Entity
public class Course {
    @Id
    @GeneratedValue(strategy = GenerationType.IDENTITY)
    private Long id;

    @Column(nullable = false)
    private String title;

    @ManyToMany(mappedBy = "courses")
    private Set<Student> students = new HashSet<>();

    // Getters and setters
}
```

In the Course entity, the @ManyToMany annotation is placed on the students field, with the mappedBy attribute set to "courses". This indicates that the students field is the inverse side of the relationship and refers to the courses field in the Student entity.

Managing the Relationship

When managing a @ManyToMany relationship, it is important to handle both sides of the association to maintain consistency. This typically involves adding or removing entities from the collections in both associated entities. Here's how the enrollment of a student into a course can be managed:

```
public void enrollStudentInCourse(Student student, Course course) {
    student.getCourses().add(course);
    course.getStudents().add(student);
}
```

By ensuring both collections are updated, the bidirectional relationship remains consistent. Depending on the use case, it may be prudent to encapsulate these operations within methods on the entities themselves, thus adhering to object-oriented principles and promoting encapsulation.

Fetching and Querying Many-to-Many Associations

Lazy loading is the default fetching strategy for @ManyToMany associations, meaning that the related entities are not fetched until accessed. To customize the fetching strategy, the fetch attribute can be specified in the @ManyToMany annotation:

```
@ManyToMany(fetch = FetchType.EAGER)
private Set<Course> courses = new HashSet<>();
```

With FetchType.EAGER, the related Course entities are fetched immediately along with the Student entity. This can have performance implications, so it should be used judiciously based on the application's requirements.

Example Query

Consider a repository method to fetch all students enrolled in a particular course:

```
@Query("SELECT s FROM Student s JOIN s.courses c WHERE c.title = :courseTitle"
    )
List<Student> findStudentsByCourseTitle(@Param("courseTitle") String courseTitle);
```

This query uses JPQL to join the Student and Course entities based on the join table and retrieves students enrolled in the specified course.

Cascade Operations

Cascading operations such as persist, merge, remove, refresh, and detach may be applied to @ManyToMany relationships through the cascade attribute:

```
@ManyToMany(cascade = {CascadeType.PERSIST, CascadeType.MERGE})
private Set<Course> courses = new HashSet<>();
```

In this case, when a Student entity is persisted or merged, the associated Course entities are also persisted or merged, respectively.

By leveraging the @ManyToMany annotation effectively, complex associations between entities can be mapped and managed within the JPA framework, ensuring consistent and reliable interactions with the underlying database.

3.9 Mapping Inheritance in Entities

Inheritance is a fundamental pillar of object-oriented programming (OOP), and Java Persistence API (JPA) provides robust mechanisms to map an inheritance hierarchy to a relational database. In this section, we explore the primary strategies JPA offers for mapping inheritance: the single table strategy, the joined table strategy, and the table-per-class strategy. We will delve into the intricacies of each strategy, illustrate their implementation with examples, and discuss their advantages and drawbacks.

To map inheritance in JPA, the @Inheritance annotation is used along with the @DiscriminatorColumn and @DiscriminatorValue annotations where applicable. The choice of strategy significantly impacts the database design and query performance.

1. Single Table Strategy

The single table strategy maps an entire class hierarchy to a single database table. This approach involves using a discriminator column to differentiate between different entity types in the hierarchy.

Example:

```
@Entity
@Inheritance(strategy = InheritanceType.SINGLE_TABLE)
@DiscriminatorColumn(name = "type", discriminatorType = DiscriminatorType.
    STRING)
public abstract class Vehicle {
    @Id
    @GeneratedValue(strategy = GenerationType.IDENTITY)
    private Long id;
    private String manufacturer;

    // getters and setters
}

@Entity
@DiscriminatorValue("Car")
public class Car extends Vehicle {
    private int seats;

    // getters and setters
}

@Entity
@DiscriminatorValue("Truck")
public class Truck extends Vehicle {
    private int payloadCapacity;

    // getters and setters
}
```

In this example, the Vehicle class is marked with @Inheritance and @DiscriminatorColumn. The Car and Truck subclasses use the @DiscriminatorValue annotation to specify the value stored in the discriminator column to differentiate between the types.

The resulting SQL table schema will look something like:

```
CREATE TABLE vehicle (
   id BIGINT AUTO_INCREMENT PRIMARY KEY,
   manufacturer VARCHAR(255),
   type VARCHAR(31),
   seats INTEGER, -- only used for Car entities
   payloadCapacity INTEGER -- only used for Truck entities
);
```

This strategy is simple to implement and can offer substantial performance benefits, particularly for polymorphic queries. However, it can lead to sparsely populated columns when entities in the hierarchy have distinct fields.

2. Joined Table Strategy

The joined table strategy maps each class in an inheritance hierarchy to its own database table. The tables are joined together, typically using a foreign key constraint.

Example:

```
@Entity
@Inheritance(strategy = InheritanceType.JOINED)
public abstract class Payment {
    @Id
    @GeneratedValue(strategy = GenerationType.IDENTITY)
    private Long id;
    private double amount;

    // getters and setters
}

@Entity
public class CreditCardPayment extends Payment {
    private String cardNumber;

    // getters and setters
}

@Entity
public class PayPalPayment extends Payment {
    private String paypalAccount;

    // getters and setters
}
```

In this setup, each subclass extends the Payment class and has its own table where specific fields for the subclass are stored.

The SQL table schema will be:

```
CREATE TABLE payment (
   id BIGINT AUTO_INCREMENT PRIMARY KEY,
   amount DOUBLE
);

CREATE TABLE credit_card_payment (
   id BIGINT PRIMARY KEY,
   cardNumber VARCHAR(255),
   FOREIGN KEY (id) REFERENCES payment(id)
);

CREATE TABLE paypal_payment (
   id BIGINT PRIMARY KEY,
   paypalAccount VARCHAR(255),
   FOREIGN KEY (id) REFERENCES payment(id)
);
```

In the joined table strategy, polymorphic queries need to join tables, which can incur performance costs. This schema is more normalized, avoiding sparsely populated columns, and is suitable when entities have significantly differing fields.

3. Table-per-Class Strategy

The table-per-class strategy involves mapping each class in the inheritance hierarchy to a separate table, with each table containing all the fields declared by its class and its superclasses. Here, no inheritance relationship is maintained at the database level.

Example:

```
@Entity
@Inheritance(strategy = InheritanceType.TABLE_PER_CLASS)
public abstract class Animal {
    @Id
    @GeneratedValue(strategy = GenerationType.IDENTITY)
    private Long id;
    private String species;

    // getters and setters
}

@Entity
public class Dog extends Animal {
    private String breed;

    // getters and setters
}

@Entity
public class Cat extends Animal {
    private String color;

    // getters and setters
}
```

With this approach, each subclass is mapped to its own table, and no joins are involved when querying a single entity type.

The SQL table schema will include:

```
CREATE TABLE dog (
    id BIGINT AUTO_INCREMENT PRIMARY KEY,
    species VARCHAR(255),
    breed VARCHAR(255)
);

CREATE TABLE cat (
    id BIGINT AUTO_INCREMENT PRIMARY KEY,
    species VARCHAR(255),
    color VARCHAR(255)
);
```

This strategy can lead to considerable redundancy if there are many common fields across different entities in the hierarchy. Polymorphic queries in this scenario will require a UNION of queries across the multiple tables.

A thorough understanding of these inheritance mapping strategies will aid in designing a JPA-based application that is both efficient and maintainable. Each strategy has its unique advantages and trade-offs, making the choice dependent on specific application requirements and the characteristics of the data model.

3.10 Customizing Column and Table Names

In Java Persistence API (JPA), the default naming conventions for columns and tables may not always align with the requirements of the underlying database schema or the developers' preferences. The ability to customize column and table names is crucial for maintaining a coherent and understandable database design, especially when dealing with legacy databases or databases managed by multiple applications. JPA provides various annotations to facilitate this customization, including @Table and @Column.

The @Table annotation allows specifying details at the table level. This includes the name of the table, schema, and catalog to which the entity is mapped. On the other hand, the @Column annotation is used to customize the mapping at the column level. Below, we delve into the use of these annotations, providing examples and clarifications to enable effective customization.

@Table Annotation

The @Table annotation is applied at the class level. It allows you to specify the name of the table that will be used to persist the entity, along with optional schema and catalog attributes. The syntax is straightforward and is shown in the following example:

```
import javax.persistence.Entity;
import javax.persistence.Table;

@Entity
@Table(name = "employees", schema = "hr", catalog = "corporate")
public class Employee {
    // Class contents
}
```

In this example, the entity Employee is mapped to the employees table in the hr schema and the corporate catalog. If the schema and catalog attributes are omitted, the defaults defined by the persistence provider or the database will be used.

@Column Annotation

The @Column annotation provides a way to customize the column name, as well as other properties such as length, nullability, and uniqueness. Here is an example:

```
import javax.persistence.Entity;
import javax.persistence.Column;
import javax.persistence.Id;

@Entity
public class Employee {

    @Id
    private Long id;

    @Column(name = "employee_name", length = 50, nullable = false)
    private String name;

    @Column(name = "employee_age", nullable = true)
    private Integer age;

    // Getters and Setters
}
```

In this example, the Employee entity maps the name and age properties to the employee_name and employee_age columns, respectively. The length attribute sets the column length to 50, and nullable = false ensures that the name column cannot store NULL values.

Customizing Column Properties

Beyond renaming columns, the @Column annotation allows further customization:

- unique: Ensures that the column must contain unique values.
- insertable: Determines whether the column should be included in SQL INSERT statements.
- updatable: Determines whether the column should be included in SQL UPDATE statements.
- columnDefinition: Specifies the SQL fragment that is used when generating the DDL for the column.
- table: Specifies the table that contains the column. Useful for secondary tables.

Consider the following example:

```
@Entity
public class Product {

    @Id
    private Long id;

    @Column(name = "product_code", unique = true, length = 25)
    private String code;

    @Column(name = "product_description", columnDefinition = "TEXT")
    private String description;

    @Column(name = "product_price", updatable = false)
    private Double price;

    @Column(name = "created_date", insertable = false, updatable = false,
        columnDefinition = "TIMESTAMP DEFAULT CURRENT_TIMESTAMP")
    private Timestamp createdDate;

    // Getters and Setters
}
```

In this example, the Product entity demonstrates multiple customizations:

- The code field is set to be unique with a maximum length of 25 characters.
- The description field has a custom SQL type of TEXT.
- The price field is non-updatable, preventing changes after the initial insertion.
- The createdDate field has a default value and is neither insertable nor updatable by JPA.

Applying Customizations in Composite Keys

When an entity uses composite keys, it is represented by an EmbeddedId or IdClass. Each key component might need customization. This can be managed using the @Column annotation within the embeddable class.

```
import javax.persistence.Embeddable;
import javax.persistence.Column;
import javax.persistence.EmbeddedId;
import javax.persistence.Entity;

@Embeddable
public class OrderDetailKey {

    @Column(name = "order_id")
```

```
    private Long orderId;

    @Column(name = "product_id")
    private Long productId;

    // Getters and Setters
}

@Entity
public class OrderDetail {

    @EmbeddedId
    private OrderDetailKey id;

    @Column(name = "quantity")
    private Integer quantity;

    // Getters and Setters
}
```

In this example, the composite key OrderDetailKey customizes the column names for its fields.

Applying these customization techniques allows for precise control over the database schema, ensuring alignment with organizational standards or external constraints. Understanding and effectively applying these annotations is essential for expert proficiency in Java Persistence.

Chapter 4

Advanced Entity Mappings

This chapter explores advanced entity mappings in JPA, focusing on more complex and specialized mappings. It covers advanced attribute mappings using annotations like @Lob, @Temporal, and @Enumerated, and discusses mapping composite primary keys with @IdClass and @EmbeddedId. The chapter also examines bidirectional relationships and advanced inheritance mappings with @Inheritance and @DiscriminatorColumn. Additional topics include defining and using entity graphs with @NamedEntityGraph, utilizing secondary tables with @SecondaryTable, implementing optimistic locking with @Version, and handling concurrency with pessimistic locking using @Lock. Finally, it addresses mapping and using collection types effectively.

4.1 Understanding Advanced Mappings

Understanding advanced mappings in the Java Persistence API (JPA) is crucial for effectively managing and manipulating complex data structures within your application. JPA provides a robust set of annotations and configuration options to handle various mapping scenarios that go beyond the basics. This section delves into these advanced mappings to help you better structure and optimize your persistence layer.

Advanced mappings in JPA include the use of several specialized annotations such as @Lob, @Temporal, and @Enumerated, which are used to map large objects, date/time values, and enumerated types respectively. These mappings allow you to represent complex data types appropriately within your database schema.

Consider the following example where we use the @Lob annotation to map a large object. This can be particularly useful when dealing with large text or binary data:

```
@Entity
public class Document {
    @Id
    @GeneratedValue(strategy = GenerationType.AUTO)
    private Long id;

    @Lob
    private String content;

    // getters and setters
}
```

In this example, the content field is mapped as a large object (LOB) in the database, allowing the storage of large amounts of text without constraints imposed by standard VARCHAR columns.

Temporal data types pose another challenge in persistence. JPA provides the @Temporal annotation to map Java java.util.Date or java.util.Calendar types to database DATE, TIME, or TIMESTAMP types, depending on the temporal precision needed:

```
@Entity
public class Event {
    @Id
    @GeneratedValue(strategy = GenerationType.AUTO)
    private Long id;

    @Temporal(TemporalType.DATE)
    private Date eventDate;

    @Temporal(TemporalType.TIMESTAMP)
    private Date eventTimestamp;

    // getters and setters
}
```

The @Temporal annotation ensures that eventDate is mapped to a DATE column and eventTimestamp is mapped to a TIMESTAMP column in the database, preserving both date-only and full timestamp precision.

Enumerated types can be mapped using the @Enumerated annotation, which allows an enum to be represented either as an ordinal (integer) or as a string (name) in the database:

```
@Entity
public class Task {
    public enum Status {
        NOT_STARTED,
        IN_PROGRESS,
        COMPLETED
    }

    @Id
    @GeneratedValue(strategy = GenerationType.AUTO)
    private Long id;

    @Enumerated(EnumType.STRING)
    private Status status;

    // getters and setters
}
```

Here, the status field is represented as a string value corresponding to the enum name, aiding in readability and maintainability of the persisted data.

Composite primary keys are another advanced aspect of entity mapping, often required in scenarios involving legacy databases or complex data relationships. JPA supports composite primary keys through the @IdClass and @EmbeddedId annotations.

The @IdClass annotation allows for the definition of a composite key in a separate class, ensuring that the primary key consists of multiple fields. The @EmbeddedId is used to embed a composite primary key class within the entity directly.

Bidirectional relationships also represent an important aspect of advanced mappings, allowing navigation in both directions between related entities. These relationships often require careful management of owning and inverse sides using @OneToMany, @ManyToOne, @OneToOne, and @ManyToMany annotations.

Inheritance mappings facilitate the representation of inheritance hierarchies in the database schema. JPA provides @Inheritance and @DiscriminatorColumn annotations to manage these hierarchies, enabling configuration of single-table, joined, or table-per-class strategies.

Entity graphs, defined via @NamedEntityGraph, optimize fetch plans by specifying which attributes and related entities should be loaded. Secondary tables (@SecondaryTable) enable the storage of an entity's attributes across multiple tables, optimizing table normalization and data organization.

Optimistic locking (@Version) and pessimistic locking (@Lock) are advanced techniques for handling concurrency, ensuring data integrity during concurrent access.

Lastly, collections such as lists, sets, maps, and arrays can be mapped effectively, providing flexibility in modeling one-to-many and many-to-many relationships.

Understanding these advanced mappings enables the development of sophisticated, efficient, and maintainable persistence layers, supporting complex application requirements and fostering robust data management.

4.2 Advanced Attribute Mappings: @Lob, @Temporal, and @Enumerated

Advanced attribute mappings provide mechanisms to efficiently manage complex data types and persist them in a relational database. These mappings include handling large objects (LOBs), date and time types, and enumerated types. This section delves into the use of @Lob, @Temporal, and @Enumerated annotations in Java Persistence API (JPA).

@Lob: The @Lob annotation is used to represent large object data types, such as BLOB (Binary Large Object) and CLOB (Character Large Object). This is particularly useful for storing large binary files (like images, videos, and other media) and large text data (such as documents or textual contents).

```
import javax.persistence.Entity;
import javax.persistence.GeneratedValue;
import javax.persistence.GenerationType;
import javax.persistence.Id;
import javax.persistence.Lob;

@Entity
public class Article {

    @Id
    @GeneratedValue(strategy = GenerationType.IDENTITY)
    private Long id;

    @Lob
    private String content;

    // Getters and setters
}
```

In this example, the content field is annotated with @Lob, indicating that it should be treated as a large object. The persistence provider maps this field to an appropriate database column type, such as CLOB for text.

Similarly, for binary data, we could use:

```
import javax.persistence.Entity;
import javax.persistence.GeneratedValue;
import javax.persistence.GenerationType;
import javax.persistence.Id;
import javax.persistence.Lob;

@Entity
public class Photo {

    @Id
    @GeneratedValue(strategy = GenerationType.IDENTITY)
    private Long id;

    @Lob
    private byte[] image;

    // Getters and setters
}
```

Here, the image field, which is a binary array, is annotated with @Lob and mapped to a BLOB column type in the database.

@Temporal: The @Temporal annotation is used to specify the exact type of a temporal field (date and time). Java provides extensive support for date and time manipulation through java.util.Date and java.sql.Date, and it's crucial to map these correctly in the database.

```
import javax.persistence.Entity;
import javax.persistence.GeneratedValue;
import javax.persistence.GenerationType;
import javax.persistence.Id;
import javax.persistence.Temporal;
import javax.persistence.TemporalType;
import java.util.Date;

@Entity
public class Event {

    @Id
    @GeneratedValue(strategy = GenerationType.IDENTITY)
    private Long id;

    @Temporal(TemporalType.DATE)
    private Date eventDate;

    @Temporal(TemporalType.TIMESTAMP)
    private Date eventTimestamp;

    // Getters and setters
}
```

In this example, eventDate is mapped to the TemporalType.DATE, meaning only the date part is stored, ignoring the time. In contrast, eventTimestamp is mapped to TemporalType.TIMESTAMP, preserving both the date and time information.

@Enumerated: The @Enumerated annotation is used to map Java enumeration types to a database. It can store either the enumeration's ordinal (integer value) or its name (string representation), depending on the specified EnumType.

```
import javax.persistence.Entity;
import javax.persistence.EnumType;
import javax.persistence.Enumerated;
import javax.persistence.GeneratedValue;
import javax.persistence.GenerationType;
import javax.persistence.Id;

@Entity
public class Task {

    public enum Status {
        PENDING, IN_PROGRESS, COMPLETED
    }

    @Id
    @GeneratedValue(strategy = GenerationType.IDENTITY)
    private Long id;

    @Enumerated(EnumType.STRING)
    private Status status;

    // Getters and setters
}
```

Here, the status field is annotated with @Enumerated(EnumType.STRING), which stores the enumeration name in the database. Alternatively, using EnumType.ORDINAL would store the ordinal value of the enumeration, which might save space but can be more error-prone if the enumeration definitions change.

Understanding how to correctly use these advanced attribute mappings—@Lob, @Temporal, and @Enumerated—ensures that complex data types are handled effectively and efficiently in JPA, enhancing the robustness and functionality of data persistence layers.

4.3 Mapping Composite Primary Keys: @IdClass and @EmbeddedId

Composite primary keys are employed when an entity's primary key comprises multiple fields. These composite keys are essential in various scenarios, such as mapping natural business keys, enforcing uniqueness across multiple columns, or when dealing with legacy databases. JPA provides two approaches for defining composite primary keys: the use of the @IdClass annotation and the @EmbeddedId annotation.

Using @IdClass: The @IdClass annotation allows entity classes to use a separate primary key class. This primary key class must be serializable and define a no-argument constructor. The primary key fields are specified within this class, and the entity class uses the @IdClass annotation to reference it.

Consider the following example of a Order entity that has a composite key consisting of orderId and productId.

```
import java.io.Serializable;
import javax.persistence.Column;
import javax.persistence.Entity;
import javax.persistence.Id;
import javax.persistence.IdClass;

@Entity
@IdClass(OrderId.class)
public class Order {

    @Id
    @Column(name = "order_id")
    private Long orderId;

    @Id
    @Column(name = "product_id")
    private Long productId;

    private int quantity;

    // Getters and Setters
}
```

The composite key class OrderId would be defined as follows:

```
import java.io.Serializable;
import java.util.Objects;

public class OrderId implements Serializable {

    private Long orderId;
    private Long productId;
```

```
    public OrderId() {}

    public OrderId(Long orderId, Long productId) {
        this.orderId = orderId;
        this.productId = productId;
    }

    @Override
    public boolean equals(Object o) {
        if (this == o) return true;
        if (o == null || getClass() != o.getClass()) return false;
        OrderId orderId1 = (OrderId) o;
        return Objects.equals(orderId, orderId1.orderId) && Objects.equals(productId,
            orderId1.productId);
    }

    @Override
    public int hashCode() {
        return Objects.hash(orderId, productId);
    }

    // Getters and Setters
}
```

In this setup, the Order class designates OrderId as the composite key class using the @IdClass annotation. The @Id annotation is used on the entity fields to mark them as part of the primary key. It is critical for the OrderId class to properly implement equals() and hashCode() methods to guarantee correct functionality within collections and JPA contexts.

Using @EmbeddedId: The @EmbeddedId annotation can be used to define the composite key directly within the entity as an embedded primary key. This embedded key class is also required to be serializable and must define a no-argument constructor.

The same Order entity example can be implemented using @EmbeddedId as follows:

```
import java.io.Serializable;
import javax.persistence.Column;
import javax.persistence.Embeddable;
import javax.persistence.EmbeddedId;
import javax.persistence.Entity;

@Entity
public class Order {

    @EmbeddedId
    private OrderId orderId;

    private int quantity;

    // Getters and Setters
}
```

With the embedded key class OrderId defined as follows:

```
import java.io.Serializable;
import java.util.Objects;
import javax.persistence.Column;
import javax.persistence.Embeddable;

@Embeddable
public class OrderId implements Serializable {

    @Column(name = "order_id")
    private Long orderId;

    @Column(name = "product_id")
    private Long productId;

    public OrderId() {}

    public OrderId(Long orderId, Long productId) {
        this.orderId = orderId;
        this.productId = productId;
    }

    @Override
    public boolean equals(Object o) {
        if (this == o) return true;
        if (o == null || getClass() != o.getClass()) return false;
        OrderId orderId1 = (OrderId) o;
        return Objects.equals(orderId, orderId1.orderId) && Objects.equals(productId,
               orderId1.productId);
    }

    @Override
    public int hashCode() {
        return Objects.hash(orderId, productId);
    }

    // Getters and Setters
}
```

In this scenario, OrderId is embedded directly within the Order entity using the @EmbeddedId annotation. This approach simplifies entity definitions by aggregating the primary key fields into a single object, making the code cleaner and easier to maintain.

Both approaches have their use-cases and choosing one over the other often depends on design preferences or specific requirements of the application. Employing the @IdClass annotation provides a straightforward mapping where primary key fields remain a part of the entity. On the other hand, @EmbeddedId encapsulates the key fields within an embeddable class, leading to a more coherent and encapsulated design.

4.4 Advanced Relationship Mappings: Bidirectional Relationships

Bidirectional relationships in JPA allow the entities to reference each other in both directions, enhancing navigational and querying capabilities. This section articulates the design and implementation techniques for creating and managing bidirectional relationships using annotations effectively, focusing on @OneToOne, @OneToMany, @ManyToOne, and @ManyToMany relationships.

- @OneToOne **Bidirectional Relationships:** A one-to-one relationship signifies that an entity is directly associated with a single instance of another entity. For instance, consider an example of a User entity and a Profile entity where each user has one profile, and each profile is associated with one user.

```
@Entity
public class User {
    @Id
    @GeneratedValue(strategy = GenerationType.IDENTITY)
    private Long id;

    @OneToOne(mappedBy = "user", cascade = CascadeType.ALL, orphanRemoval =
        true)
    private Profile profile;
    // other fields, getters and setters
}

@Entity
public class Profile {
    @Id
    @GeneratedValue(strategy = GenerationType.IDENTITY)
    private Long id;

    @OneToOne
    @JoinColumn(name = "user_id")
    private User user;
    // other fields, getters and setters
}
```

The mappedBy attribute is crucial in bidirectional relationships as it indicates that the Profile entity owns the association, implying that the User entity's mapping is subordinate. The cascade = CascadeType.ALL ensures that persist, merge, remove, refresh, and detach operations are cascaded to the associated entity. The orphanRemoval = true setting specifies that if a User entity is dissociated from the Profile, the Profile should be removed from the database.

- @OneToMany and @ManyToOne **Bidirectional Relationships:**

For an entity to be associated with multiple instances of another entity, the @OneToMany and @ManyToOne annotations come into play. Consider a Department entity that contains multiple Employee entities.

```
@Entity
public class Department {
    @Id
    @GeneratedValue(strategy = GenerationType.IDENTITY)
    private Long id;

    @OneToMany(mappedBy = "department", cascade = CascadeType.ALL,
        orphanRemoval = true)
    private List<Employee> employees = new ArrayList<>();
    // other fields, getters and setters
}

@Entity
public class Employee {
    @Id
    @GeneratedValue(strategy = GenerationType.IDENTITY)
    private Long id;

    @ManyToOne
    @JoinColumn(name = "department_id")
    private Department department;
    // other fields, getters and setters
}
```

In this scenario, the mappedBy attribute in the Department class indicates that the employees collection is mapped by the department attribute in the Employee class. Consequently, @ManyToOne within the Employee class points to the owning side of the relationship, establishing the link through the department_id foreign key column.

- @ManyToMany **Bidirectional Relationships:** When multiple entities can be associated with multiple instances of another entity, @ManyToMany relationships are employed. For instance, considering a Student entity and a Course entity where a student can enroll in multiple courses and a course can have multiple students.

```
@Entity
public class Student {
    @Id
    @GeneratedValue(strategy = GenerationType.IDENTITY)
    private Long id;

    @ManyToMany(mappedBy = "students")
    private Set<Course> courses = new HashSet<>();
    // other fields, getters and setters
}

@Entity
```

```
public class Course {
    @Id
    @GeneratedValue(strategy = GenerationType.IDENTITY)
    private Long id;

    @ManyToMany
    @JoinTable(
        name = "student_course",
        joinColumns = @JoinColumn(name = "course_id"),
        inverseJoinColumns = @JoinColumn(name = "student_id")
    )
    private Set<Student> students = new HashSet<>();
    // other fields, getters and setters
}
```

The @JoinTable annotation in the Course entity defines the join table that contains foreign keys mapping the Student and Course entities. The mappedBy attribute in the Student entity's courses collection references the students collection defined in the Course entity, firmly synchronizing the bidirectional relationship.

Bidirectional relationships necessitate careful consideration of cascading operations and orphan removal policies. Misconfigurations can lead to unintended deletions or persistence problems, emphasizing the importance of robust unit testing. Furthermore, while bidirectional relationships provide enhanced navigability and querying support, they can sometimes introduce complexity and performance overheads. Therefore, bidirectional mappings should be employed judiciously, balancing the requirements for data integrity and application performance.

4.5 Advanced Inheritance Mappings: @Inheritance and @DiscriminatorColumn

Inheritance in Java Persistence API (JPA) allows entities to be related through inheritance, leveraging object-oriented principles to model complex data hierarchies. The @Inheritance and @DiscriminatorColumn annotations facilitate mapping inheritance structures to database tables, enabling polymorphic queries and seamless data manipulation across entity subclasses. This section details the configurations and use cases for these annotations, ensuring a comprehensive understanding of advanced inheritance mappings.

The @Inheritance annotation can be applied at the entity class level to define the inheritance strategy. JPA offers three strategies: SINGLE_TABLE, JOINED, and TABLE_PER_CLASS. Each strategy has distinct advantages and trade-offs, which are elaborated below.

SINGLE TABLE Strategy

The SINGLE_TABLE strategy employs a single database table to hold all entity types within the inheritance hierarchy. A discriminator column, typically created using the @DiscriminatorColumn annotation, differentiates between entity types.

```
@Entity
@Inheritance(strategy = InheritanceType.SINGLE_TABLE)
@DiscriminatorColumn(name = "type", discriminatorType = DiscriminatorType.
    STRING)
public abstract class Vehicle {
    @Id
    private Long id;
    private String manufacturer;
    // getters and setters
}

@Entity
@DiscriminatorValue("Car")
public class Car extends Vehicle {
    private int numDoors;
    // getters and setters
}

@Entity
@DiscriminatorValue("Bike")
public class Bike extends Vehicle {
    private boolean isElectric;
    // getters and setters
}
```

The @DiscriminatorColumn annotation defines the discriminator column's name and type. The @DiscriminatorValue annotation specifies the value stored in the discriminator column to identify each entity type. The resulting table would include columns *id*, *manufacturer*, *numDoors*, *isElectric*, and *type*.

id	manufacturer	type	numDoors	isElectric
1	Ford	Car	4	null
2	Yamaha	Bike	null	true

This approach offers simplicity and performance benefits due to fewer joins being required for queries. However, it can lead to several null values in columns that are only applicable to specific subclasses.

JOINED Table Strategy

The JOINED strategy maps each entity class to its own table. The base class is represented by a table containing common attributes, and each subclass is stored in a separate table, including attributes specific to the subclass. This strategy allows for normalized data representation and avoids null columns.

```
@Entity
@Inheritance(strategy = InheritanceType.JOINED)
public abstract class Vehicle {
    @Id
    private Long id;
    private String manufacturer;
    // getters and setters
}

@Entity
public class Car extends Vehicle {
    private int numDoors;
    // getters and setters
}

@Entity
public class Bike extends Vehicle {
    private boolean isElectric;
    // getters and setters
}
```

The resulting table structure would consist of a *Vehicle* table and individual *Car* and *Bike* tables linked via primary key.

Vehicle Table:

id	manufacturer
1	Ford
2	Yamaha

Car Table:

id	numDoors
1	4

Bike Table:

id	isElectric
2	true

Queries against the inheritance hierarchy require joins between the tables, which could impact performance, especially as the number of entities grows.

TABLE PER CLASS Strategy

The TABLE_PER_CLASS strategy maps each concrete entity to its own table, with each table containing all inherited and subclass-specific fields. There is no discriminator column, and no table is created for the abstract base class.

```
@Entity
@Inheritance(strategy = InheritanceType.TABLE_PER_CLASS)
public abstract class Vehicle {
    @Id
    private Long id;
    private String manufacturer;
```

```
    // getters and setters
}

@Entity
public class Car extends Vehicle {
    private int numDoors;
    // getters and setters
}

@Entity
public class Bike extends Vehicle {
    private boolean isElectric;
    // getters and setters
}
```

Here, the *id* attribute serves as the primary key in each table, and each table independently holds its entity-specific attributes.

```
Car Table:
| id  | manufacturer | numDoors |
|-----|--------------|----------|
| 1   | Ford         | 4        |

Bike Table:
| id  | manufacturer | isElectric |
|-----|--------------|------------|
| 2   | Yamaha       | true       |
```

While this strategy avoids nullable columns and reduces complexity, it can result in duplication of schema definitions for common fields and complicates query operations that traverse the inheritance hierarchy.

By comprehensively understanding @Inheritance and @DiscriminatorColumn, JPA users can effectively model their domain data structures, balancing between performance, normalization, and complexity to meet their application's specific needs.

4.6 Entity Graphs: Defining and Using @NamedEntityGraph

The Java Persistence API (JPA) provides mechanisms to define and use entity graphs for controlling entity fetching strategies. An entity graph specifies a blueprint of entities and their attributes to be fetched during a query. This feature is particularly beneficial for performance optimization, as it minimizes the number of queries and the amount of data transferred by explicitly defining which associations should be eagerly loaded.

Defining an Entity Graph

An entity graph can be defined using the @NamedEntityGraph annotation, which can be placed on an entity class. The @NamedEntityGraph annotation accepts several parameters including name, attributeNodes, and subgraphs. It is essential to precisely define an entity graph reflecting the necessary associations and fields required for a given operation.

Consider an example entity class, Order, which has a many-to-one relationship to Customer and a one-to-many relationship with OrderItem:

```
@Entity
@NamedEntityGraph(
    name = "Order.withCustomerAndItems",
    attributeNodes = {
        @NamedAttributeNode("customer"),
        @NamedAttributeNode(value = "items", subgraph = "itemsGraph")
    },
    subgraphs = {
        @NamedSubgraph(
            name = "itemsGraph",
            attributeNodes = {
                @NamedAttributeNode("product")
            }
        )
    }
)
public class Order {
    @Id
    private Long id;

    @ManyToOne
    private Customer customer;

    @OneToMany(mappedBy = "order")
    private List<OrderItem> items;

    // Getters and setters omitted for brevity
}
```

In the above example, the entity graph named Order.withCustomerAndItems instructs the JPA provider to fetch the customer and items attributes eagerly whenever this graph is applied. Additionally, within the items attribute, the product attribute of OrderItem is also eagerly fetched through the subgraph mechanism.

Using an Entity Graph in Queries

Once an entity graph is defined, it can be utilized in JPA queries to fetch the entities and their associations based on the graph definition. The EntityManager interface provides methods to specify the entity graph during query construction.

Below is an example of how to use the previously defined entity graph in a JPQL query:

```
EntityManager em = ...; // Obtain EntityManager instance
EntityGraph<?> entityGraph = em.createEntityGraph("Order.withCustomerAndItems
    ");

TypedQuery<Order> query = em.createQuery("SELECT o FROM Order o WHERE o.
    id = :id", Order.class);
query.setParameter("id", 1L);
query.setHint("javax.persistence.loadgraph", entityGraph);

Order order = query.getSingleResult();
```

Here, the entity graph Order.withCustomerAndItems is applied to the query through the javax.persistence.loadgraph hint. This instructs the JPA provider to follow the fetching strategy outlined in the entity graph when executing the query.

Differences between fetchgraph and loadgraph

JPA distinguishes between two types of graph hints: fetchgraph and loadgraph.

- **fetchgraph**: When this hint is used, attributes specified in the entity graph are treated as EAGER, and all other attributes are treated as LAZY.
- **loadgraph**: When this hint is used, attributes specified in the entity graph are treated as EAGER, and other attributes follow the default fetch type defined in the entity's mapping.

In practical use, loadgraph is generally more flexible since it respects the default fetch strategies for unspecified attributes. The following example demonstrates the use of the fetchgraph hint:

```
TypedQuery<Order> query = em.createQuery("SELECT o FROM Order o WHERE o.
    id = :id", Order.class);
query.setParameter("id", 1L);
query.setHint("javax.persistence.fetchgraph", entityGraph);

Order order = query.getSingleResult();
```

This behavior ensures that only the attributes described in the entity graph are eagerly fetched, making fetchgraph advantageous when strict control over fetch behavior is necessary.

Programmatic Definition of Entity Graphs

In addition to annotations, entity graphs can be defined programmatically using the EntityManager's createEntityGraph method. This approach offers dynamic flexibility when the entity graph configuration needs to vary based on runtime conditions.

Below is an example demonstrating the programmatic creation of an entity graph:

```
EntityGraph<Order> entityGraph = em.createEntityGraph(Order.class);
entityGraph.addAttributeNodes("customer");
entityGraph.addSubgraph("items").addAttributeNodes("product");

TypedQuery<Order> query = em.createQuery("SELECT o FROM Order o WHERE o.
    id = :id", Order.class);
query.setParameter("id", 1L);
query.setHint("javax.persistence.loadgraph", entityGraph);

Order order = query.getSingleResult();
```

The above example illustrates creating an entity graph for the Order entity and adding attribute nodes for customer and items. A subgraph is added to explicitly include the product attribute within items. This constructed entity graph is then applied to the query using the javax.persistence.loadgraph hint.

Utilization Scenarios

Entity graphs are particularly useful in scenarios requiring fine-grained control over fetching strategies, such as:

- Reducing N+1 select problem by explicitly specifying associations to be fetched in a single query.
- Optimizing performance for complex queries where specific associations need to be eagerly loaded.
- Implementing different fetching strategies for various use cases within the same entity class.

Effectively defining and using entity graphs can substantially improve the performance and efficiency of data retrieval operations, making them a powerful tool in the JPA toolkit. Properly leveraging entity graphs can lead to more maintainable code by keeping fetching logic encapsulated in a single, reusable definition.

4.7 Using Secondary Tables: @SecondaryTable and @PrimaryKeyJoinColumn

Secondary tables in JPA provide a mechanism to split entity information across multiple tables. This is often necessary in scenarios where different columns of an entity should be stored in different tables, either for performance reasons or due to legacy database designs. When an entity spans multiple tables, the @SecondaryTable annotation is used in conjunction with the @PrimaryKeyJoinColumn annotation to define the primary key relationship between these tables.

The @SecondaryTable annotation allows you to specify the secondary table and the mapping of the primary key column. This works in tandem with the primary table (usually defined by the @Table annotation or by default the table named after the entity). To demonstrate the use of secondary tables, consider an example with an entity named Employee, spanning two tables: employee and employee_details.

The employee table stores basic employee information such as id, first_name, and last_name, while the employee_details table contains additional employee details such as address and phone_number. Here is how you can define this entity in JPA:

```
import javax.persistence.Entity;
import javax.persistence.Id;
import javax.persistence.Column;
import javax.persistence.SecondaryTable;
import javax.persistence.PrimaryKeyJoinColumn;
import javax.persistence.Table;

@Entity
@Table(name = "employee")
@SecondaryTable(name = "employee_details",
            pkJoinColumns = @PrimaryKeyJoinColumn(name = "emp_id"))
public class Employee {

    @Id
    @Column(name = "id")
    private Long id;

    @Column(name = "first_name")
    private String firstName;

    @Column(name = "last_name")
    private String lastName;

    @Column(table = "employee_details", name = "address")
    private String address;

    @Column(table = "employee_details", name = "phone_number")
    private String phoneNumber;

    // Getters and setters
}
```

In this example, the @SecondaryTable annotation specifies that the employee_details table is a secondary table for the Employee entity. The pkJoinColumns element defines the joining columns between the primary table (employee) and the secondary table (employee_details).

Specifically, it specifies that the emp_id column in the employee_details table is the foreign key that references the id column in the employee table.

The @Column annotations with the table attribute indicate that the address and phone_number fields are stored in the employee_details table.

Consider the following SQL script used to create these tables:

```
CREATE TABLE employee (
    id BIGINT NOT NULL,
    first_name VARCHAR(50),
    last_name VARCHAR(50),
    PRIMARY KEY (id)
);

CREATE TABLE employee_details (
    emp_id BIGINT NOT NULL,
    address VARCHAR(255),
    phone_number VARCHAR(20),
    PRIMARY KEY (emp_id),
    FOREIGN KEY (emp_id) REFERENCES employee(id)
);
```

When persisting an Employee entity, JPA will handle the insertion of data across these tables seamlessly:

```
EntityManagerFactory emf = Persistence.createEntityManagerFactory("example-unit");
EntityManager em = emf.createEntityManager();
EntityTransaction tx = em.getTransaction();

tx.begin();
Employee employee = new Employee();
employee.setId(1L);
employee.setFirstName("John");
employee.setLastName("Doe");
employee.setAddress("1234 Elm Street");
employee.setPhoneNumber("555-1234");

em.persist(employee);
tx.commit();

em.close();
emf.close();
```

The corresponding SQL output might look like:

```
INSERT INTO employee (id, first_name, last_name) VALUES (1, 'John', 'Doe');
INSERT INTO employee_details (emp_id, address, phone_number) VALUES (1, '1234 Elm Street', '555-1234');
```

In addition to splitting data across multiple tables, secondary tables also support more advanced configurations. For example, you can define multiple secondary tables for a single entity:

```
@Entity
@Table(name = "employee")
@SecondaryTables({
```

```
    @SecondaryTable(name = "employee_details",
                    pkJoinColumns = @PrimaryKeyJoinColumn(name = "emp_id")),
    @SecondaryTable(name = "employee_salary",
                    pkJoinColumns = @PrimaryKeyJoinColumn(name = "emp_id"))
})
public class Employee {

    @Id
    @Column(name = "id")
    private Long id;

    @Column(name = "first_name")
    private String firstName;

    @Column(name = "last_name")
    private String lastName;

    @Column(table = "employee_details", name = "address")
    private String address;

    @Column(table = "employee_details", name = "phone_number")
    private String phoneNumber;

    @Column(table = "employee_salary", name = "salary")
    private BigDecimal salary;

    // Getters and setters
}
```

This configuration specifies that the Employee entity spans three tables: employee, employee_details, and employee_salary. The pkJoinColumns attribute ensures proper linkage among the tables based on their primary keys.

Understanding and utilizing secondary tables can greatly enhance your capacity to manage and organize complex data structures in JPA. By leveraging annotations like @SecondaryTable and @PrimaryKeyJoinColumn, you can efficiently map an entity to multiple tables, adhering to both design and performance considerations.

4.8 Optimistic Locking: @Version

Optimistic locking is a concurrency control mechanism used to prevent conflicting updates in a multi-user environment without the use of database locks. The principle behind optimistic locking is that conflicts between concurrent transactions are rare, so transactions can proceed without locking resources. The JPA implementation detects conflicts at the time of the transaction commit by verifying that no other transaction has modified the data since it was read. This verification is implemented in JPA using the @Version annotation.

The @Version annotation is applied to a field in an entity class, which serves as the version control attribute. This field is incremented every time an update is made to the entity. If a conflicting update by another transaction is detected during the commit, an OptimisticLockException is thrown.

```
@Entity
public class Product {
    @Id
    @GeneratedValue(strategy = GenerationType.IDENTITY)
    private Long id;

    private String name;
    private BigDecimal price;

    @Version
    private int version;

    // Getters and Setters
}
```

In this example, the Product entity has a version field annotated with @Version. Each time the Product entity is updated, the version field is automatically incremented. When an update transaction is about to be committed, JPA checks the version field to ensure it matches the version in the database. If the versions do not match, it indicates that another transaction has modified the entity, and thus, an OptimisticLockException is raised.

Consider two transactions attempting to update the same Product entity concurrently:

1. Transaction A reads a Product entity with version 1. 2. Transaction B reads the same Product entity (version 1). 3. Transaction A updates the Product entity and commits the transaction, incrementing the version to 2. 4. Transaction B attempts to update the Product entity and commit the transaction. Since the version in Transaction B (version 1) does not match the current version in the database (version 2), JPA raises an OptimisticLockException.

The versioning mechanism ensures data consistency without locking resources. If a conflict is detected, the application can choose to retry the transaction or take alternative measures to resolve the conflict.

To illustrate this, let's look at a possible service layer implementation that handles optimistic locking.

```
@Service
public class ProductService {

    @Autowired
```

```
    private ProductRepository productRepository;

    @Transactional
    public void updateProductPrice(Long productId, BigDecimal newPrice) {
        try {
            Product product = productRepository.findById(productId)
                                    .orElseThrow(() -> new EntityNotFoundException("
                                        Product not found"));
            product.setPrice(newPrice);
            productRepository.save(product);
        } catch (OptimisticLockException e) {
            // Handle the optimistic locking failure
            throw new ConcurrentModificationException("The product was concurrently
                    modified", e);
        }
    }
}
```

In this service layer, we attempt to update a product's price. If an OptimisticLockException is caught, it throws a ConcurrentModificationException, providing a mechanism to inform the caller about the conflict. Handling such exceptions gracefully is crucial for making applications robust in concurrent environments.

Let's demonstrate the corresponding transactional actions and the generated SQL for optimistic locking:

1. Transaction A reads the product:

```
SELECT id, name, price, version FROM product WHERE id = 1

id  | name       | price | version
----|------------|-------|--------
1   | Widget     | 10.00 | 1
```

2. Transaction B reads the same product:

```
SELECT id, name, price, version FROM product WHERE id = 1
```

3. Transaction A updates and commits the product:

```
UPDATE product SET price = 12.00, version = version + 1 WHERE id = 1 AND version = 1
```

4. Transaction B attempts to update and commit the product:

```
UPDATE product SET price = 11.00, version = version + 1 WHERE id = 1 AND version = 1

- This statement fails as version = 1 no longer matches the current version.
```

The efficiency of optimistic locking makes it suitable for applications where the likelihood of concurrent updates to the same entity is relatively low. However, in scenarios with high contention, it may lead to frequent conflicts that need resolution.

While optimistic locking provides a robust and lightweight mechanism for consistency, understanding its nuances and handling potential conflicts ensures data integrity and a smooth user experience in concurrent operations.

4.9 Concurrency Control with Pessimistic Locking: @Lock

Concurrency control is a critical aspect of database management systems, ensuring that concurrent transactions can execute without leading to inconsistent data states. The pessimistic locking mechanism provided in Java Persistence API (JPA) is vital for scenarios where the risk of concurrent data modification conflicts is high.

In pessimistic locking, the database prevents other transactions from accessing the locked data until the current transaction is completed. This mechanism uses explicit locks applied to the database rows, tables, or other structures being accessed. JPA's @Lock annotation is utilized to facilitate pessimistic locks within the entity manager.

Pessimistic Locking Types

JPA defines three types of pessimistic locks, which can be specified using the javax.persistence.LockModeType enumeration:

- PESSIMISTIC_READ: Acquires a shared lock on the data. Other transactions can read the data but cannot modify it until the lock is released.
- PESSIMISTIC_WRITE: Acquires an exclusive lock on the data. Other transactions cannot read or modify the data until the lock is released.
- PESSIMISTIC_FORCE_INCREMENT: Similar to PESSIMISTIC_WRITE, but additionally increments the version attribute of the entity, forcing other transactions to reload the entity.

Usage of @Lock Annotation

The @Lock annotation can be applied to queries at both the method and the entity manager level to specify the desired locking type. Below is an example illustrating the use of @Lock in a repository method:

```
@Entity
public class Product {
```

```
    @Id
    @GeneratedValue(strategy = GenerationType.IDENTITY)
    private Long id;

    private String name;
    private int quantity;

    // Getters and setters
}

public interface ProductRepository extends JpaRepository<Product, Long> {

    @Lock(LockModeType.PESSIMISTIC_WRITE)
    @Query("SELECT p FROM Product p WHERE p.id = :id")
    Product findProductByIdPessimisticWrite(@Param("id") Long id);
}
```

This example indicates that the Product entity should be locked with a pessimistic write lock when accessed by the findProductByIdPessimisticWrite method.

Programmatic Locking

In addition to using the @Lock annotation, JPA also allows for programmatic locking via the EntityManager.lock method. This is useful when dynamic lock usage is required. Below is an example demonstrating how to acquire a pessimistic lock programmatically:

```
EntityManager em = entityManagerFactory.createEntityManager();
em.getTransaction().begin();

try {
    Product product = em.find(Product.class, 1L, LockModeType.
        PESSIMISTIC_WRITE);
    product.setQuantity(product.getQuantity() - 1);
    em.persist(product);

    em.getTransaction().commit();
} catch (Exception e) {
    em.getTransaction().rollback();
    throw e;
} finally {
    em.close();
}
```

In this example, a PESSIMISTIC_WRITE lock is acquired on the Product entity with ID 1L, ensuring exclusive access until the transaction completes.

Considerations and Best Practices

Pessimistic locking should be used judiciously as it can lead to deadlocks and reduced concurrency. Transactions holding locks should be committed or rolled back promptly to minimize lock contention and resource blocking.

- Ensure that locks are held for the shortest duration necessary. - Avoid long-running transactions when using pessimistic locks. - Use the appropriate pessimistic lock type based on the operation requirements (read or write conflict prevention). - Monitor and manage locking strategies to prevent deadlocks.

Deadlocks occur when multiple transactions are waiting indefinitely for each other to release locks. Proper transactional boundaries and locking order can minimize the occurrence of deadlocks.

Optimizations and Handling Lock Timeouts

Timeouts can be specified to manage how long a transaction should wait to acquire a lock. This minimizes the impact of lock contention by aborting attempts that take too long. JPA allows setting lock timeouts through query hints. Below is an example:

```
Map<String, Object> properties = new HashMap<>();
properties.put("javax.persistence.lock.timeout", 3000);

EntityManager em = entityManagerFactory.createEntityManager();
em.getTransaction().begin();

try {
    Product product = em.find(Product.class, 1L, LockModeType.
          PESSIMISTIC_WRITE, properties);
    product.setQuantity(product.getQuantity() - 1);
    em.persist(product);

    em.getTransaction().commit();
} catch (Exception e) {
    em.getTransaction().rollback();
    throw e;
} finally {
    em.close();
}
```

In this scenario, the transaction will wait for up to 3000 milliseconds (3 seconds) to acquire a lock before timing out. This facilitates controlled resource allocation and improves overall system responsiveness.

By effectively managing pessimistic locks, JPA applications can ensure data integrity in concurrent environments, albeit with careful consideration of performance and potential deadlocks.

4.10 Mapping and Using Collection Types

In Java Persistence API (JPA), handling collection types is essential for representing various relationships and aggregations within entity classes. JPA provides robust mechanisms to map collections such as List, Set, Map, and Collection. These collection types can be either basic types or entity types. Properly mapping collections enables efficient and effective data retrieval and manipulation, ensuring that relationships are consistently maintained in the database.

Collection Mappings: When mapping collections, it is crucial to understand the associated JPA annotations and their implications. The most frequently used annotations for collection mappings include @OneToMany, @ManyToMany, and @ElementCollection. Each annotation serves a different purpose and is tailored to the specific type of relationship or collection being handled.

@OneToMany is used to define a one-to-many relationship between two entities, where one entity can relate to multiple instances of another entity. For example, consider an Order entity that can have multiple OrderItems.

```
@Entity
public class Order {

    @Id
    private Long id;

    @OneToMany(mappedBy = "order", cascade = CascadeType.ALL, orphanRemoval
         = true)
    private List<OrderItem> orderItems;

    // getters and setters
}

@Entity
public class OrderItem {

    @Id
    private Long id;

    @ManyToOne
    @JoinColumn(name = "order_id")
    private Order order;

    // getters and setters
}
```

@ManyToMany defines a many-to-many relationship between entities, where each entity can relate to multiple instances of the other entity. It is common to use a join table to manage such relationships. For example, consider a Student entity and a Course entity where students can enroll in multiple courses and courses can have multiple students.

```
@Entity
public class Student {
```

```
    @Id
    private Long id;

    @ManyToMany
    @JoinTable(name = "student_course",
            joinColumns = @JoinColumn(name = "student_id"),
            inverseJoinColumns = @JoinColumn(name = "course_id"))
    private List<Course> courses;

    // getters and setters
}

@Entity
public class Course {

    @Id
    private Long id;

    @ManyToMany(mappedBy = "courses")
    private List<Student> students;

    // getters and setters
}
```

@ElementCollection is used for mapping collections of basic or embeddable types. This is particularly useful when storing a collection of values that are not entities but still need to be part of an entity's state. For example, consider an Employee entity that stores a collection of phone numbers.

```
@Entity
public class Employee {

    @Id
    private Long id;

    @ElementCollection
    @CollectionTable(name = "employee_phone", joinColumns = @JoinColumn(name
        = "employee_id"))
    @Column(name = "phone_number")
    private List<String> phoneNumbers;

    // getters and setters
}
```

Handling Collections Efficiently: Efficient collection handling involves understanding and applying the appropriate fetch strategies provided by JPA. The FetchType can be either EAGER or LAZY.

LAZY fetching is typically preferred for large collections, as it avoids unnecessary loading of data until it is explicitly accessed. For instance, in the Order and OrderItem example, the fetching could be defined as:

```
@Entity
public class Order {

    @Id
```

```
    private Long id;

    @OneToMany(mappedBy = "order", fetch = FetchType.LAZY, cascade =
         CascadeType.ALL, orphanRemoval = true)
    private List<OrderItem> orderItems;

    // getters and setters
}
```

EAGER fetching can be beneficial for smaller collections or when immediate access to the entire collection is required.

```
@Entity
public class Student {

    @Id
    private Long id;

    @ManyToMany(fetch = FetchType.EAGER)
    @JoinTable(name = "student_course",
              joinColumns = @JoinColumn(name = "student_id"),
              inverseJoinColumns = @JoinColumn(name = "course_id"))
    private List<Course> courses;

    // getters and setters
}
```

Best Practices in Collection Mappings: The design and mapping of collections should adhere to several best practices to ensure optimal performance and maintainability. These include:

- Carefully choosing between LAZY and EAGER fetching based on the context and expected usage patterns.
- Using the appropriate collection interface (List, Set, etc.) to reflect the type of data and required operations.
- Managing cascading operations responsibly with CascadeType, particularly for orphan removal or dependent entity lifecycle management.
- Considering the use of join tables for ManyToMany relationships to avoid excessive data duplication and complexity.
- Leveraging the power of JPA Criteria API or JPQL for advanced queries involving collections to maintain efficient data retrieval.

Example of Advanced Collection Query using JPQL:

```
@Entity
public class Library {
```

```
    @Id
    private Long id;

    @OneToMany(mappedBy = "library", fetch = FetchType.LAZY, cascade =
        CascadeType.ALL)
    private Set<Book> books;

    // getters and setters
}

@Entity
public class Book {

    @Id
    private Long id;

    @ManyToOne
    @JoinColumn(name = "library_id")
    private Library library;

    private String title;

    // getters and setters
}

public List<Library> findLibrariesWithBookTitle(EntityManager em, String title) {
    TypedQuery<Library> query = em.createQuery(
        "SELECT l FROM Library l JOIN l.books b WHERE b.title = :title", Library.
            class);
    query.setParameter("title", title);
    return query.getResultList();
}
```

This example demonstrates how one can leverage JPQL to query entities with specific collection elements, enhancing the interaction and data manipulation within JPA.

By comprehensively understanding the above concepts, developers can effectively map and manage collection types in JPA, ensuring that relationships between entities are expressed accurately and efficiently within the database.

Chapter 5

Querying with JPQL and Criteria API

This chapter provides an in-depth look at querying in JPA using JPQL (Java Persistence Query Language) and the Criteria API. It covers the basics of JPQL, including SELECT, WHERE, and ORDER BY clauses, as well as functions and expressions. The chapter also discusses using named queries with @NamedQuery and @NamedQueries, and parameter binding in JPQL. Dynamic query creation with JPQL is explored, followed by an introduction to the Criteria API for building queries programmatically. It concludes with advanced topics like creating complex queries using Criteria API and combining both JPQL and Criteria API in applications.

5.1 Introduction to Querying in JPA

Understanding how to interact with the database using Java Persistence API (JPA) is a foundational aspect of modern enterprise Java applications. JPA abstracts the complexities of data access, allowing developers to write database operations in a domain-driven, object-oriented manner. This section provides a comprehensive introduction to querying in JPA, setting the stage for more advanced topics discussed later in this chapter.

JPA offers several mechanisms to query and manipulate data. The three most prominent are JPQL (Java Persistence Query Language), the Criteria API, and native SQL queries. Each of these has its strengths and use cases, catering to different needs within an application.

JPQL is a powerful query language similar to SQL (Structured Query Language) but designed specifically for JPA. Unlike SQL, which directly operates on relational database tables, JPQL operates on the entity objects defined within JPA. This makes JPQL both expressive and intuitive for Java developers, as it eliminates the impedance mismatch between object-oriented application code and relational data models.

Criteria API offers a type-safe way to construct queries programmatically. As it is built on top of JPQL, any JPQL construct can be expressed using the Criteria API. The primary advantage of the Criteria API is that it allows for dynamic query construction. This is particularly useful for complex queries that need to be built based on runtime conditions.

There are scenarios where neither JPQL nor the Criteria API suffices, especially when dealing with database-specific features or performance optimizations. In such cases, JPA allows for **native SQL queries**, enabling developers to execute plain SQL queries directly.

To execute queries in JPA, we typically work with the EntityManager, which is the primary interface for interacting with the persistence context. The EntityManager provides methods to create and execute both JPQL and native SQL queries.

Here is a basic example of using the EntityManager to execute a JPQL query:

```
@Entity
public class Employee {
    @Id
    private Long id;
    private String name;
    private Double salary;
    // getters and setters
}

EntityManager em = entityManagerFactory.createEntityManager();
List<Employee> employees = em.createQuery("SELECT e FROM Employee e",
      Employee.class).getResultList();
```

This example demonstrates a simple SELECT query that retrieves all employees from the database. JPQL syntax is similar to SQL, but it operates on the Employee entity rather than a database table.

Parameters can be bound to queries to make them more dynamic and reusable. Consider the following example, which finds employees by their name:

```
String jpql = "SELECT e FROM Employee e WHERE e.name = :name";
TypedQuery<Employee> query = em.createQuery(jpql, Employee.class);
query.setParameter("name", "John Doe");
List<Employee> employees = query.getResultList();
```

By using the setParameter method, the query dynamically binds the name parameter, demonstrating a basic form of parameter binding in JPQL.

The Criteria API is more verbose but offers a type-safe, programmatic way to build queries. Below is an example equivalent to the previous JPQL query using the Criteria API:

```
CriteriaBuilder cb = em.getCriteriaBuilder();
CriteriaQuery<Employee> cq = cb.createQuery(Employee.class);
Root<Employee> employee = cq.from(Employee.class);
cq.select(employee).where(cb.equal(employee.get("name"), "John Doe"));
TypedQuery<Employee> query = em.createQuery(cq);
List<Employee> employees = query.getResultList();
```

This example illustrates the steps to build and execute a Criteria query. The CriteriaBuilder constructs the various parts of the query, ensuring type safety at compile time.

In scenarios where JPQL and Criteria API cannot achieve the desired result, native SQL queries come into play. Here's an example of executing a native SQL query through JPA:

```
String sql = "SELECT * FROM employee WHERE name = 'John Doe'";
Query query = em.createNativeQuery(sql, Employee.class);
List<Employee> employees = query.getResultList();
```

This example uses a SQL query directly against the database, bypassing the abstraction provided by JPQL and Criteria API. Native queries are useful for leveraging database-specific features or optimizations that are not abstracted by JPA.

The versatility and flexibility provided by JPQL, Criteria API, and native SQL queries make JPA a powerful tool for data access in Java applications. The following sections will delve deeper into each of these querying mechanisms, offering detailed explanations and advanced examples to equip you with the expertise to utilize JPA effectively in real-world scenarios.

5.2 Understanding JPQL: Java Persistence Query Language

Java Persistence Query Language (JPQL) is a platform-independent query language used in the Java Persistence API (JPA) for retrieving objects from a relational database. While it resembles SQL in many ways, JPQL operates on the object-oriented entities and relationships defined in a JPA application rather than directly on database tables. This section aims to elucidate the syntax and semantics of JPQL, offering readers a robust understanding of how to formulate queries that interact with the underlying database through the JPA entities.

JPQL allows developers to craft queries from the entity model, which translates into SQL queries executed against the relational database. An entity in the JPA context refers to a lightweight, persistent domain object. JPQL abstracts the complexity of raw SQL queries, making the querying process more intuitive and aligned with the domain model of the application.

Basic JPQL syntax mirrors SQL but with significant differences in how entities and their attributes are referenced. For instance, consider a typical entity class in JPA:

```
@Entity
public class Employee {
    @Id
    private Long id;
    private String name;
    private Double salary;

    // Getters and setters omitted for brevity
}
```

To query all employees with a salary greater than a certain amount using JPQL, the query would look as follows:

```
SELECT e FROM Employee e WHERE e.salary > :salary
```

Here, Employee is the entity name, e is the alias for the entity, and e.salary refers to the salary attribute of the Employee entity. Unlike SQL, JPQL works with the entity model directly.

Key Components of JPQL

Several key components constitute the JPQL syntax that is crucial for formulating queries:

- **Entity Names:** JPQL queries use entity names defined in the JPA context rather than database table names. For the Employee entity, the JPQL query references Employee and not the underlying table in the database.

- **Select Clause:** The SELECT clause specifies the entities or entity attributes to be retrieved. For example:

```
SELECT e.name FROM Employee e
```

retrieves only the name attribute of each Employee.

- **Where Clause:** The WHERE clause filters results based on specified conditions. Conditions can be constructed using entity attributes and various supported operators (=, >, <, LIKE, etc.).

- **Order By Clause:** The ORDER BY clause specifies the ordering of the query results. For example, to retrieve employees ordered by their name:

```
SELECT e FROM Employee e ORDER BY e.name
```

JPQL Functions and Expressions

JPQL supports several built-in functions and expressions for operations analogous to SQL. Some commonly used functions include:

- CONCAT: Concatenates two strings. - UPPER, LOWER: Converts the case of a string. - LENGTH: Returns the length of a string.

Expressions enhance querying by providing the ability to perform operations on entity attributes. For instance:

```
SELECT e FROM Employee e WHERE UPPER(e.name) = 'JOHN DOE'
```

Combines the UPPER function to ensure the comparison is case-insensitive.

Joins in JPQL

Like SQL, JPQL supports joins but based on entity relationships rather than foreign key constraints. Suppose the Employee entity has a relationship with a Department entity:

```
@Entity
public class Department {
    @Id
    private Long id;
    private String name;

    @OneToMany(mappedBy = "department")
    private List<Employee> employees;
```

```
    // Getters and setters omitted for brevity
}

@Entity
public class Employee {
    @Id
    private Long id;
    private String name;
    private Double salary;

    @ManyToOne
    @JoinColumn(name = "department_id")
    private Department department;

    // Getters and setters omitted for brevity
}
```

To retrieve employees along with their department names, a JPQL join is used:

```
SELECT e.name, d.name FROM Employee e JOIN e.department d
```

Named Queries

JPQL queries can be statically defined through the @NamedQuery annotation for repeated use, improving code readability and performance:

```
@Entity
@NamedQuery(name = "Employee.findAll",
            query = "SELECT e FROM Employee e")
public class Employee {
    @Id
    private Long id;
    private String name;
    private Double salary;

    // Getters and setters omitted for brevity
}
```

With the above definition, the named query Employee.findAll can be reused across different parts of the application.

Parameter Binding in JPQL

JPQL supports both positional and named parameter binding for injecting parameters into queries safely. Named parameters (:parameterName) are preferred for their readability:

```
SELECT e FROM Employee e WHERE e.salary > :salary
```

Positional parameters use question marks and positions starting from one:

```
SELECT e FROM Employee e WHERE e.salary > ?1
```

To set parameter values dynamically, the setParameter method is used:

```
Query query = entityManager.createQuery("SELECT e FROM Employee e WHERE e.
    salary > :salary");
query.setParameter("salary", 50000);
List<Employee> employees = query.getResultList();
```

This thorough examination into the core aspects of JPQL equips readers with the necessary skills to efficiently query JPA entities, leveraging an object-oriented approach to handle the intricacies of database interactions.

5.3 Basic JPQL Queries: SELECT, WHERE, ORDER BY

The Java Persistence Query Language (JPQL) is a powerful query language designed for working with data in the context of Java Persistence API (JPA). It allows developers to interact with the database in an object-oriented manner, making use of entity classes rather than directly dealing with database tables. This section delves into the foundational elements of JPQL, specifically focusing on the SELECT, WHERE, and ORDER BY clauses.

The SELECT clause forms the core of retrieving data in JPQL. It specifies the entity attributes or objects that should be returned from the query. Below is a basic example of a SELECT query that fetches all rows from the Employee entity:

```
String jpql = "SELECT e FROM Employee e";
TypedQuery<Employee> query = entityManager.createQuery(jpql, Employee.class);
List<Employee> results = query.getResultList();
```

In this example, the query retrieves all instances of the Employee entity. The result is stored in a list of Employee objects.

The WHERE clause applies conditions to filter the results returned by the SELECT clause. The WHERE clause can use different types of expressions and functions to achieve precise filtering. For instance, the following query retrieves Employee entities that have a salary greater than a specified amount:

```
String jpql = "SELECT e FROM Employee e WHERE e.salary > :minSalary";
TypedQuery<Employee> query = entityManager.createQuery(jpql, Employee.class);
query.setParameter("minSalary", 50000);
List<Employee> results = query.getResultList();
```

Here, :minSalary is a named parameter that the query uses to filter employees based on their salary. The setParameter method binds the value 50000 to :minSalary.

Suppose multiple conditions need to be applied. In that case, the WHERE clause can incorporate logical operators such as AND and OR. For example, to find employees with a salary greater than 50000 and a department ID of 10:

```
String jpql = "SELECT e FROM Employee e WHERE e.salary > :minSalary AND e.
    department.id = :deptId";
TypedQuery<Employee> query = entityManager.createQuery(jpql, Employee.class);
query.setParameter("minSalary", 50000);
query.setParameter("deptId", 10);
List<Employee> results = query.getResultList();
```

The final key element in basic JPQL queries covered here is the ORDER BY clause. This clause is used to sort the query results based on one or more entity attributes. Sorting can be performed in ascending (ASC) or descending (DESC) order. Consider the following example, which retrieves all Employee entities and sorts them by salary in descending order:

```
String jpql = "SELECT e FROM Employee e ORDER BY e.salary DESC";
TypedQuery<Employee> query = entityManager.createQuery(jpql, Employee.class);
List<Employee> results = query.getResultList();
```

In cases where multiple sorting criteria are required, the ORDER BY clause can include multiple attributes. For example, to sort employees first by department ID in ascending order and then by salary in descending order:

```
String jpql = "SELECT e FROM Employee e ORDER BY e.department.id ASC, e.
    salary DESC";
TypedQuery<Employee> query = entityManager.createQuery(jpql, Employee.class);
List<Employee> results = query.getResultList();
```

To summarize these basic JPQL commands, the SELECT clause allows for data retrieval, the WHERE clause enables filtering, and the ORDER BY clause provides sorting capabilities. Each of these components can be combined to form more complex queries tailored to specific data retrieval needs within a JPA-managed application. Through leveraging these foundational JPQL constructs, developers can efficiently query and manipulate entity data in a type-safe manner.

5.4 JPQL Functions and Expressions

In Java Persistence Query Language (JPQL), functions and expressions play a critical role in constructing queries that are both flexible and powerful. This section explores various built-in functions provided by JPQL and illustrates their application in filtering, transforming, and aggregating data efficiently.

JPQL includes a variety of standard functions that are similar to those found in SQL. These functions can be categorized into several groups, including string functions, numeric functions, date-time functions, and others such as null-related functions. Detailed understanding of each category facilitates the construction of sophisticated queries.

String Functions

String functions are used for operations on string data. The following are some of the most commonly used string functions in JPQL:

- CONCAT(string1, string2): Concatenates two strings.
- SUBSTRING(string, start, length): Extracts a substring from a given string starting at a specified position and of a specified length.
- TRIM([LEADING/TRAILING/BOTH] [character] FROM string): Removes leading, trailing, or both leading and trailing characters from a string. If no character is specified, whitespace is trimmed.
- LOWER(string): Converts a string to lowercase.
- UPPER(string): Converts a string to uppercase.
- LENGTH(string): Returns the length of a string.
- LOCATE(substring, string[, start]): Returns the position of the first occurrence of a substring in a string, optionally starting from a specified position.

Example Usage of String Functions

Consider the following entity definition for illustration:

```
@Entity
public class Employee {
    @Id
```

```
    private Long id;
    private String firstName;
    private String lastName;
    private String email;
    // getters and setters
}
```

To concatenate the first name and last name of employees, one can use the CONCAT function as shown:

```
TypedQuery<String> query = em.createQuery(
    "SELECT CONCAT(e.firstName, ' ', e.lastName) FROM Employee e", String.class);

List<String> fullNames = query.getResultList();
```

This query concatenates the firstName and lastName fields of the Employee entity, separated by a space.

Numeric Functions

JPQL also supports several numeric functions, including:

- ABS(number): Returns the absolute value of a number.
- SQRT(number): Returns the square root of a number.
- MOD(number, divisor): Returns the remainder of the division of one number by another.

Example Usage of Numeric Functions

Assume an Order entity with a double type amount field:

```
@Entity
public class Order {
    @Id
    private Long id;
    private double amount;
    // getters and setters
}
```

To fetch the absolute values of order amounts, the ABS function is used as follows:

```
TypedQuery<Double> query = em.createQuery(
    "SELECT ABS(o.amount) FROM Order o", Double.class);
List<Double> absoluteAmounts = query.getResultList();
```

Date-Time Functions

JPQL includes several functions for operations on date-time data. These functions often depend on the underlying database support:

- CURRENT_DATE: Returns the current date.
- CURRENT_TIME: Returns the current time.
- CURRENT_TIMESTAMP: Returns the current timestamp (date and time).

Example Usage of Date-Time Functions

To fetch orders placed on the current date, one can use the CURRENT_DATE function:

```
TypedQuery<Order> query = em.createQuery(
    "SELECT o FROM Order o WHERE o.orderDate = CURRENT_DATE", Order.
        class);
List<Order> orders = query.getResultList();
```

Aggregation Functions

Aggregation functions allow performing calculations across collections of data. The primary aggregation functions in JPQL are:

- COUNT(expression): Returns the number of values.
- SUM(expression): Returns the sum of values.
- AVG(expression): Returns the average of values.
- MAX(expression): Returns the maximum value.
- MIN(expression): Returns the minimum value.

Example Usage of Aggregation Functions

To count the number of orders, the COUNT function is utilized as follows:

```
TypedQuery<Long> query = em.createQuery(
    "SELECT COUNT(o) FROM Order o", Long.class);
Long orderCount = query.getSingleResult();
```

Similarly, calculating the average order amount can be achieved using the AVG function:

```
TypedQuery<Double> query = em.createQuery(
    "SELECT AVG(o.amount) FROM Order o", Double.class);
Double averageAmount = query.getSingleResult();
```

Conditional Expressions

JPQL supports conditional expressions such as CASE and COALESCE:

- CASE: Implements conditional logic, similar to IF-THEN-ELSE.
- COALESCE(expression1, expression2, ..., n): Returns the first non-null expression in the list.

Example Usage of Conditional Expressions

To categorize orders based on their amount, one might use the CASE expression:

```
TypedQuery<String> query = em.createQuery(
    "SELECT CASE "
    + "WHEN o.amount > 1000 THEN 'HIGH VALUE' "
    + "WHEN o.amount > 500 THEN 'MEDIUM VALUE' "
    + "ELSE 'LOW VALUE' "
    + "END "
    + "FROM Order o", String.class);
List<String> categories = query.getResultList();
```

COALESCE can be employed to provide a default value when dealing with potentially null fields:

```
TypedQuery<String> query = em.createQuery(
    "SELECT COALESCE(e.email, 'No Email Address') FROM Employee e", String.
        class);
List<String> emails = query.getResultList();
```

This query ensures that if an employee does not have an email address, the string No Email Address is returned instead of a null value.

These functions and expressions enhance the capability of JPQL, enabling developers to write more effective queries for data retrieval and manipulation. The ability to apply operations directly within queries significantly reduces the need for additional processing in application logic.

5.5 Using Named Queries: @NamedQuery and @NamedQueries

Named queries in JPA offer a robust way to define static queries, which can be pre-compiled and reused across the application. This mechanism enhances readability, maintainability, and potentially performance, as the Named Queries can be compiled only once by the EntityManager. Named queries are defined via the @NamedQuery and @NamedQueries annotations.

The @NamedQuery annotation is used to define a single query, while @NamedQueries is used to group multiple @NamedQuery annotations.

```
@Entity
@NamedQueries({
    @NamedQuery(
        name = "Employee.findByName",
        query = "SELECT e FROM Employee e WHERE e.name = :name"
    ),
    @NamedQuery(
        name = "Employee.findAll",
        query = "SELECT e FROM Employee e"
    )
})
public class Employee {
    @Id
    @GeneratedValue(strategy=GenerationType.AUTO)
    private Long id;

    private String name;

    // Constructors, getters, and setters
}
```

In the example above, two named queries are defined. The query with the name Employee.findByName retrieves employees by their name, while Employee.findAll fetches all employees.

To use these named queries in code, one can use the EntityManager.createNamedQuery method and set parameters if required.

```
public List<Employee> getEmployeesByName(String employeeName) {
    EntityManager em = emf.createEntityManager();
    List<Employee> employees = em.createNamedQuery("Employee.findByName",
          Employee.class)
                                 .setParameter("name", employeeName)
                                 .getResultList();
    em.close();
    return employees;
}

public List<Employee> getAllEmployees() {
    EntityManager em = emf.createEntityManager();
    List<Employee> employees = em.createNamedQuery("Employee.findAll", Employee
          .class)
                                 .getResultList();
    em.close();
    return employees;
}
```

The @NamedQuery annotation contains two main elements:

- **name**: This specifies the name of the query, which will be used to access it programmatically.
- **query**: This is the actual JPQL (Java Persistence Query Language) query string.

Parameters in named queries are set via the setParameter method of the Query interface. This can be done using named parameters (prefixed with a colon, e.g., :name) or positional parameters (using numeric placeholders).

Named queries provide several advantages:

- **Pre-compilation**: The query string is parsed and validated once, rather than each time it is executed.
- **Centralized Management**: Queries can be managed in one place, which helps reduce duplication and maintenance efforts.
- **Improved Readability**: The query logic is not scattered across the codebase, making it easier to understand the data access layer.

However, there are a few considerations when using named queries:

- Modifying a query implies modifying the entity class, which can lead to code being less modular.
- Named queries are static; hence, they might not be suitable for more dynamic requirements.
- It is essential to make sure that all named queries are tested properly, as JPA will validate them during the startup phase.

Consider this use case: Suppose we need a more complex query that fetches employees based on their department and a range of salaries. This can be managed using named queries effectively:

```
@Entity
@NamedQueries({
    @NamedQuery(
        name = "Employee.findByDepartmentAndSalary",
        query = "SELECT e FROM Employee e WHERE e.department = :department
              AND e.salary BETWEEN :minSalary AND :maxSalary"
    )
})
public class Employee {
    // Class body remains the same
}
```

This query is more sophisticated and demonstrates how flexible named queries can be while maintaining performance benefits and readability.

```
public List<Employee> getEmployeesByDepartmentAndSalary(String department,
        double minSalary, double maxSalary) {
    EntityManager em = emf.createEntityManager();
    List<Employee> employees = em.createNamedQuery("Employee.
            findByDepartmentAndSalary", Employee.class)
                                    .setParameter("department", department)
                                    .setParameter("minSalary", minSalary)
                                    .setParameter("maxSalary", maxSalary)
                                    .getResultList();
    em.close();
    return employees;
}
```

In the provided method, the named parameters :department, :minSalary, and :maxSalary are set dynamically at runtime. This approach combines the benefits of static query compilation with runtime flexibility.

To ensure optimal application performance, it is advisable to analyze the necessity and schema of the queries being declared as named queries. While they offer significant advantages, especially for static and reusable queries, the design phase should thoroughly consider the balance between static and dynamic query requirements.

5.6 Parameter Binding in JPQL

Parameter binding in JPQL (Java Persistence Query Language) is an essential technique that allows developers to dynamically pass parameters to queries at runtime. Parameter binding enhances query flexibility and security, prevents SQL injection attacks, and improves query performance by reusing compiled query plans. JPQL supports two types of parameter binding: positional parameters and named parameters.

Positional Parameters

Positional parameters are denoted by a question mark followed by an index (e.g., ?1, ?2, etc.). The index represents the parameter's position in the query. When binding a positional parameter, it is crucial to ensure the order of parameters in the query matches the order of provided values.

Example:

```
String jpql = "SELECT e FROM Employee e WHERE e.departmentId = ?1 AND e.
    salary > ?2";
TypedQuery<Employee> query = entityManager.createQuery(jpql, Employee.class);
query.setParameter(1, 10);
query.setParameter(2, 50000);
List<Employee> employees = query.getResultList();
```

The above example demonstrates a JPQL query that retrieves employees from a specific department with a salary greater than a specified amount. The positional parameters ?1 and ?2 are bound to the actual values 10 and 50000 respectively.

Named Parameters

Named parameters, denoted by a colon followed by a parameter name (e.g., :deptId, :minSalary, etc.), provide a more readable and maintainable approach to parameter binding. Named parameters are especially advantageous in complex queries where the order of parameters can easily become confusing.

Example:

```
String jpql = "SELECT e FROM Employee e WHERE e.departmentId = :deptId AND
    e.salary > :minSalary";
TypedQuery<Employee> query = entityManager.createQuery(jpql, Employee.class);
query.setParameter("deptId", 10);
query.setParameter("minSalary", 50000);
List<Employee> employees = query.getResultList();
```

In this example, the named parameters :deptId and :minSalary improve query readability and reduce the chance of parameter binding errors.

Type-Safe Parameter Binding

JPQL supports type-safe parameter binding through the setParameter method. The method can automatically infer the type of the parameter based on the provided value. Additionally, developers can explicitly specify the parameter type to avoid ambiguity.

Example:

```
import javax.persistence.TemporalType;

// Using automatic type inference
query.setParameter("hireDate", new Date());

// Specifying temporal type for date parameters
query.setParameter("hireDate", new Date(), TemporalType.DATE);
```

The TemporalType enumeration allows developers to specify the desired temporal precision for date parameters, ensuring the correct handling of temporal data in JPQL queries.

Binding Collections to Parameters

JPQL allows binding collections to query parameters. This feature is beneficial when dealing with queries that involve IN predicates or involve searching within a set of values.

Example:

```
List<Integer> departmentIds = Arrays.asList(1, 2, 3, 4);
String jpql = "SELECT e FROM Employee e WHERE e.departmentId IN :deptIds";
TypedQuery<Employee> query = entityManager.createQuery(jpql, Employee.class);
query.setParameter("deptIds", departmentIds);
List<Employee> employees = query.getResultList();
```

Binding collections to parameters simplifies the construction of IN predicates and enhances query flexibility.

Advanced Parameter Binding Techniques

In addition to basic parameter binding, JPQL also offers advanced techniques such as using parameter binding in UPDATE and DELETE queries.

Example:

```
String updateJpql = "UPDATE Employee e SET e.salary = :newSalary WHERE e.
    departmentId = :deptId";
Query updateQuery = entityManager.createQuery(updateJpql);
updateQuery.setParameter("newSalary", 60000);
updateQuery.setParameter("deptId", 10);
int updatedCount = updateQuery.executeUpdate();

String deleteJpql = "DELETE FROM Employee e WHERE e.departmentId = :deptId";
Query deleteQuery = entityManager.createQuery(deleteJpql);
deleteQuery.setParameter("deptId", 10);
int deletedCount = deleteQuery.executeUpdate();
```

The example showcases how parameter binding is utilized in both UPDATE and DELETE operations, facilitating the dynamic modification and removal of records based on specified criteria.

Overall, parameter binding in JPQL provides a robust and flexible mechanism for creating dynamic queries. By supporting both positional and named parameters, JPQL enhances query readability, maintainability, and security.

5.7 Dynamic Queries with JPQL

Dynamic queries in JPQL (Java Persistence Query Language) provide a flexible mechanism for constructing queries at runtime based on various conditions and parameters. Unlike static queries, where the query structure is predefined and embedded within the code, dynamic queries allow developers to build and modify the query structure programmatically, responding to user inputs, application states, and other runtime factors.

Creating dynamic queries in JPQL involves several steps: constructing the base query, appending conditions dynamically, and finally executing the constructed query. The following code snippets and examples illustrate these steps in detail.

To begin constructing a dynamic JPQL query, we utilize the EntityManager interface, which provides the createQuery method. This method allows us to specify a JPQL string to form the basic structure of the query. The base JPQL query typically includes only the SELECT clause, with WHERE clauses and other conditions added dynamically as needed.

```
EntityManager em = ...;
StringBuilder jpql = new StringBuilder("SELECT e FROM Employee e");
boolean isFirstCondition = true;

if (department != null) {
    if (isFirstCondition) {
        jpql.append(" WHERE");
        isFirstCondition = false;
    } else {
        jpql.append(" AND");
    }
    jpql.append(" e.department = :department");
}

if (salary > 0) {
    if (isFirstCondition) {
        jpql.append(" WHERE");
        isFirstCondition = false;
    } else {
        jpql.append(" AND");
    }
    jpql.append(" e.salary > :salary");
}

Query query = em.createQuery(jpql.toString());

if (department != null) {
    query.setParameter("department", department);
}

if (salary > 0) {
    query.setParameter("salary", salary);
}

List<Employee> employees = query.getResultList();
```

In the example above, the JPQL query is constructed using a StringBuilder to form the query string dynamically. The variables department and salary represent potential input parameters that dictate the conditions to be appended to the query. The boolean flag isFirstCondition ensures the proper inclusion of the WHERE clause and conjunctions (AND) as conditions are added.

After constructing the query string, the createQuery method of the EntityManager is called to create a Query instance. Parameters are then set using the setParameter method to bind the dynamic values, and the resulting list of Employee entities is fetched using the getResultList method.

Dynamic queries are particularly useful in scenarios where user inputs or application state determine query conditions. For instance, consider a search functionality where users can filter results based on various optional criteria. The flexibility of dynamic queries allows developers to build such features without the overhead of maintaining numerous static queries for each possible combination of filter criteria.

```
public List<Employee> searchEmployees(String name, String department, Double
    minSalary, Double maxSalary) {
    EntityManager em = ...;
    StringBuilder jpql = new StringBuilder("SELECT e FROM Employee e");
    boolean isFirstCondition = true;

    if (name != null && !name.isEmpty()) {
        if (isFirstCondition) {
            jpql.append(" WHERE");
            isFirstCondition = false;
        } else {
            jpql.append(" AND");
        }
        jpql.append(" e.name LIKE :name");
    }

    if (department != null && !department.isEmpty()) {
        if (isFirstCondition) {
            jpql.append(" WHERE");
            isFirstCondition = false;
        } else {
            jpql.append(" AND");
        }
        jpql.append(" e.department = :department");
    }

    if (minSalary != null) {
        if (isFirstCondition) {
            jpql.append(" WHERE");
            isFirstCondition = false;
        } else {
            jpql.append(" AND");
        }
        jpql.append(" e.salary >= :minSalary");
    }

    if (maxSalary != null) {
        if (isFirstCondition) {
            jpql.append(" WHERE");
            isFirstCondition = false;
        } else {
            jpql.append(" AND");
        }
        jpql.append(" e.salary <= :maxSalary");
    }
```

```
    Query query = em.createQuery(jpql.toString());

    if (name != null && !name.isEmpty()) {
        query.setParameter("name", "%" + name + "%");
    }

    if (department != null && !department.isEmpty()) {
        query.setParameter("department", department);
    }

    if (minSalary != null) {
        query.setParameter("minSalary", minSalary);
    }

    if (maxSalary != null) {
        query.setParameter("maxSalary", maxSalary);
    }

    return query.getResultList();
}
```

The searchEmployees method demonstrates how dynamic queries can handle multiple optional criteria seamlessly. It builds the JPQL query string by checking each criterion and conditionally appending the appropriate clauses. Parameters are then bound based on the provided values, allowing for a flexible and efficient search mechanism.

Dynamic queries also support complex expressions, JOIN operations, and other JPQL features. The following example showcases a more advanced usage involving a LEFT JOIN to retrieve employees along with their department details, conditional on various dynamic parameters.

```
public List<Object[]> searchEmployeesWithDepartments(String name, Integer
    minDepartmentSize) {
    EntityManager em = ...;
    StringBuilder jpql = new StringBuilder("SELECT e, d FROM Employee e LEFT
        JOIN e.department d");
    boolean isFirstCondition = true;

    if (name != null && !name.isEmpty()) {
        if (isFirstCondition) {
            jpql.append(" WHERE");
            isFirstCondition = false;
        } else {
            jpql.append(" AND");
        }
        jpql.append(" e.name LIKE :name");
    }

    if (minDepartmentSize != null) {
        if (isFirstCondition) {
            jpql.append(" WHERE");
            isFirstCondition = false;
        } else {
            jpql.append(" AND");
        }
        jpql.append(" (SELECT COUNT(emp) FROM Employee emp WHERE emp.
            department = d) >= :minDepartmentSize");
```

```
    }

    Query query = em.createQuery(jpql.toString());

    if (name != null && !name.isEmpty()) {
        query.setParameter("name", "%" + name + "%");
    }

    if (minDepartmentSize != null) {
        query.setParameter("minDepartmentSize", minDepartmentSize);
    }

    return query.getResultList();
}
```

This example illustrates the incorporation of a LEFT JOIN along with subqueries to filter departments by size, demonstrating the versatile capabilities of dynamic JPQL queries.

5.8 Introduction to Criteria API

The Criteria API in Java Persistence API (JPA) allows for building queries in a programmatic and type-safe manner, providing an alternative to writing queries in JPQL. It leverages Java objects for query definition, which leads to better integration with the IDE and compile-time syntax checking. This section explores the essential concepts, structures, and syntax involved in utilizing the Criteria API effectively.

The primary entry point for creating Criteria queries is through the javax.persistence.criteria.CriteriaBuilder interface. This interface provides factory methods for constructing various elements of a query, such as the CriteriaQuery, Predicate, and Expression instances. The Criteria API aims to create queries that are both flexible and maintainable.

Creating a Criteria Query

A typical Criteria query process involves the following steps: 1. Obtain an instance of CriteriaBuilder from the EntityManager. 2. Create a CriteriaQuery instance using the CriteriaBuilder. 3. Define the query roots, which are the starting points for querying, using the from method on the CriteriaQuery. 4. Use the CriteriaQuery to construct a query by chaining various methods, such as select, where, and orderBy. 5. Get the TypedQuery object from the EntityManager and execute the query to obtain results.

```
EntityManager entityManager = entityManagerFactory.createEntityManager();
```

```
CriteriaBuilder criteriaBuilder = entityManager.getCriteriaBuilder();
CriteriaQuery<Person> criteriaQuery = criteriaBuilder.createQuery(Person.class);
Root<Person> personRoot = criteriaQuery.from(Person.class);
criteriaQuery.select(personRoot);

TypedQuery<Person> query = entityManager.createQuery(criteriaQuery);
List<Person> results = query.getResultList();
```

In the example above, the from method defines the query root, which is the Person entity. The select method designates that all instances of Person are to be selected. The resulting list, results, contains all Person entities in the database.

Applying Conditions with Predicates

The CriteriaBuilder interface is equipped with a variety of methods to generate Predicate instances used to impose conditions on the query. These predicates are passed to the where method of CriteriaQuery. Below is an example of a query that retrieves persons whose age is greater than 30.

```
CriteriaBuilder criteriaBuilder = entityManager.getCriteriaBuilder();
CriteriaQuery<Person> criteriaQuery = criteriaBuilder.createQuery(Person.class);
Root<Person> personRoot = criteriaQuery.from(Person.class);

Predicate ageGreaterThan = criteriaBuilder.greaterThan(personRoot.get("age"), 30);
criteriaQuery.select(personRoot).where(ageGreaterThan);

TypedQuery<Person> query = entityManager.createQuery(criteriaQuery);
List<Person> results = query.getResultList();
```

In this case, the greaterThan method from CriteriaBuilder generates a Predicate that represents the condition "age > 30." This predicate is then passed to the where method to filter the results accordingly.

Ordering the Results

The Criteria API also supports specifying the order of query results. The orderBy method in CriteriaQuery takes one or more Order objects, which can be created using the asc or desc methods from CriteriaBuilder.

```
CriteriaBuilder criteriaBuilder = entityManager.getCriteriaBuilder();
CriteriaQuery<Person> criteriaQuery = criteriaBuilder.createQuery(Person.class);
Root<Person> personRoot = criteriaQuery.from(Person.class);

criteriaQuery.select(personRoot).orderBy(criteriaBuilder.asc(personRoot.get("lastName
    ")));

TypedQuery<Person> query = entityManager.createQuery(criteriaQuery);
List<Person> results = query.getResultList();
```

This example demonstrates ordering the results by the lastName attribute in ascending order.

Using Path Expressions

The Criteria API allows navigation of entity relationships using path expressions. A path expression refers to an attribute of an entity or an association from the root.

```
CriteriaBuilder criteriaBuilder = entityManager.getCriteriaBuilder();
CriteriaQuery<Order> criteriaQuery = criteriaBuilder.createQuery(Order.class);
Root<Order> orderRoot = criteriaQuery.from(Order.class);
Join<Order, Customer> customerJoin = orderRoot.join("customer");

Predicate customerNameCondition = criteriaBuilder.equal(customerJoin.get("name"), "
    John Doe");
criteriaQuery.select(orderRoot).where(customerNameCondition);

TypedQuery<Order> query = entityManager.createQuery(criteriaQuery);
List<Order> results = query.getResultList();
```

In this snippet, the join method is used to navigate the relationship between Order and Customer. The query fetches all Order instances where the Customer's name is "John Doe."

Combining Multiple Predicates

The Criteria API supports combining multiple predicates using logical operators like and and or. This enables the construction of composite conditions.

```
CriteriaBuilder criteriaBuilder = entityManager.getCriteriaBuilder();
CriteriaQuery<Person> criteriaQuery = criteriaBuilder.createQuery(Person.class);
Root<Person> personRoot = criteriaQuery.from(Person.class);

Predicate agePredicate = criteriaBuilder.greaterThan(personRoot.get("age"), 30);
Predicate cityPredicate = criteriaBuilder.equal(personRoot.get("city"), "New York");
Predicate finalPredicate = criteriaBuilder.and(agePredicate, cityPredicate);

criteriaQuery.select(personRoot).where(finalPredicate);

TypedQuery<Person> query = entityManager.createQuery(criteriaQuery);
List<Person> results = query.getResultList();
```

This example combines an age condition and a city condition with an and operator, ensuring that only persons older than 30 and residing in New York are selected.

By providing a type-safe and programmatic approach, the Criteria API ensures that queries are more maintainable and less prone to runtime errors. This helps bridge the gap between object-oriented paradigms and relational databases. The following sections build upon this foundation, introducing more advanced uses and optimizations of the Criteria API in JPA.

5.9 Building Criteria Queries Dynamically

Dynamic query construction using the Criteria API offers flexibility and type-safety, making it a robust alternative to JPQL for constructing complex queries programmatically. This section examines the essential components and techniques to build criteria queries dynamically in JPA.

The Criteria API leverages a metamodel and fluent API style to construct queries dynamically in a type-safe manner. We start with importing the necessary JPA classes:

```
import javax.persistence.criteria.CriteriaBuilder;
import javax.persistence.criteria.CriteriaQuery;
import javax.persistence.criteria.Root;
import javax.persistence.criteria.Predicate;
import javax.persistence.EntityManager;
import javax.persistence.EntityManagerFactory;
import javax.persistence.Persistence;
```

Here, we make use of the CriteriaBuilder, CriteriaQuery, Root, and Predicate classes, essential for constructing dynamic queries.

A criteria query is initiated by obtaining an instance of CriteriaBuilder from the EntityManager. This builder is used to create the constituents of the query: the criteria query itself, the query root, predicates, and the selection criteria.

```
EntityManagerFactory emf = Persistence.createEntityManagerFactory("example-unit");
EntityManager em = emf.createEntityManager();
CriteriaBuilder cb = em.getCriteriaBuilder();
CriteriaQuery<Person> cq = cb.createQuery(Person.class);
Root<Person> person = cq.from(Person.class);
```

In this example, Person.class is the entity type for which the query is being created. The Root<Person> defines a range variable in the FROM clause.

Basic Criteria Query Construction

A basic query would select all entities of a particular type. For example, to select all entries from the Person table:

```
cq.select(person);
List<Person> result = em.createQuery(cq).getResultList();
```

The select(person) method specifies that the query's result should contain instances of the Person entity.

Adding Predicates to Criteria Queries

Adding a WHERE clause involves constructing Predicate instances.

For example, to filter persons by age:

```
Predicate agePredicate = cb.greaterThan(person.get("age"), 25);
cq.where(agePredicate);
List<Person> result = em.createQuery(cq).getResultList();
```

Here, cb.greaterThan(person.get("age"), 25) creates a predicate where the age of the person must be greater than 25.

Combining Multiple Predicates

Multiple predicates can be combined using logical operators. For example, to filter by age and name:

```
Predicate agePredicate = cb.greaterThan(person.get("age"), 25);
Predicate namePredicate = cb.equal(person.get("name"), "John");
cq.where(cb.and(agePredicate, namePredicate));
List<Person> result = em.createQuery(cq).getResultList();
```

Here, cb.and(agePredicate, namePredicate) combines the two predicates with a logical AND operation.

Ordering Results

To order the results, the orderBy method is utilized in conjunction with CriteriaBuilder's sorting methods. For example, to order by age in ascending order:

```
cq.orderBy(cb.asc(person.get("age")));
List<Person> result = em.createQuery(cq).getResultList();
```

Selecting Specific Fields

To select specific fields rather than entire entities, the multiselect method can be utilized:

```
CriteriaQuery<Object[]> cq = cb.createQuery(Object[].class);
Root<Person> person = cq.from(Person.class);
cq.multiselect(person.get("name"), person.get("age"));
List<Object[]> result = em.createQuery(cq).getResultList();
```

Paging Results

To implement pagination, the setFirstResult and setMaxResults methods of TypedQuery are employed:

```
TypedQuery<Person> query = em.createQuery(cq);
query.setFirstResult(0);
query.setMaxResults(10);
List<Person> result = query.getResultList();
```

This code retrieves the first 10 results from the query.

Joining Tables

Joining related entities involves using the join method. For example, to join the Person and Address entities:

```
Root<Person> p = cq.from(Person.class);
Join<Person, Address> address = p.join("address");
cq.where(cb.equal(address.get("city"), "New York"));
List<Person> result = em.createQuery(cq).getResultList();
```

In this example, the query joins the Person entity with the Address entity and filters by the city name.

The Criteria API empowers developers to construct complex queries programmatically, ensuring type-safety and dynamic query generation. When both flexibility and maintainability are critical, the Criteria API serves as a potent tool in JPA's query arsenal.

5.10 Using Criteria Queries for Complex Queries

The Criteria API in JPA provides a powerful framework for building complex queries programmatically. Unlike JPQL, which relies on static query strings, the Criteria API leverages the type-safety and dynamic nature of Java to construct queries. This section will cover the use of Criteria API to formulate intricate query hierarchies and demonstrate its capabilities through practical examples.

Understanding how to construct complex queries using the Criteria API begins with mastering the core components: CriteriaBuilder, CriteriaQuery, and Root.

1. Setting Up CriteriaQuery

The first step in constructing any Criteria API query is to obtain an instance of CriteriaBuilder from the EntityManager. Subsequently, a CriteriaQuery object is created by invoking the createQuery method. The Root object is then defined to specify the entity class involved in the query. The following code snippet illustrates this setup:

```
EntityManager em = entityManagerFactory.createEntityManager();
CriteriaBuilder cb = em.getCriteriaBuilder();
CriteriaQuery<Person> cq = cb.createQuery(Person.class);
Root<Person> personRoot = cq.from(Person.class);
```

2. Combining Multiple Predicates

Complex queries often require combining multiple criteria or predicates. The Criteria API facilitates this using the Predicate interface along with logical operators like and and or. Example:

```
Predicate agePredicate = cb.greaterThan(personRoot.get("age"), 30);
Predicate namePredicate = cb.like(personRoot.get("name"), "J%");
cq.where(cb.and(agePredicate, namePredicate));
```

3. Using Joins in Criteria Queries

Joining tables or entities is a crucial aspect of formulating complex queries. The Criteria API supports inner and outer joins using the Join object. Here's how to join two entities:

```
Root<Order> orderRoot = cq.from(Order.class);
Join<Order, Customer> customerJoin = orderRoot.join("customer");
cq.select(orderRoot).where(cb.equal(customerJoin.get("status"), "active"));
```

4. Applying Grouping and Aggregation

Adding groupBy and having clauses enhances queries with aggregation functions. These clauses are utilized for summarizing information. Example:

```
cq.select(cb.construct(OrderSummary.class,
        personRoot.get("id"), cb.count(personRoot)))
  .groupBy(personRoot.get("id"))
  .having(cb.greaterThan(cb.count(personRoot), 5));
```

5. Sorting the Query Result

Ordering query results can be achieved by employing the orderBy method. The Criteria API supports multiple sorting criteria using Order objects. Example:

```
cq.orderBy(cb.desc(personRoot.get("registrationDate")), cb.asc(personRoot.get("name"
    )));
```

6. Subqueries in Criteria API

The Criteria API allows embedding subqueries within the main query. Subqueries can be utilized to perform further filtering or calculations:

```
Subquery<Integer> subquery = cq.subquery(Integer.class);
Root<Order> subOrder = subquery.from(Order.class);
subquery.select(cb.count(subOrder))
        .where(cb.equal(subOrder.get("customerId"), personRoot.get("id")));
cq.where(cb.equal(subquery, 10));
```

7. Executing the Criteria Query

Once a complex query is fully constructed, it is executed by creating a

TypedQuery instance and invoking query execution methods:

```
TypedQuery<Person> query = em.createQuery(cq);
List<Person> results = query.getResultList();
```

Through these examples, it becomes evident how the Criteria API can be employed to construct highly flexible and intricate queries. Utilizing these techniques ensures that complex query requirements can be met efficiently.

5.11 Combining JPQL and Criteria API in Applications

Effective use of both JPQL and the Criteria API can enhance the flexibility and maintainability of applications, making it easier to implement complex queries and business logic. Sometimes, the constraints of static query strings (declarative style with JPQL) and the dynamic nature of query construction (programmatic style with Criteria API) complement each other well and can be integrated to achieve optimized querying solutions in Java Persistence API (JPA). This section demonstrates strategies for combining both JPQL and Criteria API effectively.

When an application requires dynamic query construction while leveraging predefined JPQL query strings, combining these approaches can yield powerful results. Consider an example query requirement where a dynamic filter is applied to a base JPQL query string.

To illustrate this, we will define a context where we need to retrieve a list of employees from the database with a dynamically constructed filter for their department. The static nature of the base query can be leveraged in JPQL, while the dynamic filtering criteria can be constructed using the Criteria API.

```
@Entity
public class Employee {
    @Id
    private Long id;
    private String name;
    private String department;
    private double salary;
    // Getters and Setters
}
```

Suppose we have a base JPQL query string defined to fetch employees:

```
@NamedQuery(
    name = "Employee.findAll",
    query = "SELECT e FROM Employee e"
)
```

Then, from a service or a repository layer, we might want to dynamically apply additional conditions to this base query.

```
public List<Employee> findEmployeesWithDynamicFilter(String departmentFilter) {
    // 1. Get the EntityManager from the entity manager factory
    EntityManager em = entityManagerFactory.createEntityManager();

    // 2. Begin with the named JPQL query
    Query baseQuery = em.createNamedQuery("Employee.findAll");
    StringBuilder queryString = new StringBuilder(baseQuery.unwrap(Query.class).
        getQueryString());

    // 3. Append a dynamic WHERE clause if filters are provided
    if (departmentFilter != null && !departmentFilter.isEmpty()) {
        queryString.append(" WHERE e.department = :department");
    }

    // 4. Create a new Query with the dynamically constructed query string
    Query dynamicQuery = em.createQuery(queryString.toString());

    // 5. Set parameters dynamically
    if (departmentFilter != null && !departmentFilter.isEmpty()) {
        dynamicQuery.setParameter("department", departmentFilter);
    }

    // 6. Execute the query and return results
    @SuppressWarnings("unchecked")
    List<Employee> employees = (List<Employee>) dynamicQuery.getResultList();
    em.close();
    return employees;
}
```

This approach allows combining the static structure of a named JPQL query with the flexibility of dynamic query construction, facilitating ease of maintenance and dynamic behavior.

Another scenario where combining JPQL and Criteria API is beneficial is when certain parts of the query logic are more straightforward to express in JPQL and other parts require the dynamic capabilities of Criteria API. For instance, we might start with a Criteria API query and subsequently use JPQL for operations that are cumbersome to construct programmatically.

Consider a case where we need to calculate the average salary of employees dynamically per department:

```
public double findAverageSalaryByDepartment(String department) {
    EntityManager em = entityManagerFactory.createEntityManager();
    CriteriaBuilder cb = em.getCriteriaBuilder();

    // Construct Criteria query structure for base conditions
```

```
    CriteriaQuery<Double> cq = cb.createQuery(Double.class);
    Root<Employee> employee = cq.from(Employee.class);
    cq.select(cb.avg(employee.get("salary")));

    if (department != null && !department.isEmpty()) {
        cq.where(cb.equal(employee.get("department"), department));
    }

    TypedQuery<Double> criteriaQuery = em.createQuery(cq);

    try {
        return criteriaQuery.getSingleResult();
    } catch (NoResultException nre) {
        return 0.0;
    } finally {
        em.close();
    }
}
```

This example leverages the Criteria API for flexible query construction based on dynamic conditions, while the JPQL could be utilized to fetch static parts of the result set or predefine certain parts of the query logic.

Interweaving JPQL and Criteria API allows developers to leverage the strengths of both approaches, crafting solutions that are both maintainable and performant in real-world applications. This combined usage not only simplifies query construction under complex business requirements but also optimizes performance by preventing the recomputation of static parts of queries.

Chapter 6

Spring Data JPA Overview

This chapter offers a comprehensive overview of Spring Data JPA, starting with its integration into your project. It explains the concept of Spring Data repositories and the creation of derived query methods. Custom repository methods are also introduced, alongside configuration options for Spring Data JPA. The chapter covers essential features like pagination and sorting, details the process of query creation, and demonstrates the use of @Query for custom queries. It concludes with a discussion on integrating Spring Data JPA with Spring Boot to streamline application development.

6.1 Introduction to Spring Data JPA

Spring Data JPA is a fundamental component of the larger Spring Data project, designed to simplify the implementation of data access layers by reducing the amount of boilerplate code and providing a consistent approach to data access. At its core, Spring Data JPA facilitates the creation, execution, and management of database operations in Java applications, leveraging the Java Persistence API (JPA) for object-relational mapping (ORM).

Spring Data JPA offers a repository abstraction over the underlying data store, allowing developers to focus on the domain and its interactions rather than on the tedious, lower-level details of database operations. It enhances application development by allowing developers to build repositories and query methods using just their method names, eliminating the need for verbose query language syntax.

The JPA standard, which Spring Data JPA builds upon, is a Java specification for managing relational data. It allows applications to interact with relational databases through Java objects in a platform-independent manner. JPA includes features such as the entity manager, repositories, transactions, and query capabilities, all of which are gracefully integrated with Spring Data JPA.

Spring Data JPA significantly reduces the boilerplate code required for performing basic CRUD (Create, Read, Update, Delete) operations. By defining an interface that extends one of the Spring Data repository interfaces, complete implementations for common operations are provided at runtime. Consider the following example:

```
public interface PersonRepository extends JpaRepository<Person, Long> {
}
```

In this example, *PersonRepository* is an interface extending JpaRepository. The JpaRepository interface provides several methods for CRUD operations, such as save(), delete(), and findAll(). Spring Data JPA enables the implementation and injection of this repository, thus eliminating the need for writing the tedious SQL or JPQL code.

Spring Data JPA supports a wide variety of databases without requiring special configuration or code adjustments. It integrates seamlessly with Spring Framework, providing support for declarative transactions and simplifying the use of Dependency Injection (DI). Developers can use Spring's @Transactional annotation to manage transaction boundaries declaratively, as shown below:

```
@Service
public class PersonService {

    @Autowired
    private PersonRepository personRepository;

    @Transactional
    public void savePerson(Person person) {
        personRepository.save(person);
    }
}
```

The @Transactional annotation ensures that the savePerson method runs within a transaction context, committing all or none of the operations within its scope, thereby preserving data integrity.

Spring Data JPA also offers powerful query capabilities through method name conventions and the @Query annotation. For instance, developers can define methods in the repository interface using predefined keywords to perform queries on entity properties:

```
public interface PersonRepository extends JpaRepository<Person, Long> {
    List<Person> findByLastName(String lastName);
}
```

The above method findByLastName will automatically generate and execute the appropriate query to retrieve instances of Person with the specified lastName. Such derived query methods simplify the codebase, increase readability, and reduce the likelihood of errors.

For more complex queries beyond the capabilities of method name derivation, the @Query annotation can be utilized to define custom queries using JPQL or native SQL:

```
public interface PersonRepository extends JpaRepository<Person, Long> {

    @Query("SELECT p FROM Person p WHERE p.firstName = :firstName")
    List<Person> findByFirstName(@Param("firstName") String firstName);
}
```

The @Query annotation provides a means to write and manage more sophisticated queries when required. Integrating such features into the repository interface allows for a clear and structured approach to data operations.

In addition to simplifying CRUD operations and query creation, Spring Data JPA provides mechanisms for pagination and sorting, facilitating the handling of large datasets efficiently. The Pageable and Sort interfaces are pivotal in this context:

```
Page<Person> findAll(Pageable pageable);
List<Person> findAll(Sort sort);
```

The Pageable parameter allows the method to return data in a paginated format, thus optimizing performance and user experience. Similarly, the Sort parameter enables the sorting of query results based on specific criteria.

To utilize Spring Data JPA effectively, one must also configure the Spring application context correctly. This involves setting up the data source, JPA provider, and enabling Spring Data repositories. An example configuration in a Spring Boot application typically resides in the application.properties file:

```
spring.datasource.url=jdbc:h2:mem:testdb
spring.datasource.driverClassName=org.h2.Driver
```

```
spring.datasource.username=sa
spring.datasource.password=password
spring.jpa.database-platform=org.hibernate.dialect.H2Dialect
```

This configuration connects to an in-memory H2 database and specifies Hibernate as the JPA provider. In Spring Boot applications, enabling Spring Data JPA repositories is as simple as including the @EnableJpaRepositories annotation in a configuration class or the main application class:

```
@SpringBootApplication
@EnableJpaRepositories(basePackages = "com.example.repository")
public class Application {
    public static void main(String[] args) {
        SpringApplication.run(Application.class, args);
    }
}
```

The @EnableJpaRepositories annotation activates the scanning of repository interfaces within the specified package, facilitating the auto-configuration of Spring Data JPA components.

By leveraging Spring Data JPA, developers can focus more on business logic and domain modeling rather than on the intricacies of data access layers. This holistic integration with the Spring ecosystem enables streamlined development processes and enhances maintainability, scalability, and readability of enterprise-level applications.

6.2 Setting Up Spring Data JPA in Your Project

A well-structured setup is crucial for leveraging the advantages of Spring Data JPA in your project. This section details the steps required to integrate Spring Data JPA into a Java application, ensuring a seamless transition from configuration to execution. Follow each step meticulously to establish a robust foundation for utilizing Spring Data JPA.

Step 1: Add Dependencies

The first step in setting up Spring Data JPA is to add the necessary dependencies to your project's build configuration file. For a Maven-based project, include the following dependencies in the pom.xml file.

```
<dependencies>
    <dependency>
        <groupId>org.springframework.boot</groupId>
        <artifactId>spring-boot-starter-data-jpa</artifactId>
```

```
    </dependency>
    <dependency>
        <groupId>org.springframework.boot</groupId>
        <artifactId>spring-boot-starter-web</artifactId>
    </dependency>
    <dependency>
        <groupId>com.h2database</groupId>
        <artifactId>h2</artifactId>
        <scope>runtime</scope>
    </dependency>
    <dependency>
        <groupId>org.springframework.boot</groupId>
        <artifactId>spring-boot-starter-test</artifactId>
        <scope>test</scope>
    </dependency>
</dependencies>
```

If you are using Gradle, add the following dependencies to the build.gradle file.

```
dependencies {
    implementation 'org.springframework.boot:spring-boot-starter-data-jpa'
    implementation 'org.springframework.boot:spring-boot-starter-web'
    runtimeOnly 'com.h2database:h2'
    testImplementation 'org.springframework.boot:spring-boot-starter-test'
}
```

Step 2: Configure the Data Source

Next, configure the data source in your project's application.properties file. This configuration defines the database connection parameters and JPA-specific properties.

```
spring.datasource.url=jdbc:h2:mem:testdb
spring.datasource.driverClassName=org.h2.Driver
spring.datasource.username=sa
spring.datasource.password=password

spring.jpa.hibernate.ddl-auto=update
spring.jpa.show-sql=true
spring.jpa.database-platform=org.hibernate.dialect.H2Dialect
```

This example uses H2, an in-memory database, for demonstration purposes. For production, replace these settings with your actual database configuration parameters.

Step 3: Enable JPA Repositories

Enabling JPA repositories in your project involves annotating the main application class with @EnableJpaRepositories. This annotation triggers the scanning of Spring Data repositories.

```
import org.springframework.boot.SpringApplication;
import org.springframework.boot.autoconfigure.SpringBootApplication;
import org.springframework.data.jpa.repository.config.EnableJpaRepositories;
```

```
@SpringBootApplication
@EnableJpaRepositories(basePackages = "com.example.repository")
public class JpaDemoApplication {
    public static void main(String[] args) {
        SpringApplication.run(JpaDemoApplication.class, args);
    }
}
```

Ensure the basePackages attribute points to the package containing your repository interfaces.

Step 4: Define the Entity Classes

Define entity classes representing the database tables. Annotate these classes with @Entity and @Table to map them to corresponding database tables.

```
import javax.persistence.Entity;
import javax.persistence.GeneratedValue;
import javax.persistence.GenerationType;
import javax.persistence.Id;
import javax.persistence.Table;

@Entity
@Table(name = "users")
public class User {
    @Id
    @GeneratedValue(strategy = GenerationType.IDENTITY)
    private Long id;
    private String name;
    private String email;

    // Getters and Setters
}
```

Step 5: Create Repository Interfaces

Create repository interfaces by extending the JpaRepository interface from Spring Data JPA. These interfaces enable CRUD operations and query method execution on your entities.

```
import org.springframework.data.jpa.repository.JpaRepository;
import org.springframework.stereotype.Repository;

@Repository
public interface UserRepository extends JpaRepository<User, Long> {
}
```

Step 6: Configure the Main Application Class

Ensure the main application class is correctly annotated and configured to start the application context. This class is the entry point of your Spring Boot application.

```
import org.springframework.boot.SpringApplication;
import org.springframework.boot.autoconfigure.SpringBootApplication;
```

```
@SpringBootApplication
public class JpaDemoApplication {
    public static void main(String[] args) {
        SpringApplication.run(JpaDemoApplication.class, args);
    }
}
```

Step 7: Verify the Setup

Finally, verify the correct setup by running your application. The following snippet runs a simple test to check if the context loads successfully.

```
import org.junit.jupiter.api.Test;
import org.springframework.boot.test.context.SpringBootTest;

@SpringBootTest
class JpaDemoApplicationTests {
    @Test
    void contextLoads() {
    }
}
```

This comprehensive step-by-step setup ensures that Spring Data JPA is correctly configured and ready to manage data access within your Java application.

6.3 Understanding Spring Data Repositories

Spring Data repositories are pivotal in simplifying data access within Spring-based applications. They provide a higher-level abstraction over data access layers, which mitigates the need for boilerplate code typically associated with data access logic.

At the core of Spring Data repositories lies the *Repository* interface, which serves as a marker interface. The Spring Data framework detects and automatically configures the repository instances from the interface definitions during the application context initialization phase. This mechanism allows developers to focus on implementing application-specific logic without managing data access boilerplate code.

Spring Data JPA provides several repository interfaces that inherit from the base *Repository* interface:

- **CrudRepository**: Provides CRUD (Create, Read, Update, Delete) functionality.

- **PagingAndSortingRepository**: Extends *CrudRepository* to add pagination and sorting capabilities.
- **JpaRepository**: Extends *PagingAndSortingRepository* and adds specific JPA-related methods such as `flush` and `saveAndFlush`.

To illustrate the usage of these repositories, consider the following *User* entity defined with JPA annotations:

```
@Entity
public class User {
    @Id
    @GeneratedValue(strategy = GenerationType.IDENTITY)
    private Long id;

    private String name;

    private String email;

    // Getters and setters omitted for brevity
}
```

Here, a *UserRepository* can be created by extending one of the aforementioned repository interfaces. For instance, extending *JpaRepository*:

```
public interface UserRepository extends JpaRepository<User, Long> {

    // Additional query methods can be defined here
}
```

By extending *JpaRepository*, *UserRepository* inherits several methods that allow basic query operations:

- `save(S entity)`: Saves a given entity.
- `findById(ID id)`: Retrieves an entity by its id.
- `findAll()`: Returns all entities.
- `deleteById(ID id)`: Deletes the entity with the given id.
- `deleteAll()`: Deletes all entities.
- `existsById(ID id)`: Returns whether an entity with the given id exists.
- `findAll(Pageable pageable)`: Returns a page of entities meeting the paging restriction provided in the *Pageable* object.

In addition to pre-defined CRUD operations, Spring Data JPA allows creating customized query methods based on method naming conventions. The framework parses the method name and constructs a query accordingly. For example:

```
public interface UserRepository extends JpaRepository<User, Long> {

    List<User> findByName(String name);

    List<User> findByEmailContaining(String keyword);

    List<User> findByNameOrEmail(String name, String email);

    Long countByEmail(String email);

    void deleteByName(String name);
}
```

With these derived query methods in place, executing a query becomes a straightforward task. For instance, to find users by name in a service class:

```
@Service
public class UserService {

    @Autowired
    private UserRepository userRepository;

    public List<User> getUsersByName(String name) {
        return userRepository.findByName(name);
    }
}
```

Certain situations may require more complex queries that cannot be expressed through method name derivation. To handle such cases, custom queries can be defined using the `@Query` annotation in the repository interface, which will be discussed later in this chapter.

Spring Data repositories support extensive customization through various configurations. Considerations include customizing repository base classes, using custom base repositories, or creating custom implementations for specific methods. These advanced configurations enable seamless integration and enhanced functionality tailored to application needs.

The role of Spring Data repositories in managing data access cannot be overstated. They abstract the complexities of data manipulation, repository creation, and configuration, thus enabling developers to deliver robust, high-performance applications with reduced effort. Integrating Spring Data repositories effectively leverages JPA's power while preserving the flexibility and scalability required in modern application development.

6.4 Derived Query Methods

Derived query methods in Spring Data JPA allow developers to define database queries directly through method names in the repository interfaces. This approach enhances readability and reduces boilerplate code, seamlessly integrating with the type-safe nature of Java. The method names append conditions and query structure, which Spring Data JPA parses to generate the appropriate SQL queries automatically.

Understanding Method Naming

Spring Data JPA relies on method name conventions to derive the appropriate query. The key elements include the entity's property names and the keywords that define the query behavior such as findBy, queryBy, countBy, etc. To illustrate, consider an 'Employee' entity with fields 'id', 'firstName', 'lastName', and 'age'. Below are examples of derived query methods utilizing these fields:

```
public interface EmployeeRepository extends JpaRepository<Employee, Long> {
    List<Employee> findByLastName(String lastName);
    List<Employee> findByAgeGreaterThanEqual(int age);
}
```

Here, Spring Data JPA identifies 'findByLastName' as a query searching for employees by 'lastName' and 'findByAgeGreaterThanEqual' as a query fetching employees with an 'age' greater than or equal to a specified value.

Keywords and Query Generation

Below is a non-exhaustive list of keywords and their purpose:

- And - Concatenates two criteria.
- Or - Specifies alternative criteria.
- Between - Specifies a range (requires two parameters).
- LessThan - Values less than the specified value.
- GreaterThan - Values greater than the specified value.
- Like - Performs wildcard searches.

- IsNull/IsNotNull - Checks for null values.
- OrderBy - Sorts the results (can combine with the properties like Asc, Desc).

Examples integrating these keywords:

```
List<Employee> findByLastNameAndAge(String lastName, int age);
List<Employee> findByFirstNameOrLastName(String firstName, String lastName);
List<Employee> findByAgeBetween(int startAge, int endAge);
List<Employee> findByFirstNameLike(String firstNamePattern);
List<Employee> findByAgeIsNull();
List<Employee> findByLastNameOrderByFirstNameAsc(String lastName);
```

Handling Nested Properties

Spring Data JPA supports querying by properties of nested entities using property path notation. Assume an 'Employee' entity has a nested 'Address' entity with a 'zipcode' field:

```
public class Employee {
    private Address address;
    // getters and setters
}

public class Address {
    private String zipcode;
    // getters and setters
}
```

Query methods can then access nested properties:

```
List<Employee> findByAddressZipcode(String zipcode);
```

Using Pagination and Sorting

Derived query methods integrate with pagination and sorting by utilizing the Pageable and Sort parameters. Utilizing these allows returning only a subset of results tailored by offset and limit constraints or ordered via specific properties. Consider the following example combining pagination with a derived query method:

```
Page<Employee> findByLastName(String lastName, Pageable pageable);
```

When calling this method, a Pageable object encapsulates pagination information:

```
Pageable pageable = PageRequest.of(0, 10, Sort.by("firstName").ascending());
Page<Employee> employees = employeeRepository.findByLastName("Smith", pageable
    );
```

Transactional Safety

As derived queries deal with database operations, ensuring transactional integrity is paramount. Spring's @Transactional annotation can apply to repository methods, controlling transaction boundaries:

```
@Transactional(readOnly = true)
List<Employee> findByLastName(String lastName);
```

Read-only transactions optimize performance by hinting to the database that no modifications will occur, allowing specific database engines to perform optimizations.

Derived query methods represent an expressive, type-safe method of defining queries, leveraging Spring Data JPA's powerful parsing capabilities. They enhance codebase readability while maintaining the necessary level of detail and complexity in interacting with persistent storage efficiently.

6.5 Custom Repository Methods

Spring Data JPA provides substantial convenience for implementing database operations through repository interfaces. Beyond the predefined query methods and derived query methods, there are scenarios where complex queries or specific custom logic must be included in the repository layer. Custom repository methods offer flexibility by allowing the definition of bespoke logic in repositories. This section elucidates the process of creating and using custom repository methods in Spring Data JPA, reinforcing understanding with detailed examples.

Creating a Custom Repository Interface

To begin with, define a custom repository interface. This interface includes the signature of the custom method that you want to implement. Typically, the custom repository interface extends the main repository interface. Here is an example of defining a custom repository interface for an entity User:

```
public interface UserRepositoryCustom {
    List<User> findUsersByStatus(String status);
}
```

In this example, the UserRepositoryCustom interface declares a method findUsersByStatus to find users based on their status.

Implementing the Custom Repository Interface

Next, you need to provide the implementation of the custom repository interface. This is achieved by creating a class that implements the custom interface. This class should also include the @Repository annotation to denote it as a repository bean. Here's the implementation of the custom repository interface:

```
@Repository
public class UserRepositoryCustomImpl implements UserRepositoryCustom {

    @PersistenceContext
    private EntityManager entityManager;

    @Override
    public List<User> findUsersByStatus(String status) {
        String hql = "FROM User WHERE status = :status";
        return entityManager.createQuery(hql, User.class)
                            .setParameter("status", status)
                            .getResultList();
    }
}
```

In the above code snippet:

- The UserRepositoryCustomImpl class implements the UserRepositoryCustom interface.
- The @PersistenceContext annotation is used to inject the EntityManager instance. This EntityManager is crucial for executing JPA queries.
- The findUsersByStatus method uses HQL (Hibernate Query Language) to construct and execute the query for retrieving users based on their status.

Integrating the Custom Repository with the Main Repository

To use custom repository methods within your main repository interface, extend your main repository interface with the custom repository interface. Here is an example of integrating the custom repository into the UserRepository:

```
public interface UserRepository extends JpaRepository<User, Long>,
    UserRepositoryCustom {
}
```

By extending UserRepositoryCustom, the UserRepository now inherits the custom method findUsersByStatus and can be used seamlessly in service layers or elsewhere in your application.

Using the Custom Repository Method

Finally, the custom method can be utilized in your service or controller layer for performing the defined operation. Here is an example of using the custom repository method in a service class:

```
@Service
public class UserService {

    @Autowired
    private UserRepository userRepository;

    public List<User> getUsersByStatus(String status) {
        return userRepository.findUsersByStatus(status);
    }
}
```

This service class:

- Utilizes the @Autowired annotation to inject an instance of UserRepository.
- Defines the getUsersByStatus method which delegates the task to the custom repository method findUsersByStatus.

When executed, this setup retrieves users based on the specific status by leveraging the custom method defined in the repository. Custom repository methods thus ensure that complex or specific queries can be handled efficiently without resorting to convoluted or less maintainable code. This integration showcases the seamless extensibility of Spring Data JPA in handling advanced querying requirements.

6.6 Configuring Spring Data JPA

Efficient and precise configuration of Spring Data JPA is critical for tailoring the persistence layer of an application to its specific needs. Here, we'll delve into various configuration techniques and parameters that enhance the functionality and performance of Spring Data JPA.

Project Setup and Dependencies

To start, ensure that the necessary dependencies are included in your project's build configuration file. For a Maven project, dependencies for Spring Data JPA and a chosen database need to be included in the pom.xml file. Illustrated below is the essential configuration:

```
<dependency>
    <groupId>org.springframework.boot</groupId>
    <artifactId>spring-boot-starter-data-jpa</artifactId>
```

```
</dependency>
<dependency>
    <groupId>com.h2database</groupId>
    <artifactId>h2</artifactId>
    <scope>runtime</scope>
</dependency>
```

For Gradle users, dependencies are added in the build.gradle file as shown:

```
dependencies {
    implementation 'org.springframework.boot:spring-boot-starter-data-jpa'
    runtimeOnly 'com.h2database:h2'
}
```

Primary Configuration File

The primary configuration for Spring Data JPA is typically done in the application.properties or application.yml file. These files contain settings that are automatically used by Spring Boot during startup.

Here is an example of application.properties for H2 database configuration:

```
spring.datasource.url=jdbc:h2:mem:testdb
spring.datasource.driverClassName=org.h2.Driver
spring.datasource.username=sa
spring.datasource.password=password
spring.jpa.database-platform=org.hibernate.dialect.H2Dialect
spring.jpa.show-sql=true
spring.jpa.hibernate.ddl-auto=update
```

Alternatively, if using application.yml:

```
spring:
  datasource:
    url: jdbc:h2:mem:testdb
    driverClassName: org.h2.Driver
    username: sa
    password: password
  jpa:
    database-platform: org.hibernate.dialect.H2Dialect
    show-sql: true
    hibernate:
      ddl-auto: update
```

Here, spring.datasource.url specifies the JDBC URL, spring.datasource.driverClassName defines the driver class, and the username and password configurations are for database authentication. The spring.jpa.database-platform property specifies the Hibernate dialect, which is necessary for the correct SQL generation for the underlying database. Setting spring.jpa.show-sql to true activates the SQL logging in the console, which is useful during development, and spring.jpa.hibernate.ddl-auto handles the schema generation, here set to update.

Advanced Configuration Properties

Beyond the basic setup, several advanced configuration properties can fine-tune the JPA behavior, such as:

- spring.jpa.properties.hibernate.cache.use_second_level_cache controls whether the second-level cache is used.
- spring.jpa.properties.hibernate.enable_lazy_load_no_trans allows the loading of lazy-loaded data without a transactional context.
- spring.jpa.hibernate.naming.physical-strategy sets the physical naming strategy.

These parameters, set within application.properties or application.yml, can significantly affect the performance and behavior of the persistence layer.

Entity Manager Configuration

The EntityManager is pivotal in JPA. Configuring it correctly ensures efficient resource management. You can explicitly configure the EntityManagerFactory bean:

```
import javax.persistence.EntityManagerFactory;
import org.springframework.context.annotation.Bean;
import org.springframework.orm.jpa.JpaTransactionManager;
import org.springframework.orm.jpa.LocalContainerEntityManagerFactoryBean;
import org.springframework.context.annotation.Configuration;
import org.springframework.transaction.PlatformTransactionManager;
import org.springframework.data.jpa.repository.config.EnableJpaRepositories;

@Configuration
@EnableJpaRepositories(basePackages = "com.example.repository")
public class JpaConfig {

    @Bean
    public LocalContainerEntityManagerFactoryBean entityManagerFactory(
            EntityManagerFactoryBuilder builder) {
        return builder.dataSource(dataSource())
                      .packages("com.example.model")
                      .persistenceUnit("examplePU")
                      .build();
    }

    @Bean
    public PlatformTransactionManager transactionManager(EntityManagerFactory
            entityManagerFactory) {
        return new JpaTransactionManager(entityManagerFactory);
    }

    // Define DataSource bean here
}
```

In this configuration, the LocalContainerEntityManagerFactoryBean is set up with the data source and package scan for entity classes. The transactionManager bean is required for managing transactions.

Customizing the Repository Configuration

Spring Data JPA can be customized using the @EnableJpaRepositories annotation's attributes, such as basePackages, repositoryFactoryBeanClass, queryLookupStrategy, and entityManagerFactoryRef. For instance:

```
@EnableJpaRepositories(
    basePackages = "com.example.repository",
    repositoryFactoryBeanClass = MyCustomRepositoryFactoryBean.class,
    queryLookupStrategy = QueryLookupStrategy.Key.CREATE_IF_NOT_FOUND,
    entityManagerFactoryRef = "entityManagerFactory")
```

This setup customizes the repository scanning location, specifies a custom factory bean, establishes a strategy for query lookup, and references a specific EntityManagerFactory.

Through these meticulous configurations, Spring Data JPA facilitates tailored persistence operations, enhancing both performance and functionality of the Java application.

6.7 Pagination and Sorting

Pagination and sorting are crucial features for efficiently managing large datasets within your database. Spring Data JPA offers robust support for these operations, ensuring your applications can retrieve and display data in a performant manner. This section delves into the mechanisms provided by Spring Data JPA for implementing pagination and sorting, enhancing the efficiency of your data retrieval processes.

Spring Data JPA provides a flexible and easy-to-use 'Pageable' interface, which encapsulates information about the requested page such as page number, page size, and sorting information. To utilize pagination in repository methods, you need to pass an instance of 'Pageable' to a query method that returns a 'Page<T>' object.

Consider the following repository interface method:

```
import org.springframework.data.domain.Page;
import org.springframework.data.domain.Pageable;
import org.springframework.data.jpa.repository.JpaRepository;

public interface UserRepository extends JpaRepository<User, Long> {
    Page<User> findAll(Pageable pageable);
```

```
}
```

In this example, the 'findAll' method returns a 'Page<User>', which contains not just the list of users, but also metadata about the total number of elements, number of total pages, and the current page index. To execute the query with pagination, you need to create a 'PageRequest' object, which is a concrete implementation of 'Pageable' interface:

```
import org.springframework.data.domain.PageRequest;
import org.springframework.data.domain.Pageable;

Pageable pageable = PageRequest.of(0, 10); // Page index starts at 0, with a page size
    of 10
Page<User> resultPage = userRepository.findAll(pageable);

List<User> users = resultPage.getContent(); // List of users in the requested page
```

This example requests the first page (index 0) with a size of 10. The 'Page<User>' result allows you to extract the paginated list of users and provides methods such as 'getTotalElements()', 'getTotalPages()', 'getNumber()', and 'hasNext()', which help in navigating through the paginated data.

Sorting is equally essential and can be seamlessly incorporated into the pagination process. The 'PageRequest' class provides an overloaded version of the 'of' method that accepts sorting parameters. For instance, to sort users by their username in ascending order, the code looks like this:

```
import org.springframework.data.domain.Sort;
import org.springframework.data.domain.Sort.Order;

Pageable pageable = PageRequest.of(0, 10, Sort.by(Order.asc("username")));
Page<User> resultPage = userRepository.findAll(pageable);

List<User> users = resultPage.getContent();
```

In this snippet, the 'Sort.by' method constructs a 'Sort' object that specifies the sort order for the 'username' attribute. You can chain multiple sort orders by passing additional 'Order' instances to the 'Sort.by' method.

Moreover, 'Sort' also permits specifying the direction of sorting using the 'Direction' enum. Here is how to sort users by their usernames in descending order and their IDs in ascending order:

```
import org.springframework.data.domain.Sort;
import org.springframework.data.domain.Sort.Direction;

Pageable pageable = PageRequest.of(0, 10, Sort.by(Direction.DESC, "username")
                                        .and(Sort.by(Direction.ASC, "id")));
```

```
Page<User> resultPage = userRepository.findAll(pageable);

List<User> users = resultPage.getContent();
```

In advanced scenarios, you might want to apply pagination and sorting on more complex queries. Spring Data JPA allows you to combine these features with custom query methods. When defining a custom query method using the '@Query' annotation, you can include 'Pageable' parameter to enable pagination and sorting:

```
import org.springframework.data.domain.Page;
import org.springframework.data.domain.Pageable;
import org.springframework.data.jpa.repository.Query;
import org.springframework.data.repository.query.Param;

public interface UserRepository extends JpaRepository<User, Long> {
    @Query("SELECT u FROM User u WHERE u.email LIKE %:email%")
    Page<User> findByEmailContaining(@Param("email") String email, Pageable
         pageable);
}
```

This example demonstrates a custom query that searches for users based on their email addresses. By including the 'Pageable' parameter, you enable pagination and sorting for the result set. To execute this query, you would use:

```
Pageable pageable = PageRequest.of(0, 10, Sort.by(Direction.ASC, "email"));
Page<User> resultPage = userRepository.findByEmailContaining("example", pageable)
     ;

List<User> users = resultPage.getContent();
```

Such flexibility in combining custom queries with pagination and sorting lets you manage large datasets effectively while maintaining concise and readable code. Understanding and leveraging these features within Spring Data JPA significantly enhances the performance and user experience of your applications.

6.8 Spring Data JPA Query Creation

Spring Data JPA provides robust query creation mechanisms that cater to a wide range of query needs, from simple to complex ones. The framework simplifies the process of crafting queries by leveraging method naming conventions in the repository interface. This section delves into the intricacies of Spring Data JPA query creation, ensuring a precise understanding of the concepts and practical applications.

The creation of queries using Spring Data JPA revolves primarily around method names. By following specific conventions, the framework can automatically interpret and provide the underlying SQL for you, reducing the need to manually write SQL statements. This feature becomes especially powerful when dealing with frequently occurring queries.

Method Naming Conventions

The first step in creating queries in Spring Data JPA is understanding the method naming conventions. These conventions are based on a declarative approach where the method name itself contains keywords that map to specific query operations.

Common keywords include:

- findBy: Finds records by specific attributes.
- readBy: Provides a read-only mechanism similar to findBy.
- queryBy: Similar to findBy but indicates query type clearly.
- countBy: Returns the count of records matching specific criteria.
- deleteBy: Deletes records that match specific criteria.
- removeBy: Synonym for deleteBy.

Consider an entity class User with attributes id, username, and email. A simple query method to find a user by username can be defined as:

```
public interface UserRepository extends JpaRepository<User, Long> {
    User findByUsername(String username);
}
```

The method name findByUsername informs Spring Data JPA to generate a query similar to:

```
SELECT u FROM User u WHERE u.username = ?1
```

Combining Conditions

Spring Data JPA allows combining multiple conditions using logical operators like And and Or in method names.

```
User findByUsernameAndEmail(String username, String email);
```

This method name translates to:

```
SELECT u FROM User u WHERE u.username = ?1 AND u.email = ?2
```

Similarly, the Or operator can be used:

```
List<User> findByUsernameOrEmail(String username, String email);
```

Which corresponds to:

SELECT u FROM User u WHERE u.username = ?1 OR u.email = ?2

Handling Query Return Types

Spring Data JPA supports various return types for query methods, including:

- Entity types (e.g., User)
- Optional<T>
- List<T>
- Page<T> for paginated results
- Slice<T> for more efficient paging
- Stream<T> for processing large datasets

Sorting Results

To sort query results, append the OrderBy keyword followed by the property name and sorting direction (Asc for ascending and Desc for descending).

```
List<User> findByUsernameOrderByEmailAsc(String username);
```

This method generates the following query:

SELECT u FROM User u WHERE u.username = ?1 ORDER BY u.email ASC

Paging Through Results

Paging is supported through method signatures that include a Pageable parameter. The Pageable interface provides pagination information, such as page number and size.

```
Page<User> findByEmail(String email, Pageable pageable);
```

The corresponding query includes the pagination details provided by the Pageable parameter:

SELECT u FROM User u WHERE u.email = ?1

Spring Data JPA appends LIMIT and OFFSET based on the Pageable information.

Using Native Queries

Although derived query methods can cover a wide array of use cases, there are instances where native queries are necessary, such as for complex SQL operations or database-specific features. This can be accomplished using the @Query annotation with the nativeQuery attribute set to true.

```
@Query(value = "SELECT * FROM users WHERE username = ?1", nativeQuery =
    true)
User findByUsernameNative(String username);
```

Native queries should be used judiciously to maintain database portability and avoid coupling application logic with specific SQL dialects.

Understanding these concepts of query creation with Spring Data JPA enhances the ability to write efficient and readable database interaction code. This seamless and declarative approach simplifies querying and maintains consistency and readability in database operations.

6.9 Using @Query for Custom Queries

The dynamic nature of query creation provided by Spring Data JPA is a powerful feature, but there are scenarios where more control is necessary over the queries being executed. In such cases, the @Query annotation is employed. The @Query annotation allows the definition of JPQL (Java Persistence Query Language) or native SQL queries directly in the repository interface. This enables the execution of sophisticated queries and optimizations tailored to specific needs.

The @Query annotation is placed above the method definition in the repository interface. There are several possible configurations and options for @Query, including both JPQL and native queries, as well as named parameters, positional parameters, and pagination features.

Basic Usage of @Query with JPQL

The Java Persistence Query Language (JPQL) provides a way to define database queries based on the entity model. Here's an example of a basic JPQL query using the @Query annotation:

```
public interface EmployeeRepository extends JpaRepository<Employee, Long> {

    @Query("SELECT e FROM Employee e WHERE e.department = ?1 AND e.salary
        > ?2")
    List<Employee> findByDepartmentAndSalaryGreaterThan(String department,
        double salary);
```

```
}
```

In this example, the method findByDepartmentAndSalaryGreaterThan is annotated with @Query, specifying a JPQL query that selects employees from a particular department with a salary exceeding a given amount. The ?1 and ?2 are positional parameters.

Using Named Parameters in @Query

Named parameters enhance query readability by associating specific names with parameters. Here's an example demonstrating the use of named parameters:

```
public interface EmployeeRepository extends JpaRepository<Employee, Long> {

    @Query("SELECT e FROM Employee e WHERE e.department = :department
          AND e.salary > :salary")
    List<Employee> findByDepartmentAndSalaryGreaterThan(@Param("department")
          String department, @Param("salary") double salary);

}
```

In this example, named parameters :department and :salary are used in the query, improving the clarity of parameter mapping.

Executing Native SQL Queries

There are cases where JPQL is insufficient, and you need to leverage native SQL for more complex operations or performance reasons. For such instances, setting the nativeQuery element to true in the @Query annotation allows the execution of native SQL queries:

```
public interface EmployeeRepository extends JpaRepository<Employee, Long> {

    @Query(value = "SELECT * FROM employees e WHERE e.department = :
          department", nativeQuery = true)
    List<Employee> findByDepartmentNative(@Param("department") String
          department);

}
```

Here, the findByDepartmentNative method uses a native SQL query to find employees in a specified department. The nativeQuery attribute instructs Spring Data JPA to treat the query string as a native SQL query.

Pagination and Sorting with @Query

The @Query annotation also supports integration with pagination and sorting functionality. For instance, the following example demonstrates how to paginate query results:

```
public interface EmployeeRepository extends JpaRepository<Employee, Long> {

    @Query("SELECT e FROM Employee e WHERE e.department = :department")
    Page<Employee> findByDepartmentWithPagination(@Param("department") String
          department, Pageable pageable);

}
```

When executing this query, a Pageable parameter is passed to the method. This allows the results to be paginated according to the specifications enclosed in the Pageable object.

Modifying Queries with @Modifying

For update and delete operations, the @Modifying annotation is used in combination with @Query. Here's an example of an update operation:

```
public interface EmployeeRepository extends JpaRepository<Employee, Long> {

    @Modifying
    @Query("UPDATE Employee e SET e.salary = :salary WHERE e.department = :
          department")
    int updateSalaryByDepartment(@Param("salary") double salary, @Param("
          department") String department);

}
```

In this example, the updateSalaryByDepartment method updates the salary of employees in the specified department. The @Modifying annotation is mandatory for update and delete queries to indicate that the method will modify the database state.

Handling Nullability with @Query

The result type of a custom query can be managed to handle nullable returns. When a method is expected to return a single result but may encounter no data, the return type can be an Optional:

```
public interface EmployeeRepository extends JpaRepository<Employee, Long> {

    @Query("SELECT e FROM Employee e WHERE e.id = :id")
    Optional<Employee> findByIdOptional(@Param("id") Long id);

}
```

This ensures that the method findByIdOptional gracefully handles cases where no employee is found for the provided id by returning an Optional<Employee>.

These various ways to use the @Query annotation facilitate the creation of customized queries tailored to complex and specific application requirements. By leveraging JPQL, native queries, named parameters, pagination, and sorting, one can achieve precise and efficient data retrieval and manipulation. Furthermore, the inclusion of @Modifying operations ensures that update and delete actions are straightforward and implicitly understood, enhancing the robustness and maintainability of the codebase.

6.10 Integration with Spring Boot

Integrating Spring Data JPA with Spring Boot streamlines development by simplifying configuration and enhancing productivity. Spring Boot automates configuration and thus reduces boilerplate code commonly associated with setting up Spring applications. This section will elucidate the steps and key concepts necessary for effectively integrating Spring Data JPA within a Spring Boot application.

To begin, ensure that your project is set up with Spring Boot and that you have the necessary dependencies. In your project's pom.xml file, include the following dependencies:

```
<dependency>
    <groupId>org.springframework.boot</groupId>
    <artifactId>spring-boot-starter-data-jpa</artifactId>
</dependency>
<dependency>
    <groupId>org.springframework.boot</groupId>
    <artifactId>spring-boot-starter-web</artifactId>
</dependency>
<dependency>
    <groupId>com.h2database</groupId>
    <artifactId>h2</artifactId>
    <scope>runtime</scope>
</dependency>
```

In this example, the spring-boot-starter-data-jpa dependency includes Spring Data JPA along with Hibernate as the default JPA provider, while the spring-boot-starter-web is included for building web applications. The h2 database dependency is used for an in-memory database, which is convenient for development and testing.

Next, configure the database connection in the application.properties file located in the src/main/resources directory. Below are sample properties for an H2 database:

```
spring.datasource.url=jdbc:h2:mem:testdb
spring.datasource.driverClassName=org.h2.Driver
spring.datasource.username=sa
spring.datasource.password=password
spring.jpa.database-platform=org.hibernate.dialect.H2Dialect
```

These properties configure the datasource URL, driver, and credentials for the database, as well as the Hibernate dialect that matches the database type.

Define your JPA entities by annotating your classes with @Entity, @Table, and relevant JPA annotations. For instance, consider the following entity class:

```
import javax.persistence.Entity;
import javax.persistence.GeneratedValue;
import javax.persistence.GenerationType;
import javax.persistence.Id;
import javax.persistence.Table;

@Entity
@Table(name = "users")
public class User {
    @Id
    @GeneratedValue(strategy = GenerationType.IDENTITY)
    private Long id;

    private String name;
    private String email;

    // getters and setters
}
```

In this example, the @Entity annotation marks the User class as a JPA entity. The @Table annotation specifies the table name in the database. The @Id and @GeneratedValue annotations define the primary key and its generation strategy.

Next, create a repository interface for your entity by extending the JpaRepository interface provided by Spring Data JPA:

```
import org.springframework.data.jpa.repository.JpaRepository;

public interface UserRepository extends JpaRepository<User, Long> {
    // Additional query methods, if needed
}
```

By extending JpaRepository, the UserRepository interface inherits several CRUD methods, such as save, findById, findAll, deleteById, and many more. You can also define additional query methods based on entity attributes.

Implement a service layer to handle business logic. For example:

```
import org.springframework.beans.factory.annotation.Autowired;
import org.springframework.stereotype.Service;
import java.util.List;

@Service
public class UserService {
    private final UserRepository userRepository;
```

```
    @Autowired
    public UserService(UserRepository userRepository) {
        this.userRepository = userRepository;
    }

    public List<User> findAllUsers() {
        return userRepository.findAll();
    }

    public User saveUser(User user) {
        return userRepository.save(user);
    }

    // Additional service methods as needed
}
```

In the UserService class, the @Service annotation denotes that it is a service component in the Spring context. Through dependency injection, the UserRepository is autowired into the service class, allowing access to repository methods.

Finally, create a controller to handle web requests, for example:

```
import org.springframework.beans.factory.annotation.Autowired;
import org.springframework.web.bind.annotation.*;

import java.util.List;

@RestController
@RequestMapping("/users")
public class UserController {
    private final UserService userService;

    @Autowired
    public UserController(UserService userService) {
        this.userService = userService;
    }

    @GetMapping
    public List<User> getAllUsers() {
        return userService.findAllUsers();
    }

    @PostMapping
    public User createUser(@RequestBody User user) {
        return userService.saveUser(user);
    }

    // Additional endpoints as needed
}
```

The UserController class uses the @RestController annotation, indicating that it is a web controller. The @RequestMapping annotation at the class level maps requests to /users. The @GetMapping and @PostMapping annotations correspond to HTTP GET and POST operations, respectively, facilitating interaction with the UserService methods.

Executing the Spring Boot application can be achieved through the main application class annotated with @SpringBootApplication:

```
import org.springframework.boot.SpringApplication;
import org.springframework.boot.autoconfigure.SpringBootApplication;

@SpringBootApplication
public class Application {
    public static void main(String[] args) {
        SpringApplication.run(Application.class, args);
    }
}
```

Running this main class launches the Spring Boot application, initializes the Spring context, and sets up the embedded server. You can then access the various endpoints defined in your controllers, allowing for seamless interaction with the data managed by Spring Data JPA.

Through this practical integration of Spring Data JPA with Spring Boot, developers benefit from automated configuration, reduced boilerplate, and a more streamlined development workflow, enabling efficient management of JPA entities and repositories in modern Java applications.

Chapter 7

CRUD Operations with Spring Data JPA

This chapter focuses on implementing CRUD (Create, Read, Update, Delete) operations using Spring Data JPA. It begins with creating and configuring repositories and demonstrates how to save entities using save() and saveAll() methods. The chapter covers retrieving entities with findById() and findAll(), updating entities using save() with existing entities, and deleting entities with deleteById() and deleteAll(). It also addresses handling relationships in CRUD operations, employing pagination and sorting, managing error handling and validation, and best practices for efficient and effective CRUD operations using Spring Data JPA.

7.1 Introduction to CRUD Operations with Spring Data JPA

CRUD operations constitute the foundational activities for any Java application interacting with a database. CRUD is an acronym that stands for Create, Read, Update, and Delete, and these operations encapsulate the basic data manipulation functions that are essential for persistent storage. Spring Data JPA, a part of the larger Spring Data family, simplifies the implementation of these operations by providing a repository abstraction for a relational database.

Spring Data JPA allows the developer to focus more on the application's business logic rather than boilerplate code, as it handles many repetitive tasks associated with data access. By using interfaces and annotations, developers can efficiently perform CRUD operations with minimal explicit SQL, as Spring Data JPA generates the necessary SQL under the hood.

Create Operation:

Creating a new entity in the database involves mapping an instance of a user-defined class to a corresponding database table record. The primary method for achieving this in Spring Data JPA is the save() method that is provided by the repository interface.

```
@Entity
public class User {
    @Id
    @GeneratedValue(strategy = GenerationType.IDENTITY)
    private Long id;
    private String name;
    private String email;

    // Getters and Setters
}

public interface UserRepository extends JpaRepository<User, Long> { }

public class UserService {
    @Autowired
    private UserRepository userRepository;

    public void createUser(String name, String email) {
        User user = new User();
        user.setName(name);
        user.setEmail(email);
        userRepository.save(user);
    }
}
```

Executing the createUser method results in an SQL INSERT operation to store the new User entity in the database.

Read Operation:

Reading involves retrieving entity data from the database. The repository interface provides the findById() and findAll() methods for this purpose. These methods issue SQL queries to fetch data based on the primary key or retrieve all records, respectively.

```
public User getUser(Long id) {
    return userRepository.findById(id).orElse(null);
}

public List<User> getAllUsers() {
    return userRepository.findAll();
```

```
}
```

Given a 'UserService' object, invoking getUser(1L) fetches the user with id 1, and getAllUsers() retrieves all user records from the database.

Update Operation:

Updating an entity entails modifying the existing record in the database. The save() method is versatile and also handles updates, not just inserts. When an existing entity with a valid identifier is passed to save(), the corresponding record is updated.

```
public void updateUser(Long id, String newName, String newEmail) {
    User user = userRepository.findById(id).orElse(null);
    if (user != null) {
        user.setName(newName);
        user.setEmail(newEmail);
        userRepository.save(user);
    }
}
```

When updateUser(1L, "Updated Name", "newemail@example.com") is executed, it performs an SQL UPDATE to modify the existing record.

Delete Operation:

Deleting an entity removes the corresponding record from the database. The repository provides methods like deleteById() and deleteAll() to facilitate this operation.

```
public void deleteUser(Long id) {
    userRepository.deleteById(id);
}

public void deleteAllUsers() {
    userRepository.deleteAll();
}
```

The method call deleteUser(1L) results in an SQL DELETE for the user with id 1, while invoking deleteAllUsers() clears all user records from the database.

Spring Data JPA harnesses the power of Spring Framework and Java Persistence API (JPA), making CRUD operations both intuitive and flexible. Developers can focus on defining their domain models and the essential business logic, while Spring Data JPA takes care of generating efficient database interactions. This not only enhances productivity but also ensures that the persistence layer remains consistent, maintainable, and aligned with best practices.

7.2 Creating and Configuring Repositories

To efficiently manage database interactions in a Spring Data JPA application, repositories provide the necessary abstraction layer. Repositories offer a clean way to encapsulate data access code, thereby improving maintainability and simplicity in code structure. This section delves into the creation and configuration of repositories, ensuring that they are optimally set up for CRUD operations.

Spring Data JPA repositories are interfaces which can be instantiated and used by Spring without requiring any implementation code. The framework generates implementations at runtime. This feature significantly reduces boilerplate code and lets developers focus on business logic.

Define Repository Interfaces:

To begin, annotate the repository interface with @Repository. This informs Spring that the interface is a repository bean and eligible for component scanning:

```
import org.springframework.data.repository.CrudRepository;
import org.springframework.stereotype.Repository;

@Repository
public interface UserRepository extends CrudRepository<User, Long> {
}
```

In the example above, UserRepository extends CrudRepository, which provides basic CRUD functionality. The type parameters, User and Long, indicate the entity type and its primary key type, respectively.

Enabling JPA Repositories:

To enable repository support, annotate the configuration class with @EnableJpaRepositories. This ensures Spring auto-detects interfaces extending Repository:

```
import org.springframework.context.annotation.Configuration;
import org.springframework.data.jpa.repository.config.EnableJpaRepositories;

@Configuration
@EnableJpaRepositories(basePackages = "com.example.project.repository")
public class JpaConfig {
}
```

The basePackages attribute specifies the packages to scan for repository interfaces.

Customizing Repository Base Classes:

While CrudRepository suffices for many applications, custom base classes can be used to add common methods across multiple repositories. Define a custom base interface:

```
import org.springframework.data.repository.NoRepositoryBean;
import org.springframework.data.repository.Repository;

@NoRepositoryBean
public interface BaseRepository<T, ID> extends Repository<T, ID> {
    T findOne(ID id);
    Iterable<T> findAll();
    // additional common methods
}
```

Next, create concrete repository interfaces extending the custom base interface:

```
import org.springframework.stereotype.Repository;

@Repository
public interface ProductRepository extends BaseRepository<Product, Long> {
    // repository-specific methods
}
```

Configuring Repository Properties:

Spring Data JPA repositories can be fine-tuned using properties in application.properties or application.yml. The following properties control repository behavior:

```
spring.jpa.show-sql=true
spring.jpa.hibernate.ddl-auto=update
spring.jpa.properties.hibernate.format_sql=true
```

show-sql enables SQL statement logging. ddl-auto dictates how the Hibernate schema update tool should manipulate the database schema. format_sql improves log readability.

Custom Repository Implementations:

For logic that cannot be contained within custom base interfaces or existing repository methods, custom implementations may be necessary. First, create an implementation class:

```
import javax.persistence.EntityManager;
import javax.persistence.PersistenceContext;
import org.springframework.stereotype.Repository;

@Repository
public class CustomUserRepositoryImpl implements CustomUserRepository {

    @PersistenceContext
    private EntityManager em;

    @Override
```

```
    public List<User> findUsersByStatus(String status) {
        String query = "FROM User WHERE status = :status";
        return em.createQuery(query, User.class)
                .setParameter("status", status)
                .getResultList();
    }
}
```

Then, extend the repository interface with the custom interface:

```
import org.springframework.data.repository.CrudRepository;

public interface UserRepository extends CrudRepository<User, Long>,
      CustomUserRepository {
}
```

Finally, configure Spring to use the custom implementation:

```
import org.springframework.context.annotation.Configuration;
import org.springframework.data.jpa.repository.config.EnableJpaRepositories;

@Configuration
@EnableJpaRepositories(repositoryBaseClass = CustomUserRepositoryImpl.class)
public class JpaConfig {
}
```

This instructs Spring to employ CustomUserRepositoryImpl for custom methods in the repository.

The correct setup of repositories plays a pivotal role in ensuring smooth data access operations, enabling developers to efficiently implement CRUD functionalities. Through proper interface definition, configuration, and customization, repositories in Spring Data JPA can be a powerful tool for application development.

7.3 Saving Entities: Using save() and saveAll()

In Spring Data JPA, saving entities to the database is a fundamental operation. The framework provides two principal methods for this purpose: save() and saveAll(). Understanding their proper usage and behavior is essential for managing data persistence effectively.

The save() method is used for saving a single entity. When invoking this method, Spring Data JPA either inserts a new row or updates an existing row in the database, based on the identifier's presence and value. The identifier is typically annotated with @Id in the entity class. The process of saving an entity can be illustrated with the following

example:

```
@Entity
public class Employee {
    @Id
    @GeneratedValue(strategy = GenerationType.IDENTITY)
    private Long id;

    private String firstName;
    private String lastName;
    private String email;

    // Getters and setters
}
```

Here, the Employee class defines an entity with various attributes. The EmployeeRepository interface extends JpaRepository:

```
public interface EmployeeRepository extends JpaRepository<Employee, Long> {
}
```

To save an instance of the Employee entity, a typical usage of the save() method is shown below:

```
@Service
public class EmployeeService {
    @Autowired
    private EmployeeRepository employeeRepository;

    public Employee createOrUpdateEmployee(Employee employee) {
        return employeeRepository.save(employee);
    }
}
```

In this code, createOrUpdateEmployee method accepts an Employee object and passes it to the save() method of EmployeeRepository. If the entity's id is null, Spring Data JPA performs an insert operation. If the id is present and matches an existing row, it performs an update operation. The save() method returns the persisted entity, which includes any changes made by the persistence context, such as assigned identifier values.

The behavior of saveAll() is similar but operates on collections:

```
public List<Employee> saveEmployees(List<Employee> employees) {
    return employeeRepository.saveAll(employees);
}
```

Here, saveEmployees method saves a collection of Employee entities in a single operation. The saveAll() method iterates over each Employee entity in the collection and applies the same logic used by save(). Utilizing saveAll() can be more efficient than calling save() multiple times, as it allows the persistence provider to optimize batched database writes.

Considerations must be made when dealing with large datasets. Inserting a significant number of entities in a single transaction can exhaust the persistence context's memory, potentially leading to out-of-memory errors. A common strategy is processing entities in batches:

```
@Transactional
public void saveEmployeesInBatches(List<Employee> employees, int batchSize) {
    for (int i = 0; i < employees.size(); i++) {
        employeeRepository.save(employees.get(i));
        if ((i + 1) % batchSize == 0 && i > 0) {
            employeeRepository.flush();
            employeeRepository.clear();
        }
    }
}
```

This method saves entities in segments defined by batchSize. After each batch, the persistence context, or session, is flushed and cleared to free up memory. While Transactional annotation ensures that multiple operations within a single batch are treated as an atomic unit, the flush() method forces the persistence context to synchronize with the database, and clear() detaches all entities, preventing memory overhead.

It is also critical to handle exceptions during save operations. Spring Data JPA can throw exceptions like DataIntegrityViolationException if constraints are violated. Implementing appropriate error handling mechanisms ensures robustness:

```
public Employee createEmployeeWithExceptionHandling(Employee employee) {
    try {
        return employeeRepository.save(employee);
    } catch (DataIntegrityViolationException e) {
        // Handle exception, e.g., log error and rethrow a custom exception
        throw new CustomDatabaseException("Error creating employee", e);
    }
}
```

In this example, potential DataIntegrityViolationException is caught, logged, and rethrown as a custom application-specific exception. This approach provides clearer semantics and facilitates debugging.

Leveraging the save() and saveAll() methods effectively requires understanding their default behavior, efficiency in handling large datasets, and implementing robust exception handling.

7.4 Retrieving Entities: Using findById() and findAll()

In this section, we will delve into the retrieval of entities using the findById() and findAll() methods with Spring Data JPA, offering detailed insights into their practical applications and advantages. Understanding these methods is essential for efficiently querying the database and managing the data persistence layer in a Java application.

The findById() method is designed to retrieve a single entity from the database by its primary key. It returns an Optional<T> where T is the entity type. Utilizing this method allows handling the presence or absence of an entity fluidly without risking null reference exceptions. Consider the following interface snippet for a repository handling User entities:

```
// UserRepository.java
public interface UserRepository extends JpaRepository<User, Long> {
}
```

To use the findById() method, one would invoke it as follows:

```
Optional<User> optionalUser = userRepository.findById(1L);
if (optionalUser.isPresent()) {
    User user = optionalUser.get();
    System.out.println(user.getName());
} else {
    System.out.println("User with ID 1 not found.");
}
```

The findById() method leverages the repository pattern to encapsulate database access logic, promoting cleaner and more maintainable code. The use of Optional provides a robust way to handle cases where the entity may not exist, circumventing the pitfalls of directly dealing with nulls.

The findAll() method is employed to retrieve all entities managed by the repository. It returns a List<T>, where T represents the entity type. Invoking this method typically looks like the following:

```
List<User> allUsers = userRepository.findAll();
for (User user : allUsers) {
    System.out.println(user.getName());
}
```

findAll() is particularly useful for operations requiring the processing of comprehensive data sets, like generating reports or performing bulk updates. However, one must consider the performance implications of loading large numbers of entities into memory. In such scenarios, it is often prudent to combine findAll() with pagination methods, which we will discuss in a subsequent section.

Spring Data JPA also facilitates custom query derivation based on method names. Consequently, one can define methods for more specific retrievals without writing explicit JPQL or SQL queries. For example:

```
// UserRepository.java
public interface UserRepository extends JpaRepository<User, Long> {
    List<User> findByLastName(String lastName);
}
```

Retrieve users by their last name as follows:

```
List<User> smiths = userRepository.findByLastName("Smith");
for (User smith : smiths) {
    System.out.println(smith.getName());
}
```

This feature leverages Spring Data JPA's parsing mechanism, interpreting method names to generate the appropriate queries dynamically.

Additionally, it's critical to acknowledge the advantages of proper entity annotations in retrieval operations. For instance, using the @Entity and @Id annotations correctly ensures efficient entity management and retrieval:

```
// User.java
@Entity
public class User {
    @Id
    @GeneratedValue(strategy = GenerationType.IDENTITY)
    private Long id;

    private String firstName;
    private String lastName;

    // getters and setters
}
```

Proper indexing and primary key management contribute significantly to the performance and efficiency of retrieval operations. Employing annotations such as @Indexed for frequently queried fields can optimize database performance further.

The findById() and findAll() methods form the cornerstone of basic data retrieval in Spring Data JPA, facilitating efficient and straightforward interactions with the database. The robustness of these methods, coupled with Spring Data JPA's powerful query derivation capabilities, provides developers with a solid foundation for data access operations. As we proceed, we'll explore more advanced retrieval techniques, including pagination and sorting, to enhance the efficiency of our data access layer.

7.5 Updating Entities: Using save() with Existing Entities

Updating entities is a critical aspect of CRUD operations, ensuring that the persisted state reflects the latest modifications. This section delves into employing the save() method for updating existing entities with Spring Data JPA.

The save() method serves dual purposes—it can insert new entities and update existing ones. When updating, save() distinguishes new entities from existing entities based on the entity's identifier (ID) field. If the entity has an ID that matches an existing record in the database, save() will perform an update. Otherwise, it will proceed with an insertion.

```
@Entity
public class User {
    @Id
    @GeneratedValue(strategy = GenerationType.IDENTITY)
    private Long id;
    private String username;
    private String email;

    // getters and setters
}
```

In the context of our example, the User entity defined above possesses an ID generated automatically. Let's consider a situation where we need to update a user's email address.

Firstly, we create a repository interface for the User entity, extending the JpaRepository interface:

```
public interface UserRepository extends JpaRepository<User, Long> {
}
```

To update an entity, fetch the existing entity, make the necessary changes to its fields, and save it back to the repository:

```
@Service
public class UserService {
    @Autowired
    private UserRepository userRepository;
```

```
    public User updateUserEmail(Long userId, String newEmail) {
        // Fetch the user entity by ID
        User user = userRepository.findById(userId)
                .orElseThrow(() -> new EntityNotFoundException("User not found"));

        // Update the email field
        user.setEmail(newEmail);

        // Save the updated entity
        return userRepository.save(user);
    }
}
```

In the above example, the findById() method retrieves the user entity. If the entity doesn't exist, an EntityNotFoundException is thrown. Upon fetching the entity, the email is updated, and the modified entity is saved again using the save() method, which performs an update operation since the entity exists.

Below is a corresponding unit test to verify the update operation:

```
@RunWith(SpringRunner.class)
@SpringBootTest
public class UserServiceTests {

    @Autowired
    private UserService userService;

    @Autowired
    private UserRepository userRepository;

    @Test
    public void testUpdateUserEmail() {
        // Create and save a user entity
        User user = new User();
        user.setUsername("john_doe");
        user.setEmail("john.doe@example.com");
        user = userRepository.save(user);

        // Update the user's email
        User updatedUser = userService.updateUserEmail(user.getId(), "john.
            doe@newdomain.com");

        // Verify the update
        assertThat(updatedUser.getEmail()).isEqualTo("john.doe@newdomain.com");
        assertThat(userRepository.findById(user.getId()).get().getEmail())
                .isEqualTo("john.doe@newdomain.com");
    }
}
```

The above test case creates a new user entity, updates the email, and verifies the update operation by asserting that the email field is modified, both in the returned entity and in the persisted state.

Transactional context is vital for update operations. By default, Spring Data JPA methods are transactional. However, ensure to handle transactions appropriately when implementing custom persisting logic.

A common scenario might require the simultaneous update of multiple fields. This can be seamlessly managed by amending the relevant fields before invoking save():

```
public User updateUserDetails(Long userId, String newUsername, String newEmail) {
    User user = userRepository.findById(userId)
            .orElseThrow(() -> new EntityNotFoundException("User not found"));
    user.setUsername(newUsername);
    user.setEmail(newEmail);
    return userRepository.save(user);
}
```

Additional care is required when updating entities with nested relationships. When modifying relationships, ensure that the corresponding entity states are managed correctly. For example, when updating a User entity's address:

```
@Entity
public class Address {
    @Id
    @GeneratedValue(strategy = GenerationType.IDENTITY)
    private Long id;
    private String street;
    private String city;

    // getters and setters
}

@Entity
public class User {
    @Id
    @GeneratedValue(strategy = GenerationType.IDENTITY)
    private Long id;
    private String username;
    private String email;

    @OneToOne(cascade = CascadeType.ALL)
    private Address address;

    // getters and setters
}
```

```
public User updateUserAddress(Long userId, Address newAddress) {
    User user = userRepository.findById(userId)
            .orElseThrow(() -> new EntityNotFoundException("User not found"));
    user.setAddress(newAddress);
    return userRepository.save(user);
}
```

In the case above, the User entity's Address is updated by setting a new Address object. The cascade type ALL ensures that updates to the User entity propagate to its Address.

```
{
   "username": "jane_doe",
   "email": "jane.doe@newdomain.com",
   "address": {
      "street": "123 Main St",
      "city": "Anytown"
   }
}
```

This JSON representation illustrates the updated state of a User entity, inclusive of the nested Address entity. The save() method ensures holistic persistence of all associated state changes.

Updating entities via the save() method in Spring Data JPA encapsulates a balance of simplicity and robustness, serving as a core mechanism for maintaining data integrity within the persistent context.

7.6 Deleting Entities: Using deleteById() and deleteAll()

Deleting entities in Spring Data JPA is fundamentally important for maintaining the integrity of your database by removing obsolete or unnecessary records. Spring Data JPA provides two primary methods for deleting entities: deleteById() and deleteAll(). This section details the use of these methods, their practical applications, and considerations for effective deletion operations.

The deleteById() method is used to delete a single entity based on its identifier. It is defined in the CrudRepository interface as follows:

```
void deleteById(ID id);
```

Here is an example usage of deleteById():

```
import org.springframework.beans.factory.annotation.Autowired;
import org.springframework.stereotype.Service;
import org.springframework.transaction.annotation.Transactional;

@Service
public class EmployeeService {

    @Autowired
    private EmployeeRepository employeeRepository;

    @Transactional
    public void removeEmployee(Long employeeId) {
        employeeRepository.deleteById(employeeId);
    }
}
```

In this example, the EmployeeService class defines the removeEmployee method, which calls employeeRepository.deleteById(employeeId) to delete an employee by its ID. Notice the use of the @Transactional annotation, which ensures that the deletion operation is executed within a transaction context.

It's imperative to handle scenarios where the entity to be deleted does not exist. The deleteById() method will throw an EmptyResultDataAccessException if an entity with the specified ID doesn't exist. To manage such cases gracefully, you might want to incorporate exception handling as demonstrated below:

```
import org.springframework.dao.EmptyResultDataAccessException;

@Transactional
public void removeEmployee(Long employeeId) {
    try {
        employeeRepository.deleteById(employeeId);
    } catch (EmptyResultDataAccessException e) {
        System.out.println("No employee found with ID: " + employeeId);
    }
}
```

For batch deletion, Spring Data JPA provides the deleteAll() method, which can be used to remove all records from the repository. It is defined as:

```
void deleteAll();
```

Here is an example of its application:

```
@Transactional
public void removeAllEmployees() {
    employeeRepository.deleteAll();
}
```

The deleteAll() method will remove every entity managed by the repository. This operation should be used judiciously, particularly in production environments, to avoid accidental loss of data.

Another variant of the deleteAll() method allows for the deletion of entities in batches:

```
void deleteAll(Iterable<? extends T> entities);
```

This can be useful when you need to delete a subset of entities efficiently:

```
@Transactional
public void removeEmployees(List<Employee> employees) {
    employeeRepository.deleteAll(employees);
}
```

In this example, the removeEmployees method deletes the specified employees in a batch operation. The input is a list of Employee entities to be removed.

Performance considerations are essential for deletion operations, especially when dealing with a large number of records. Direct use of deleteAll() can trigger the deletion of each entity individually, leading to a high number of database interactions. To mitigate performance impacts, consider writing custom deletion queries using the @Modifying and @Query annotations:

```
import org.springframework.data.jpa.repository.Modifying;
import org.springframework.data.jpa.repository.Query;
import org.springframework.transaction.annotation.Transactional;

public interface EmployeeRepository extends JpaRepository<Employee, Long> {

    @Modifying
    @Transactional
    @Query("DELETE FROM Employee e WHERE e.department = ?1")
    void deleteByDepartment(String department);
}
```

In this custom method, deleteByDepartment, a JPQL query deletes all employees belonging to a specific department with a single query, improving performance considerably.

In deletion operations, it is also crucial to consider integrity constraints and cascades. For entities involved in relationships, the cascade type defined will influence how deletions propagate. For instance, using CascadeType.REMOVE ensures that deleting an entity will also remove related entities automatically:

```
@Entity
public class Department {

    @OneToMany(mappedBy = "department", cascade = CascadeType.REMOVE)
    private List<Employee> employees;
}
```

In this example, deleting a Department entity will also result in the deletion of associated Employee entities, maintaining referential integrity.

Finally, soft deletions can be implemented as an alternative to physically deleting records. This approach involves marking records as deleted without actually removing them from the database. It can be achieved by adding a boolean deleted flag to the entity class and then updating repository methods to filter out records flagged as deleted.

Implementing soft deletions often involves a combination of custom queries and entity listeners, ensuring records visually disappear from the application while still retaining historical data for auditing purposes.

Through these methods, deleting entities using Spring Data JPA can be performed reliably, ensuring database integrity and application efficiency.

7.7 Handling Relationships in CRUD Operations

Handling relationships in CRUD operations is a crucial aspect of working with relational databases using Spring Data JPA. This section delves into the various types of relationships, such as one-to-one, one-to-many, many-to-one, and many-to-many, and how these can be managed efficiently using Spring Data JPA.

One-to-One Relationship

A one-to-one relationship occurs when one entity is associated with exactly one instance of another entity. This is typically implemented using the @OneToOne annotation. For example, consider a scenario where we have an Employee entity and a ParkingSpot entity.

```
@Entity
public class Employee {
    @Id
    @GeneratedValue(strategy = GenerationType.IDENTITY)
    private Long id;

    private String name;

    @OneToOne(cascade = CascadeType.ALL)
    @JoinColumn(name = "parking_spot_id", referencedColumnName = "id")
    private ParkingSpot parkingSpot;

    // getters and setters
}

@Entity
public class ParkingSpot {
    @Id
    @GeneratedValue(strategy = GenerationType.IDENTITY)
    private Long id;

    private String spot;

    @OneToOne(mappedBy = "parkingSpot")
    private Employee employee;

    // getters and setters
```

```
}
```

In this configuration, an Employee can be linked to a ParkingSpot. The @OneToOne annotation defines a one-to-one relationship and the mappedBy attribute specifies the owning side of the relationship.

One-to-Many and Many-to-One Relationship

In one-to-many and many-to-one relationships, one entity is related to multiple instances of another entity. This type of relationship is often seen between a Department and Employees. A department can have many employees, but each employee belongs to one department.

```
@Entity
public class Department {
    @Id
    @GeneratedValue(strategy = GenerationType.IDENTITY)
    private Long id;

    private String name;

    @OneToMany(mappedBy = "department", cascade = CascadeType.ALL,
         orphanRemoval = true)
    private List<Employee> employees = new ArrayList<>();

    // getters and setters
}

@Entity
public class Employee {
    @Id
    @GeneratedValue(strategy = GenerationType.IDENTITY)
    private Long id;

    private String name;

    @ManyToOne(fetch = FetchType.LAZY)
    @JoinColumn(name = "department_id")
    private Department department;

    // getters and setters
}
```

Here, a Department entity is defined to have a list of Employee entities, with the @OneToMany annotation. The inverse relationship is specified in Employee using the @ManyToOne annotation.

Many-to-Many Relationship

A many-to-many relationship occurs when multiple instances of an entity are related to multiple instances of another entity. For instance, a Student can enroll in multiple Courses, and a Course can have multiple students enrolled.

```
@Entity
```

```
public class Student {
    @Id
    @GeneratedValue(strategy = GenerationType.IDENTITY)
    private Long id;

    private String name;

    @ManyToMany
    @JoinTable(
        name = "student_course",
        joinColumns = @JoinColumn(name = "student_id"),
        inverseJoinColumns = @JoinColumn(name = "course_id"))
    private List<Course> courses = new ArrayList<>();

    // getters and setters
}

@Entity
public class Course {
    @Id
    @GeneratedValue(strategy = GenerationType.IDENTITY)
    private Long id;

    private String title;

    @ManyToMany(mappedBy = "courses")
    private List<Student> students = new ArrayList<>();

    // getters and setters
}
```

In this example, the @ManyToMany annotation is used to define a many-to-many relationship between Student and Course. The @JoinTable annotation specifies the table that joins the two entities.

Cascading and Orphan Removal

Cascade operations are crucial when dealing with relationships, allowing operations on a parent entity to be cascaded to associated child entities. These operations can be managed using the cascade attribute, available for each type of relationship annotation.

- CascadeType.PERSIST: Cascade the persist operation.
- CascadeType.MERGE: Cascade the merge operation.
- CascadeType.REMOVE: Cascade the remove operation.
- CascadeType.REFRESH: Cascade the refresh operation.
- CascadeType.DETACH: Cascade the detach operation.
- CascadeType.ALL: Cascade all operations.

Additionally, the orphanRemoval attribute can be used to remove child entities when they are removed from the relationship.

```
@OneToMany(mappedBy = "department", cascade = CascadeType.ALL,
     orphanRemoval = true)
private List<Employee> employees = new ArrayList<>();
```

This example ensures that any Employee removed from the employees list is also deleted from the database.

Fetching Strategies

Fetching strategies determine how related entities are loaded from the database. There are two primary fetching strategies: EAGER and LAZY.

- FetchType.EAGER: Related entities are loaded immediately.
- FetchType.LAZY: Related entities are loaded on-demand.

```
@ManyToOne(fetch = FetchType.LAZY)
@JoinColumn(name = "department_id")
private Department department;
```

Using FetchType.LAZY is generally recommended to enhance performance by loading related entities only when required.

CrudRepository and JpaRepository

Spring Data JPA repositories such as CrudRepository and JpaRepository provide methods to manage entity relationships. When working with relationships, the standard CRUD operations (save, findById, findAll, deleteById, deleteAll) can be utilized.

```
public interface EmployeeRepository extends JpaRepository<Employee, Long> {
}

public interface DepartmentRepository extends JpaRepository<Department, Long> {
}
```

For example, to save a Department with its related Employees:

```
Department department = new Department();
department.setName("R&D");

Employee emp1 = new Employee();
emp1.setName("John Doe");
emp1.setDepartment(department);

Employee emp2 = new Employee();
emp2.setName("Jane Doe");
emp2.setDepartment(department);
```

```
List<Employee> employees = Arrays.asList(emp1, emp2);
department.setEmployees(employees);

departmentRepository.save(department);
```

This code snippet ensures that both the Department and its associated Employees are saved due to the cascading rules defined earlier.

Handling relationships in CRUD operations requires understanding of how entities interrelate and the various JPA annotations and attributes to maintain data integrity and efficiency. Employing correct cascade types and fetch strategies ensures consistent and performant data access, aligning with the principles and capabilities of Spring Data JPA.

7.8 Pagination and Sorting in CRUD Operations

When managing large datasets, it's crucial to have efficient methods for handling data retrieval. Two fundamental techniques used to improve the performance and usability in such scenarios are pagination and sorting. Pagination allows you to fetch a specific subset of data, avoiding the performance overhead of loading the entire dataset. Sorting, on the other hand, arranges the fetched data according to one or more attributes, making it easier to organize and analyze.

In Spring Data JPA, these features are provided as part of the repository API, streamlining their usage in CRUD operations.

Pagination in Spring Data JPA

Pagination in Spring Data JPA is facilitated by the Pageable interface and the PageRequest class. The Pageable interface provides pagination information such as page number, page size, and sorting criteria. The PageRequest class is an implementation of Pageable tailored for static settings. To retrieve paginated results, we use the findAll(pageable) method provided by the repository interface.

For example, consider the following EmployeeRepository:

```
public interface EmployeeRepository extends JpaRepository<Employee, Long> {
}
```

To fetch the first page of employees, with a page size of 5, we create a PageRequest object and pass it to the findAll method:

```
Pageable firstPageWithFiveElements = PageRequest.of(0, 5);
```

```
Page<Employee> employees = employeeRepository.findAll(firstPageWithFiveElements)
    ;
```

The Page object returned provides useful methods to fetch the paginated results and metadata, such as total pages and total elements:

```
employees.getContent(); // List of employees in the first page
employees.getTotalPages(); // Total number of pages
employees.getTotalElements(); // Total number of employees
employees.getNumber(); // Current page number
```

Sorting in Spring Data JPA

Sorting can be applied standalone or combined with pagination. The Sort class in Spring Data JPA facilitates sorting. It provides multiple static methods to specify sorting criteria, like by(), descending(), and ascending().

For example, to retrieve all employees sorted by the lastName attribute in ascending order:

```
Sort sortByLastName = Sort.by("lastName").ascending();
List<Employee> employees = employeeRepository.findAll(sortByLastName);
```

Sorting can also be integrated with pagination, enhancing data management flexibility. This is achieved by providing a Sort object to the PageRequest object.

Consider the code to fetch the first page of employees sorted by their lastName attribute in descending order:

```
Pageable sortedByLastNameDesc = PageRequest.of(0, 5, Sort.by("lastName").
    descending());
Page<Employee> employees = employeeRepository.findAll(sortedByLastNameDesc);
```

Combining Pagination and Sorting

The Pageable and Sort classes can be combined to create complex and efficient data retrieval operations.

Here's an example where we fetch the second page (page index 1) of employees, each page containing 10 employees, sorted by firstName in ascending order and then by lastName in descending order:

```
Sort sortOrder = Sort.by(Sort.Order.asc("firstName"), Sort.Order.desc("lastName"));
Pageable secondPageWithSorting = PageRequest.of(1, 10, sortOrder);
Page<Employee> employees = employeeRepository.findAll(secondPageWithSorting);
```

Using pagination and sorting effectively can substantially optimize the performance and scalability of applications. It ensures data is managed efficiently, offering users a smooth interactive experience. By incorporating these features via Spring Data JPA repositories, developers can leverage straightforward, out-of-the-box solutions tailored for complex data retrieval needs.

7.9 Error Handling and Validation

Error handling and validation are crucial components of any application that interacts with a database through CRUD operations, especially when using Spring Data JPA. This section discusses strategies and techniques for effectively managing errors and validating input data to ensure system robustness and reliability.

Effective error handling in Spring Data JPA entails capturing exceptions raised during database operations and responding appropriately. Spring provides a robust exception handling mechanism that integrates seamlessly with its data access layers. Below is an example of customizing exception handling in a Spring application:

```
@RestControllerAdvice
public class GlobalExceptionHandler {

    @ExceptionHandler(EntityNotFoundException.class)
    public ResponseEntity<String> handleEntityNotFoundException(
            EntityNotFoundException ex) {
        return new ResponseEntity<>(ex.getMessage(), HttpStatus.NOT_FOUND);
    }

    @ExceptionHandler(DataIntegrityViolationException.class)
    public ResponseEntity<String> handleDataIntegrityViolationException(
            DataIntegrityViolationException ex) {
        return new ResponseEntity<>("Data Integrity Violation: " + ex.getMessage(),
                HttpStatus.BAD_REQUEST);
    }

    @ExceptionHandler(Exception.class)
    public ResponseEntity<String> handleGeneralException(Exception ex) {
        return new ResponseEntity<>("An unexpected error occurred: " + ex.
                getMessage(), HttpStatus.INTERNAL_SERVER_ERROR);
    }
}
```

In this example, a GlobalExceptionHandler class is defined with different methods to handle specific exceptions such as EntityNotFoundException and DataIntegrityViolationException. This centralized approach ensures consistency and clarity in error responses across the application.

Validation is another critical aspect of ensuring data integrity and application stability. Spring provides a rich set of annotations under the javax.validation.constraints package to facilitate input validation. Consider the following entity with various validation constraints:

```
@Entity
public class User {

    @Id
    @GeneratedValue(strategy = GenerationType.IDENTITY)
    private Long id;

    @NotNull(message = "Name cannot be null")
    @Size(min = 2, max = 50, message = "Name must be between 2 and 50 characters"
        )
    private String name;

    @Email(message = "Email should be valid")
    @NotNull(message = "Email cannot be null")
    private String email;

    @NotNull(message = "Age cannot be null")
    @Min(value = 18, message = "Age should not be less than 18")
    @Max(value = 100, message = "Age should not be greater than 100")
    private Integer age;

    // Getters and setters omitted for brevity
}
```

In this User entity, constraints such as @NotNull, @Size, @Email, @Min, and @Max ensure that only valid data is saved to the database. These constraints are checked before any CRUD operation, and violations result in a ConstraintViolationException. To validate these entities in a Spring REST controller, the @Valid annotation is used in combination with @RequestBody:

```
@RestController
@RequestMapping("/users")
public class UserController {

    @Autowired
    private UserRepository userRepository;

    @PostMapping
    public ResponseEntity<User> createUser(@Valid @RequestBody User user) {
        User savedUser = userRepository.save(user);
        return new ResponseEntity<>(savedUser, HttpStatus.CREATED);
    }

    // Other CRUD endpoints omitted for brevity
}
```

When a POST request is made to /users with an invalid User object, a MethodArgumentNotValidException is thrown. To handle these validation exceptions gracefully, an appropriate handler can be added in the GlobalExceptionHandler:

```
@ExceptionHandler(MethodArgumentNotValidException.class)
```

```
public ResponseEntity<String> handleValidationException(
        MethodArgumentNotValidException ex) {
    BindingResult bindingResult = ex.getBindingResult();
    StringBuilder errors = new StringBuilder();
    bindingResult.getAllErrors().forEach((error) -> {
        String errorMessage = error.getDefaultMessage();
        errors.append(errorMessage).append("; ");
    });
    return new ResponseEntity<>(errors.toString(), HttpStatus.BAD_REQUEST);
}
```

This handler processes each validation error and aggregates the messages into one comprehensive error response. This method provides users with clear and actionable feedback, improving the user experience when interacting with the application.

Additionally, utilizing custom validators can enforce more complex validation logic beyond built-in constraints. For example, to validate that a user's email domain is specific to a particular organization, a custom constraint annotation and validator can be implemented:

```
@Constraint(validatedBy = EmailDomainValidator.class)
@Target({ ElementType.FIELD, ElementType.METHOD, ElementType.PARAMETER,
        ElementType.ANNOTATION_TYPE })
@Retention(RetentionPolicy.RUNTIME)
@Documented
public @interface EmailDomain {
    String message() default "Invalid email domain";
    Class<?>[] groups() default {};
    Class<? extends Payload>[] payload() default {};
    String domain();
}

public class EmailDomainValidator implements ConstraintValidator<EmailDomain,
        String> {

    private String domain;

    @Override
    public void initialize(EmailDomain constraintAnnotation) {
        this.domain = constraintAnnotation.domain();
    }

    @Override
    public boolean isValid(String email, ConstraintValidatorContext context) {
        return email != null && email.endsWith("@" + domain);
    }
}
```

The @EmailDomain annotation can then be applied to the email field of the User entity:

```
@EmailDomain(domain = "example.com", message = "Email must be from example.
        com")
@Email(message = "Email should be valid")
@NotNull(message = "Email cannot be null")
private String email;
```

With this custom validation in place, any attempt to persist a User entity with an email not ending in example.com will result in a validation error.

Robust error handling and comprehensive validation improve the reliability and user experience of applications using Spring Data JPA. Implementing these practices ensures that the data managed by the application is consistent and conforms to defined business rules, resulting in a robust and maintainable system.

7.10 Best Practices for CRUD Operations with Spring Data JPA

To ensure optimal performance, maintainability, and reliability when performing CRUD operations with Spring Data JPA, adhering to certain best practices is essential. These best practices encompass a broad range of topics, including entity design, query optimization, transaction management, and proper utilization of Spring Data JPA's features. This section will explore these areas in detail.

Entity Design

A well-designed entity model lays the groundwork for efficient CRUD operations. Follow these guidelines when designing entities:

- **Use Explicit Identifiers**: Always define an explicit identifier using @Id. This approach ensures clarity and avoids potential issues with auto-generated identifiers.
- **Choose Appropriate Generation Strategies**: Utilize an appropriate generation strategy (GenerationType.IDENTITY, GenerationType.SEQUENCE, etc.) based on your database capabilities and requirements.
- **Minimize Cascading**: Use cascading rules sparingly. Excessive use can lead to unintended deletions or updates, which can cause performance issues.
- **Define Relationships Properly**: Clearly define relationships (@OneToOne, @OneToMany, @ManyToOne, @ManyToMany) using appropriate fetch types (FetchType.LAZY or FetchType.EAGER).

- **Avoid Fat Entities**: Large entities with numerous fields can become unwieldy and lead to suboptimal performance. Keep entities concise and focused.

Query Optimization

Efficient querying is crucial for performance. Adopt the following best practices for query optimization:

- **Use Projections and DTOs**: Instead of retrieving entire entities, use projections or Data Transfer Objects (DTOs) to fetch only the required fields.
- **Prefer Named Queries**: Named queries, either defined in the entity class using the @NamedQuery annotation or in an XML file, can improve readability and performance.
- **Leverage Query Methods**: Use derived query methods provided by Spring Data JPA to avoid writing boilerplate code.
- **Utilize Stream and Pagination**: For large datasets, use pagination (Pageable) to limit the number of results retrieved. Streaming (Streamable and Java Streams API) can also be employed to handle large result sets efficiently.
- **Indexing and Caching**: Ensure that frequently queried fields are indexed in the database. Utilize second-level caching judiciously to reduce database load.

Transaction Management

Proper transaction management ensures data consistency and integrity. Keep these points in mind:

- **Use @Transactional Annotation**: Mark service methods with @Transactional to manage transaction boundaries effectively.
- **Read-Only Transactions**: For read-only operations, use @Transactional(readOnly = true) to optimize transaction behavior.
- **Handle Lazy Initialization Issues**: Use @Transactional on service methods to address lazy loading issues. Alternatively, fetch the necessary data eagerly using specific queries.

Exception Handling and Validation

Effective exception handling and validation are integral for robust applications:

- **Use Custom Exceptions**: Define custom exceptions for domain-specific errors. This enhances clarity and allows for more granular error handling.
- **Handle Exceptions Properly**: Catch exceptions at appropriate layers (service or controller) and provide meaningful error messages.
- **Validate Input Data**: Use constraint annotations (@NotNull, @Size, @Pattern, etc.) to validate entity fields. Additionally, leverage Spring Validator or Bean Validation (JSR 380) for comprehensive validation.

Miscellaneous Best Practices

Additional best practices that aid in maintaining a clean and efficient codebase include:

- **Adopt a Layered Architecture**: Separate data access, service, and presentation layers to promote modularity and testability.
- **Keep Repositories Focused**: Limit the scope of repository interfaces to a specific entity or a closely related set of entities.
- **Use Specification Pattern**: For complex queries, consider using the Specification pattern provided by Spring Data JPA.
- **Avoid N + 1 Query Problem**: Use fetch joins or entity graphs to avoid the N + 1 query problem, which can significantly degrade performance.
- **Documentation and Code Comments**: Maintain clear documentation and comments, especially for complex queries and transactions, to facilitate easier maintenance and understanding.

The implementation of these best practices ensures a robust, efficient, and maintainable application when working with Spring Data JPA.

Sample Repository Interface.

```
public interface EmployeeRepository extends JpaRepository<Employee, Long> {
    @Query("SELECT e FROM Employee e WHERE e.department.id = :departmentId"
        )
    List<Employee> findEmployeesByDepartment(@Param("departmentId") Long
        departmentId);

    @Modifying
    @Transactional
    @Query("UPDATE Employee e SET e.salary = :salary WHERE e.id = :id")
    int updateEmployeeSalary(@Param("id") Long id, @Param("salary") int salary);
}
```

Sample Service Layer with Transaction.

```
@Service
public class EmployeeService {

    @Autowired
    private EmployeeRepository employeeRepository;

    @Transactional
    public Employee updateEmployeeDetails(Long id, int salary) {
        Employee employee = employeeRepository.findById(id)
                .orElseThrow(() -> new ResourceNotFoundException("Employee not
                    found"));

        employee.setSalary(salary);
        return employeeRepository.save(employee);
    }
}
```

```
Output from updateEmployeeDetails Method:
Employee{id=1, name='John Doe', department='HR', salary=5000}
```

These code examples illustrate the application of best practices in repository design, query formulation, and transaction management, ensuring that CRUD operations are performed efficiently and effectively.

Chapter 8

Building RESTful Web Services with Spring Data

This chapter discusses the process of building RESTful web services with Spring Data. It begins by setting up Spring Boot for RESTful services and defining RESTful endpoints with Spring Data REST. The chapter explores how to expose CRUD operations as RESTful APIs and customize endpoints and responses. Topics include handling validation and errors in REST APIs, securing web services, and implementing pagination and sorting. Additionally, it covers integration with front-end applications and testing RESTful web services to ensure robustness and reliability.

8.1 Introduction to RESTful Web Services

RESTful web services represent a stateless, client-server, cacheable communications protocol – typically using HTTP. REST stands for Representational State Transfer, an architectural style designed for network-based applications. In this section, we will delve into the principles of REST, its constraints, and the fundamental components that form a RESTful web service.

A **RESTful web service** provides interoperability between computer systems on the internet. This aligns with the fundamental premise of web services: the ability to establish communication between different systems irrespective of the underlying platform or language. Key characteristics of RESTful services include:

- Statelessness: No client context is stored on the server between requests. Each request from a client must contain all necessary information.
- Cacheability: Responses must be defined as cacheable or non-cacheable, enhancing performance and reducing server load.
- Uniform Interface: Simplifies and decouples the architecture, enabling each part to evolve independently.
- Layered System: The architecture is composed of layers, aiding the management and scalability of the application.
- Code on Demand (optional): Servers can extend or customize the functionality of a client via code transfer (e.g., JavaScript).
- Client-Server: A clear separation of concerns, ensuring that the client and server can evolve independently.

One of the essential aspects of RESTful web services is the use of resources. A **resource** is an object or representation of something, which can be a data entity or document. Resources are identified by URIs, and interactions with these resources are carried out using standard HTTP methods, encapsulated in the following manner:

- GET: Fetches a resource from the server. It is a read-only operation and can be safely cached.
- POST: Creates a new resource on the server. The server, upon successful creation, returns the location of the resource.
- PUT: Updates an existing resource. If the resource does not exist, the server may create it.
- DELETE: Removes a resource from the server.
- PATCH: Applies partial modifications to a resource.

These operations form the CRUD (Create, Read, Update, Delete) spectrum, providing a functional approach to perform standard database operations via HTTP requests.

Consider the following example of a RESTful web service endpoint in Java using Spring Boot:

```
import org.springframework.web.bind.annotation.*;

@RestController
@RequestMapping("/api/books")
public class BookController {

    @GetMapping("/{id}")
    public ResponseEntity<Book> getBook(@PathVariable Long id) {
        // Fetch the book from the repository
        Optional<Book> book = bookRepository.findById(id);
        return book.map(b -> ResponseEntity.ok().body(b))
                .orElse(ResponseEntity.notFound().build());
    }

    @PostMapping
    public ResponseEntity<Book> createBook(@RequestBody Book book) {
        // Save the new book to the repository
        Book savedBook = bookRepository.save(book);
        return ResponseEntity.status(HttpStatus.CREATED).body(savedBook);
    }

    @PutMapping("/{id}")
    public ResponseEntity<Book> updateBook(@PathVariable Long id, @RequestBody
        Book bookDetails) {
        // Update the book in the repository
        Book book = bookRepository.findById(id)
                                .orElseThrow(() -> new ResourceNotFoundException("
                                        Book not found"));
        book.setTitle(bookDetails.getTitle());
        book.setAuthor(bookDetails.getAuthor());
        final Book updatedBook = bookRepository.save(book);
        return ResponseEntity.ok(updatedBook);
    }

    @DeleteMapping("/{id}")
    public ResponseEntity<Map<String, Boolean>> deleteBook(@PathVariable Long
        id) {
        // Delete the book from the repository
        Book book = bookRepository.findById(id)
                                .orElseThrow(() -> new ResourceNotFoundException("
                                        Book not found"));

        bookRepository.delete(book);
        Map<String, Boolean> response = new HashMap<>();
        response.put("deleted", Boolean.TRUE);
        return ResponseEntity.ok(response);
    }
}
```

This example demonstrates the standard CRUD operations allowing for interaction with a book resource through HTTP requests. The GET, POST, PUT, and DELETE methods correspond directly to fetching, creating, updating, and deleting a book respectively.

To enhance understanding, let's examine the sample output from the GET operation on a book with id 1:

```
HTTP/1.1 200 OK
Content-Type: application/json
{
  "id": 1,
  "title": "Mastering Java Persistence",
  "author": "John Doe"
}
```

In this example, the server responds with an HTTP status code of 200 (OK) and provides the details of the book in JSON format, abiding by the principles of RESTful web services.

Understanding these principles and elements is fundamental in designing efficient and scalable RESTful web services. RESTful architecture is leveraged for its simplicity and adaptability in various applications, providing a robust foundation for building modern web services.

8.2 Setting Up Spring Boot for RESTful Services

Spring Boot dramatically simplifies the development of Java applications by providing production-ready capabilities out of the box. This section outlines the steps required to set up Spring Boot specifically for developing RESTful web services. By the end of this section, readers will have a functional Spring Boot application with configurations tailored for RESTful service development.

To create a Spring Boot application, we can use the Spring Initializr at https://start.spring.io/. It provides a web interface for generating a skeleton project. The essential steps for setting up the Spring Boot application are as follows:

- Navigate to the Spring Initializr website.
- Select the project type as Maven Project.
- Choose Java as the language.
- Choose the Spring Boot version. It is recommended to use the latest stable version.
- Provide the project metadata, such as Group, Artifact, Name, Description, and Package Name.
- In the Dependencies section, add dependencies for Spring Web and Spring Data JPA. These dependencies include libraries necessary for building REST endpoints and data persistence.

- Click on the Generate button to download the project.

Extract the downloaded ZIP file and open it in your favorite Integrated Development Environment (IDE). The project structure typically includes src/main/java for application code and src/main/resources for application configuration files.

To configure the application, start by creating a main application class annotated with @SpringBootApplication. This annotation indicates a configuration class that declares one or more @Bean methods and triggers auto-configuration, component scanning, and property support. Here is the code for the main application class:

```
package com.example.demo;

import org.springframework.boot.SpringApplication;
import org.springframework.boot.autoconfigure.SpringBootApplication;

@SpringBootApplication
public class DemoApplication {
    public static void main(String[] args) {
        SpringApplication.run(DemoApplication.class, args);
    }
}
```

Spring Boot automatically configures the application based on the dependencies specified in the pom.xml. The Spring Boot Starter Web dependency, which is part of Spring Web, includes the embedded Tomcat server, making it easier to develop and run the application without requiring external web server configurations.

The next step is to configure the application's data source in src/main/resources/application.properties. Typical properties include database URL, username, and password. Below is an example configuration for a MySQL database:

```
spring.datasource.url=jdbc:mysql://localhost:3306/demo
spring.datasource.username=root
spring.datasource.password=root
spring.jpa.hibernate.ddl-auto=update
spring.jpa.show-sql=true
```

The spring.datasource.url specifies the JDBC URL of the database. The spring.datasource.username and spring.datasource.password provide the database credentials. The spring.jpa.hibernate.ddl-auto property controls the behavior of Hibernate with respect to the database structure, set to update here to automatically update the schema as needed. The spring.jpa.show-sql property is set to true to log SQL statements for debugging purposes.

Next, define a basic REST controller to expose an endpoint. In src/-main/java/com/example/demo, create a new class called GreetingController:

```
package com.example.demo;

import org.springframework.web.bind.annotation.GetMapping;
import org.springframework.web.bind.annotation.RestController;

@RestController
public class GreetingController {

    @GetMapping("/greeting")
    public String greeting() {
        return "Hello, World!";
    }
}
```

The @RestController annotation indicates that this class handles REST API requests. Within the class, the @GetMapping("/greeting") annotation configures the endpoint to handle HTTP GET requests at the path /greeting. When accessed, it returns a simple string, "Hello, World!".

To run the application, execute the main method in DemoApplication. The Spring Boot application will start, and you can test the REST endpoint by accessing http://localhost:8080/greeting in a web browser or using tools such as curl or Postman:

```
$ curl http://localhost:8080/greeting
Hello, World!
```

Spring Boot provides various annotations and components to further customize the application. For instance, to handle custom configurations, one can utilize @Configuration classes, and for dependency injections, @Autowired can be used. Moreover, environment-specific configurations can be managed through profiles, defined in application.properties or multiple application-{profile}.properties files.

spring-boot-starter-actuator dependency can be added to expose several built-in RESTful endpoints for checking the health and metrics of your application:

```
management.endpoints.web.exposure.include=*
```

Integrating Spring Boot with additional Spring modules can be seamless. For example, integrating with Spring Security enhances security configurations, while Spring Data modules facilitate interaction with data sources beyond traditional databases, such as Redis and MongoDB.

The setup of Spring Boot for RESTful services ensures that the environment is prepared for efficient development and deployment of robust RESTful APIs. The configuration can be further customized to meet specific architectural and functional requirements such as error handling, data validation, security measures, and more sophisticated data access patterns. Additional configuration can be handled through YAML configuration files (application.yml) or programmatic configurations using Java @Configuration classes. This foundational setup acts as a springboard for further enhancements and development.

8.3 Defining RESTful Endpoints with Spring Data REST

Spring Data REST is a powerful framework that facilitates creating RESTful web services by exposing Spring Data repositories as RESTful endpoints. It provides a quick and efficient way to build RESTful APIs with minimal configuration and coding. This section delves into the process of defining RESTful endpoints using Spring Data REST.

At the core of Spring Data REST is the concept of a repository. In Spring Data, a repository is an interface that defines methods for performing CRUD operations on entities. Spring Data REST automatically generates RESTful endpoints based on these repository interfaces.

To start, ensure you have the necessary dependencies in your pom.xml file. Include spring-boot-starter-data-rest and spring-boot-starter-data-jpa:

```
<dependency>
    <groupId>org.springframework.boot</groupId>
    <artifactId>spring-boot-starter-data-rest</artifactId>
</dependency>
<dependency>
    <groupId>org.springframework.boot</groupId>
    <artifactId>spring-boot-starter-data-jpa</artifactId>
</dependency>
<dependency>
    <groupId>com.h2database</groupId>
    <artifactId>h2</artifactId>
</dependency>
```

With the dependencies in place, define your entity classes. This example uses a basic Product entity:

```
import javax.persistence.Entity;
import javax.persistence.GeneratedValue;
import javax.persistence.GenerationType;
import javax.persistence.Id;
```

```
@Entity
public class Product {

    @Id
    @GeneratedValue(strategy = GenerationType.AUTO)
    private Long id;
    private String name;
    private Double price;

    // Getters and Setters
}
```

Once the entity is defined, create a repository interface that extends one of Spring Data's repository interfaces, such as CrudRepository or PagingAndSortingRepository. Spring Data REST will expose CRUD operations at RESTful endpoints based on this interface:

```
import org.springframework.data.repository.CrudRepository;

public interface ProductRepository extends CrudRepository<Product, Long> {
}
```

After defining the entity and repository, Spring Data REST automatically generates RESTful endpoints. Start your Spring Boot application, and you can access endpoints for performing CRUD operations. For instance, using httpie to list all products:

```
http GET :8080/products
```

The response will look like:

```
{
  "_embedded": {
    "products": [
      {
        "name": "Example Product",
        "price": 25.50,
        "_links": {
          "self": {
            "href": "http://localhost:8080/products/1"
          },
          "product": {
            "href": "http://localhost:8080/products/1"
          }
        }
      }
    ]
  },
  "_links": {
    "self": {
      "href": "http://localhost:8080/products"
    }
  }
}
```

Spring Data REST also supports custom endpoints. Suppose you need an endpoint to find products by name. First, extend the repository with a new query method:

```
import org.springframework.data.repository.query.Param;
import org.springframework.data.rest.core.annotation.RepositoryRestResource;

@RepositoryRestResource
public interface ProductRepository extends CrudRepository<Product, Long> {
    List<Product> findByName(@Param("name") String name);
}
```

Now, you can access this custom endpoint to search for products by name:

```
http GET :8080/products/search/findByName?name=Example
```

This query outputs the results in a structured JSON format similar to the default CRUD operations. Parameters in the query methods are mapped to URL query parameters, allowing for flexible and powerful querying capabilities out-of-the-box.

Additionally, Spring Data REST allows customizing endpoints through configuration and annotations. For instance, to customize the base path for all endpoints, modify the application properties:

```
spring.data.rest.base-path=/api
```

Now, all endpoints will be prefixed with /api. Access the products at http://localhost:8080/api/products.

The @RepositoryRestResource annotation provides further customization. Use it to change the path and rel attributes for your repository:

```
import org.springframework.data.rest.core.annotation.RepositoryRestResource;

@RepositoryRestResource(path = "items", collectionResourceRel = "items")
public interface ProductRepository extends CrudRepository<Product, Long> {
}
```

The collection of products will now be accessible at /items, and the response attribute representing the collection will be named items instead of the default products.

Customizing entity projections enables tailoring the JSON responses. Define a projection as an interface and include which fields to expose:

```
import org.springframework.data.rest.core.config.Projection;

@Projection(name = "productSummary", types = { Product.class })
public interface ProductSummary {
    String getName();
    Double getPrice();
}
```

Apply the projection by using the ?projection parameter in requests:

```
http GET :8080/products?projection=productSummary
```

This returns only the fields defined in the ProductSummary projection, allowing clients to receive lightweight responses tailored to their needs.

Through Spring Data REST's rich feature set, defining RESTful endpoints becomes a streamlined and efficient task. By leveraging repositories, annotations, and projections, developers can quickly create robust, intuitive APIs meeting various client requirements.

8.4 Exposing CRUD Operations as RESTful APIs

Exposing CRUD (Create, Read, Update, Delete) operations as RESTful APIs is a fundamental aspect of developing web services that allow clients to interact with your application's data model over HTTP. In this section, we outline the necessary steps and provide concrete examples to illustrate how Spring Data REST facilitates the creation of these endpoints with minimal boilerplate code.

To begin, ensure that you have set up a Spring Boot project with the necessary dependencies. In your pom.xml file, include Spring Boot Starter Web and Spring Boot Starter Data JPA along with a suitable database connector:

```
<dependencies>
    <dependency>
        <groupId>org.springframework.boot</groupId>
        <artifactId>spring-boot-starter-web</artifactId>
    </dependency>
    <dependency>
        <groupId>org.springframework.boot</groupId>
        <artifactId>spring-boot-starter-data-jpa</artifactId>
    </dependency>
    <dependency>
        <groupId>com.h2database</groupId>
        <artifactId>h2</artifactId>
        <scope>runtime</scope>
    </dependency>
    <!-- Additional dependencies can be included as needed -->
</dependencies>
```

Spring Data REST automatically exposes CRUD operations as RESTful endpoints for repositories that extend Spring Data repositories such as JpaRepository. Suppose we have an entity Person as follows:

```
@Entity
public class Person {

    @Id
    @GeneratedValue(strategy = GenerationType.IDENTITY)
    private Long id;
    private String firstName;
    private String lastName;

    // Constructors, getters, setters
}
```

Next, define a repository interface for Person. By extending JpaRepository, we inherit several methods for CRUD operations:

```
public interface PersonRepository extends JpaRepository<Person, Long> {
}
```

Through Spring Data REST, the PersonRepository interface automatically generates the following RESTful endpoints:

- **Create** (POST): /persons
- **Read** (GET): /persons, /persons/{id}
- **Update** (PUT/PATCH): /persons/{id}
- **Delete** (DELETE): /persons/{id}

The detailed HTTP methods and their sample usages are as follows:

POST request to create a new Person:

```
curl -X POST http://localhost:8080/persons -H "Content-Type: application/json" -d '
    {"firstName": "John", "lastName": "Doe"}'
```

Response Example:

```
{
  "id": 1,
  "firstName": "John",
  "lastName": "Doe"
}
```

GET request to read a list of Person entities:

```
curl -X GET http://localhost:8080/persons
```

Response Example:

```
[
  {
    "id": 1,
    "firstName": "John",
    "lastName": "Doe"
  },
  {
    "id": 2,
    "firstName": "Jane",
    "lastName": "Smith"
  }
]
```

GET request to read a single Person entity by id:

```
curl -X GET http://localhost:8080/persons/1
```

Response Example:

```
{
  "id": 1,
  "firstName": "John",
  "lastName": "Doe"
}
```

PUT request to update an existing Person:

```
curl -X PUT http://localhost:8080/persons/1 -H "Content-Type: application/json" -d '
    {"firstName": "Johnny", "lastName": "Doe"}'
```

Response Example:

```
{
  "id": 1,
  "firstName": "Johnny",
  "lastName": "Doe"
}
```

PATCH request to partially update an existing Person:

```
curl -X PATCH http://localhost:8080/persons/1 -H "Content-Type: application/json" -
    d '{"lastName": "Smith"}'
```

Response Example:

```
{
  "id": 1,
  "firstName": "John",
  "lastName": "Smith"
}
```

DELETE request to remove a Person entity by id:

```
curl -X DELETE http://localhost:8080/persons/1
```

Response Example:

```
HTTP/1.1 204 No Content
```

With the basic CRUD operations exposed, it is essential to secure these endpoints and handle validation errors appropriately. Authentication and authorization mechanisms should be incorporated to ensure that only authenticated users can perform certain actions.

For instance, integrating Spring Security will enable the authentication and authorization of users:

```
@Configuration
@EnableWebSecurity
public class SecurityConfig extends WebSecurityConfigurerAdapter {

    @Override
    protected void configure(HttpSecurity http) throws Exception {
        http
            .authorizeRequests()
                .antMatchers(HttpMethod.POST, "/persons").hasRole("ADMIN")
                .antMatchers(HttpMethod.PUT, "/persons/**").hasRole("ADMIN")
                .antMatchers(HttpMethod.DELETE, "/persons/**").hasRole("ADMIN")
                .antMatchers(HttpMethod.GET, "/persons/**").permitAll()
                .and()
            .httpBasic();
    }

    @Override
    protected void configure(AuthenticationManagerBuilder auth) throws Exception {
        auth.inMemoryAuthentication()
            .withUser("user").password("{noop}password").roles("USER")
            .and()
            .withUser("admin").password("{noop}admin").roles("ADMIN");
    }
}
```

This security configuration restricts POST, PUT, and DELETE operations to users with the ‘ADMIN‘ role while allowing all users to perform GET requests.

Incorporating validation is carried out by utilizing Java Bean Validation API (JSR-380) along with Spring's validation support. For example, you can annotate the Person entity fields with validation constraints and handle validation errors in a global exception handler:

```
@Entity
public class Person {

    @Id
    @GeneratedValue(strategy = GenerationType.IDENTITY)
    private Long id;

    @NotEmpty(message = "First name must not be empty")
    private String firstName;

    @NotEmpty(message = "Last name must not be empty")
    private String lastName;

    // Constructors, getters, setters
}
```

To handle validation errors globally, you might create an exception handler:

```
@ControllerAdvice
public class GlobalExceptionHandler {

    @ExceptionHandler(MethodArgumentNotValidException.class)
    public ResponseEntity<Map<String, String>> handleValidationExceptions(
            MethodArgumentNotValidException ex) {
        Map<String, String> errors = new HashMap<>();
        ex.getBindingResult().getAllErrors().forEach((error) -> {
            String fieldName = ((FieldError) error).getField();
            String errorMessage = error.getDefaultMessage();
            errors.put(fieldName, errorMessage);
        });
        return new ResponseEntity<>(errors, HttpStatus.BAD_REQUEST);
    }
}
```

This approach ensures that validation errors are caught and meaningful error messages are returned to the client.

Developers must also consider pagination and sorting as datasets grow. Using Spring Data's Pageable and Sort parameters, you can enable clients to request paginated data and sort it accordingly:

```
public interface PersonRepository extends JpaRepository<Person, Long> {

    Page<Person> findAll(Pageable pageable);

    List<Person> findAll(Sort sort);
}
```

Clients can request paginated and sorted data by adding query parameters:

```
curl -X GET 'http://localhost:8080/persons?page=0&size=10&sort=lastName,asc'
```

Thus, exposing CRUD operations as RESTful APIs in Spring Data REST provides a straightforward, standardized way for clients to interact with the application data, ensuring secure, validated, and efficient data management.

8.5 Customizing REST Endpoints and Responses

In this section, we delve into the customization of REST endpoints and their corresponding responses in a Spring Data REST context. Customizing endpoints and responses is crucial for enabling more flexible and user-friendly API interactions. We will explore ways to modify request paths, shape data representations, and enhance the overall API experience to better suit specific application needs.

Spring Data REST offers a wealth of configuration options, ranging from modifying resource URIs to altering entity representations. Let's start by looking at how we can change the default endpoints.

Changing Default Endpoints

By default, Spring Data REST exposes repositories under paths derived from entity names. However, there may be situations where you need custom paths. This can be achieved using annotations like @RepositoryRestResource.

```
@RepositoryRestResource(collectionResourceRel = "products", path = "items")
public interface ProductRepository extends JpaRepository<Product, Long> {
   // Custom query methods can be defined here
}
```

In the example above, the ProductRepository will now be accessible under the path /items instead of the default /products. The collectionResourceRel attribute customizes the JSON field name when representing the collection resource.

Customizing Resource Representation

Customization can extend to altering how data is represented in responses. This can be essential for minimizing data payloads or aligning with specific frontend requirements. Spring Data REST leverages projections and excerpts for such tasks.

```
@Projection(name = "summary", types = { Product.class })
public interface ProductSummary {

    String getName();

    BigDecimal getPrice();
}
```

Projections define tailored views of your entities. By applying the @Projection annotation, the ProductSummary interface declares a projection for the Product entity that only includes fields name and price.

To request this projection in a client request:

```
GET /products?projection=summary
```

Customizing Response Representation with Excerpts

Excerpts provide another way to customize how entities are included within collection resources. By creating custom resource processors, developers can manipulate the default representation.

```
@Component
public class ProductProcessor implements ResourceProcessor<Resource<Product>> {

    @Override
    public Resource<Product> process(Resource<Product> resource) {
        // Modify resource representation as needed
        resource.add(new Link("http://example.com/products/" + resource.getContent
            ().getId(), "custom-link"));
        return resource;
    }
}
```

The above code defines a resource processor (ProductProcessor) that adds a custom link to the Product resource representations. Resource processors enhance the flexibility by allowing additional, dynamic content to be linked or embedded within the REST responses.

Handling Method-Level Customizations

Spring Data REST also allows for granular customizations at the method level. You can specify acceptable media types, custom handlers, and even define how endpoints should react to different HTTP methods.

```
@RepositoryRestResource(path = "orders")
public interface OrderRepository extends JpaRepository<Order, Long> {

    @RestResource(exported = false)
    @Override
    void delete(Order entity);

    @RestResource(path = "by-customer", rel = "by-customer")
    List<Order> findByCustomer(@Param("customer") String customer);
}
```

In this example, the delete method is hidden from REST endpoints by setting the exported attribute to false. Additionally, the findByCustomer method is exposed via a custom path and relationship (rel) name.

Customizing Exception Handling and Response Status Codes

Proper handling of exceptions and corresponding response status codes is vital for robust RESTful service design. Custom exception handlers ensure that clients receive meaningful error messages and appropriate HTTP status codes.

```
@ControllerAdvice
public class RestExceptionHandler extends ResponseEntityExceptionHandler {

    @ExceptionHandler(EntityNotFoundException.class)
    protected ResponseEntity<Object> handleEntityNotFound(
      EntityNotFoundException ex) {
        ApiError apiError = new ApiError(HttpStatus.NOT_FOUND);
```

```
        apiError.setMessage(ex.getMessage());
        return buildResponseEntity(apiError);
    }

    private ResponseEntity<Object> buildResponseEntity(ApiError apiError) {
        return new ResponseEntity<>(apiError, apiError.getStatus());
    }
}
```

The code above defines a custom exception handler (RestExceptionHandler) that processes EntityNotFoundException and returns a structured error response with a 404 NOT FOUND status.

Customizing REST endpoints and responses in Spring Data REST provides finer control over how RESTful services are presented and consumed. By customizing endpoints, altering resource representations, and handling exceptions gracefully, developers can create highly user-centric and robust APIs.

8.6 Handling Validation and Errors in REST APIs

In any RESTful web service, handling validation and errors effectively is crucial for ensuring robustness and user satisfaction. This section delves into methodologies for integrating validation mechanisms and creating coherent error responses in REST APIs developed using Spring Data REST and Spring Boot.

Proper validation ensures that the data being processed meets specific criteria before any further processing. Validation in Spring Boot can be achieved by leveraging Java Bean Validation (JSR-380) provided by the javax.validation package, which Spring Boot automates configuration for. Error handling, on the other hand, involves generating meaningful error responses when exceptions occur, making it easier for clients to debug issues.

Implementing Validation

To start with validation, it's essential to annotate the domain model with validation constraints. For illustration, consider an entity class User with fields username, email, and age:

```
import javax.persistence.Entity;
import javax.persistence.GeneratedValue;
import javax.persistence.GenerationType;
import javax.persistence.Id;
import javax.validation.constraints.*;
```

```
@Entity
public class User {

    @Id
    @GeneratedValue(strategy = GenerationType.AUTO)
    private Long id;

    @NotNull(message = "Username is required")
    @Size(min = 3, max = 50, message = "Username must be between 3 and 50
        characters")
    private String username;

    @Email(message = "Email should be valid")
    private String email;

    @Min(value = 18, message = "Age should not be less than 18")
    @Max(value = 150, message = "Age should not be more than 150")
    private int age;

    // Getters and setters
}
```

Here, @NotNull, @Size, @Email, @Min, and @Max are standard validation annotations that ensure the fields meet specified criteria.

When a client sends a request to create or update a User, the Spring framework will automatically validate the fields based on these annotations. If any validation constraints are violated, Spring Boot generates a MethodArgumentNotValidException, which must be caught and handled appropriately.

Custom Error Responses

To provide custom error responses, you can use a global exception handler. This handler needs a class annotated with @RestControllerAdvice:

```
import org.springframework.http.HttpStatus;
import org.springframework.http.ResponseEntity;
import org.springframework.web.bind.MethodArgumentNotValidException;
import org.springframework.web.bind.annotation.ExceptionHandler;
import org.springframework.web.bind.annotation.RestControllerAdvice;
import org.springframework.validation.FieldError;

import java.util.HashMap;
import java.util.Map;

@RestControllerAdvice
public class GlobalExceptionHandler {

    @ExceptionHandler(MethodArgumentNotValidException.class)
    public ResponseEntity<Map<String, String>> handleValidationExceptions(
            MethodArgumentNotValidException ex) {
        Map<String, String> errors = new HashMap<>();
        ex.getBindingResult().getAllErrors().forEach((error) -> {
            String fieldName = ((FieldError) error).getField();
            String errorMessage = error.getDefaultMessage();
```

```
            errors.put(fieldName, errorMessage);
        });
        return new ResponseEntity<Map<String, String>>(errors, HttpStatus.
             BAD_REQUEST);
    }
}
```

Within the handleValidationExceptions method, the BindingResult is given, which contains information about the fields causing validation errors. Each error is processed and added to a Map with the field name as the key and the error message as the value. The Map is then returned with a HttpStatus.BAD_REQUEST status, informing the client of the validation failure.

Handling Custom Exceptions

Besides standard validation errors, custom exceptions may also be defined to handle specific business logic errors. Define a custom exception class and annotate it with @ResponseStatus to set an HTTP status:

```
import org.springframework.http.HttpStatus;
import org.springframework.web.bind.annotation.ResponseStatus;

@ResponseStatus(HttpStatus.NOT_FOUND)
public class UserNotFoundException extends RuntimeException {
    public UserNotFoundException(String message) {
        super(message);
    }
}
```

To handle this custom exception globally, add a corresponding method in the GlobalExceptionHandler:

```
@ExceptionHandler(UserNotFoundException.class)
public ResponseEntity<String> handleUserNotFoundException(
      UserNotFoundException ex) {
    return new ResponseEntity<String>(ex.getMessage(), HttpStatus.NOT_FOUND);
}
```

This method catches the UserNotFoundException and returns a response entity with the exception message and HttpStatus.NOT_-FOUND status.

Here is a sample interaction that illustrates handling a validation error when creating a new User through a POST request:

```
Request:
POST /users
Content-Type: application/json

{
    "username": "a",
    "email": "invalidEmail",
    "age": 17
}

Response:
HTTP/1.1 400 Bad Request
Content-Type: application/json

{
    "username": "Username must be between 3 and 50 characters",
    "email": "Email should be valid",
    "age": "Age should not be less than 18"
}
```

The response clearly outlines the constraints violated, providing precise feedback to the client.

Incorporating these mechanisms into RESTful web services enhances their reliability and makes them more user-friendly, aiding clients in correcting their input and handling errors gracefully. By leveraging Spring Boot's validation and exception handling capabilities, operations become more predictable and significantly improve the overall experience for API consumers.

8.7 Securing RESTful Web Services

Securing RESTful web services is paramount in an era where data breaches and cyber-attacks are prevalent. Proper security ensures that sensitive data is protected and access is controlled appropriately. This section details various techniques and strategies to secure RESTful web services using Spring Security, including authentication, authorization, and best practices.

Spring Security is a powerful and customizable authentication and access control framework for the Java platform. By integrating Spring Security into a Spring Boot application, we can secure RESTful endpoints with ease.

To start, include Spring Security in the pom.xml file:

```
<dependency>
    <groupId>org.springframework.boot</groupId>
    <artifactId>spring-boot-starter-security</artifactId>
</dependency>
```

Once the dependency is included, we can proceed to configure Spring Security. Create a configuration class annotated with @EnableWebSecurity and extend WebSecurityConfigurerAdapter:

```
import org.springframework.context.annotation.Configuration;
import org.springframework.security.config.annotation.web.builders.HttpSecurity;
import org.springframework.security.config.annotation.web.configuration.
    EnableWebSecurity;
import org.springframework.security.config.annotation.web.configuration.
    WebSecurityConfigurerAdapter;

@Configuration
@EnableWebSecurity
public class SecurityConfig extends WebSecurityConfigurerAdapter {

    @Override
    protected void configure(HttpSecurity http) throws Exception {
        http
            .csrf().disable() // Disable CSRF for non-browser clients
            .authorizeRequests()
                .antMatchers("/api/public/**").permitAll()
                .anyRequest().authenticated()
                .and()
            .httpBasic(); // Use basic authentication
    }
}
```

The SecurityConfig class disables Cross-Site Request Forgery (CSRF) protection, which is not necessary for non-browser clients, and configures basic authentication. The authorizeRequests method specifies that any request matching /api/public/** is permitted, while all other requests require authentication.

Authentication can be achieved through various methods, such as basic authentication, form-based login, OAuth2, JWT (JSON Web Token), etc. This part will focus on JWT, a popular choice for securing RESTful services.

JWT is a compact, URL-safe means of representing claims between two parties. These claims are encoded as a JSON object that is digitally signed, making the token verifiable and secure.

Start by including the JWT library in your pom.xml:

```
<dependency>
    <groupId>io.jsonwebtoken</groupId>
    <artifactId>jjwt</artifactId>
    <version>0.9.1</version>
</dependency>
```

Next, create a utility class for generating and validating JWT tokens:

```
import io.jsonwebtoken.Claims;
import io.jsonwebtoken.Jwts;
import io.jsonwebtoken.SignatureAlgorithm;
```

```
import org.springframework.stereotype.Component;
import java.util.Date;

@Component
public class JwtTokenUtil {

    private final String SECRET_KEY = "mySecretKey";

    public String generateToken(String username) {
        return Jwts.builder()
                .setSubject(username)
                .setIssuedAt(new Date())
                .setExpiration(new Date(System.currentTimeMillis() + 1000 * 60 * 60 *
                    10))
                .signWith(SignatureAlgorithm.HS256, SECRET_KEY)
                .compact();
    }

    public boolean validateToken(String token, String username) {
        return username.equals(extractUsername(token)) && !isTokenExpired(token);
    }

    public String extractUsername(String token) {
        Claims claims = Jwts.parser()
                .setSigningKey(SECRET_KEY)
                .parseClaimsJws(token)
                .getBody();
        return claims.getSubject();
    }

    private boolean isTokenExpired(String token) {
        Claims claims = Jwts.parser()
                .setSigningKey(SECRET_KEY)
                .parseClaimsJws(token)
                .getBody();
        return claims.getExpiration().before(new Date());
    }
}
```

The JwtTokenUtil class handles JWT token creation and validation. Tokens are signed using the HS256 algorithm with a secret key, and expiration is set to 10 hours.

Next, create a filter to validate JWT tokens with each request:

```
import org.springframework.beans.factory.annotation.Autowired;
import org.springframework.security.authentication.
    UsernamePasswordAuthenticationToken;
import org.springframework.security.core.context.SecurityContextHolder;
import org.springframework.security.core.userdetails.User;
import org.springframework.security.web.authentication.
    WebAuthenticationDetailsSource;
import org.springframework.stereotype.Component;
import org.springframework.web.filter.OncePerRequestFilter;

import javax.servlet.FilterChain;
import javax.servlet.ServletException;
import javax.servlet.http.HttpServletRequest;
import javax.servlet.http.HttpServletResponse;
import java.io.IOException;
```

```
@Component
public class JwtRequestFilter extends OncePerRequestFilter {

    @Autowired
    private JwtTokenUtil jwtTokenUtil;

    @Override
    protected void doFilterInternal(HttpServletRequest request, HttpServletResponse
          response, FilterChain chain)
            throws ServletException, IOException {

        String authorizationHeader = request.getHeader("Authorization");

        String username = null;
        String jwt = null;

        if (authorizationHeader != null && authorizationHeader.startsWith("Bearer "))
             {
            jwt = authorizationHeader.substring(7);
            username = jwtTokenUtil.extractUsername(jwt);
        }

        if (username != null && SecurityContextHolder.getContext().getAuthentication
             () == null) {

            if (jwtTokenUtil.validateToken(jwt, username)) {

                UsernamePasswordAuthenticationToken
                        usernamePasswordAuthenticationToken =
                          new UsernamePasswordAuthenticationToken(
                                  username, null, new ArrayList<>());
                usernamePasswordAuthenticationToken
                          .setDetails(new WebAuthenticationDetailsSource().buildDetails(
                                request));
                SecurityContextHolder.getContext().setAuthentication(
                        usernamePasswordAuthenticationToken);
            }
        }
        chain.doFilter(request, response);
    }
}
```

To register this filter, modify the SecurityConfig class to include the JwtRequestFilter:

```
import org.springframework.beans.factory.annotation.Autowired;
import org.springframework.security.config.annotation.web.builders.WebSecurity;
import org.springframework.security.web.authentication.
      UsernamePasswordAuthenticationFilter;

@Configuration
@EnableWebSecurity
public class SecurityConfig extends WebSecurityConfigurerAdapter {

    @Autowired
    private JwtRequestFilter jwtRequestFilter;

    @Override
    protected void configure(HttpSecurity http) throws Exception {
        http
```

```
            .csrf().disable()
            .authorizeRequests()
                .antMatchers("/api/public/**").permitAll()
                .anyRequest().authenticated()
                .and()
            .sessionManagement()
                .sessionCreationPolicy(SessionCreationPolicy.STATELESS);

        http.addFilterBefore(jwtRequestFilter, UsernamePasswordAuthenticationFilter.
            class);
    }
}
```

Ensure that user details are retrieved and checked against a data store. Implement UserDetailsService for custom user authentication logic:

```
import org.springframework.security.core.userdetails.User;
import org.springframework.security.core.userdetails.UserDetails;
import org.springframework.security.core.userdetails.UserDetailsService;
import org.springframework.security.core.userdetails.UsernameNotFoundException;
import org.springframework.stereotype.Service;

import java.util.ArrayList;

@Service
public class MyUserDetailsService implements UserDetailsService {

    @Override
    public UserDetails loadUserByUsername(String username) throws
        UsernameNotFoundException {
        // Implement custom user validation from data store
        return new User("user", "password", new ArrayList<>());
    }
}
```

The user details are loaded from a custom data source. For initialization and testing, a static user is provided.

Finally, create an authentication controller to handle login requests and issue JWT tokens:

```
import org.springframework.beans.factory.annotation.Autowired;
import org.springframework.security.authentication.AuthenticationManager;
import org.springframework.security.authentication.
    UsernamePasswordAuthenticationToken;
import org.springframework.security.core.AuthenticationException;
import org.springframework.security.core.userdetails.UserDetails;
import org.springframework.security.core.userdetails.UserDetailsService;
import org.springframework.web.bind.annotation.*;

@RestController
public class AuthenticationController {

    @Autowired
    private AuthenticationManager authenticationManager;

    @Autowired
    private JwtTokenUtil jwtTokenUtil;
```

```
    @Autowired
    private UserDetailsService userDetailsService;

    @PostMapping("/authenticate")
    public String createAuthenticationToken(@RequestBody AuthenticationRequest
            authenticationRequest) throws Exception {
        try {
            authenticationManager.authenticate(
                new UsernamePasswordAuthenticationToken(authenticationRequest.
                        getUsername(), authenticationRequest.getPassword())
            );
        } catch (AuthenticationException e) {
            throw new Exception("Invalid username or password", e);
        }

        final UserDetails userDetails = userDetailsService.loadUserByUsername(
                authenticationRequest.getUsername());

        final String jwt = jwtTokenUtil.generateToken(userDetails.getUsername());

        return jwt;
    }
}
```

The AuthenticationController manages login requests and generates JWT tokens upon successful authentication.

```
import java.io.Serializable;

public class AuthenticationRequest implements Serializable {

    private static final long serialVersionUID = 1L;

    private String username;
    private String password;

    public AuthenticationRequest() {
    }

    public AuthenticationRequest(String username, String password) {
        this.username = username;
        this.password = password;
    }

    // Getters and Setters
}
```

8.8 Pagination and Sorting in RESTful APIs

Pagination and sorting are key features to implement in RESTful APIs to ensure efficient data retrieval and optimal user experience. These features help manage large datasets by limiting the amount of data transferred and displayed, ensuring quick load times and a manageable user interface. In this section, we delve into the principles and practical implementation of pagination and sorting using Spring Data REST.

Spring Data REST provides a seamless way to implement pagination and sorting by leveraging the Pageable and Sort interfaces. These interfaces define the parameters required for slicing and sorting through data collections. The implementation integrates effortlessly with Spring Boot's repository abstraction layer.

To demonstrate the practical aspects of pagination and sorting, consider an example in which we wish to provide an API for retrieving a list of Product entities. A Product entity might be defined as follows:

```
@Entity
public class Product {

    @Id
    @GeneratedValue(strategy = GenerationType.IDENTITY)
    private Long id;

    private String name;
    private String description;
    private double price;

    // Getters and Setters
}
```

To enable pagination and sorting in the repository, we extend the JpaRepository interface along with the PagingAndSortingRepository. Here is an example of how to define such a repository:

```
public interface ProductRepository extends PagingAndSortingRepository<Product,
     Long> {
}
```

Spring Data REST automatically exposes the RESTful endpoints for this repository, including support for pagination and sorting. When querying the /products endpoint, we can specify pagination and sorting parameters using query string parameters.

The pagination parameters include:

- page: The page number to retrieve (0-based index).
- size: The number of records per page.

The sorting parameters include:

- sort: The sorting criteria, specified as field names. Multiple sort parameters can be provided, separated by commas. Each sort parameter can have the suffix ',asc' or ',desc' to specify ascending or descending order.

For example, to retrieve the second page of products with five products per page, sorted by name in ascending order and then by price in descending order, the query might look like this:

```
/products?page=1&size=5&sort=name,asc&sort=price,desc
```

Spring Data REST handles these parameters automatically, but for custom implementations, we can manually use the Pageable and Sort objects. Here's an example of a controller method implementing custom pagination and sorting:

```
@RestController
@RequestMapping("/api/products")
public class ProductController {

    @Autowired
    private ProductRepository productRepository;

    @GetMapping
    public Page<Product> getAllProducts(Pageable pageable) {
        return productRepository.findAll(pageable);
    }
}
```

In this controller, the Pageable object encapsulates pagination information, which allows the findAll method to return a Page<Product>. The Page object contains not only the current list of products but also metadata about the pagination, such as total number of pages and records.

To further customize pagination, we can define default pagination settings using a configuration class:

```
@Configuration
public class PaginationConfig implements WebMvcConfigurer {

    @Override
    public void addArgumentResolvers(List<HandlerMethodArgumentResolver>
            argumentResolvers) {
        PageableHandlerMethodArgumentResolver resolver = new
                PageableHandlerMethodArgumentResolver();
        resolver.setFallbackPageable(PageRequest.of(0, 10));
        argumentResolvers.add(resolver);
    }
}
```

With this configuration, if no size parameter is specified, the default page size will be 10.

Sorting can also be configured programmatically. Consider adjusting the sorting logic in a controller method:

```
@GetMapping("/sorted")
public List<Product> getSortedProducts(@RequestParam String sortBy) {
    return productRepository.findAll(Sort.by(Sort.Direction.ASC, sortBy));
```

```
}
```

This method retrieves all products sorted by the specified field in ascending order.

Handling pagination and sorting not only boosts performance but also enhances user experience. By structuring data retrieval efficiently, users can navigate through data-intensive applications smoothly. Properly integrating these features into RESTful APIs ensures scalability and usability, key aspects of modern web applications.

8.9 Integrating with Front-end Applications

Integration with front-end applications is a fundamental aspect of modern web application development. The communication between the client-side and server-side must be carefully designed to ensure a seamless user experience. This section delves into how to utilize RESTful web services built with Spring Data REST in conjunction with various front-end technologies such as Angular, React, and Vue.js. By the end of this section, readers will have a thorough understanding of how to consume RESTful APIs effectively on the client side.

To illustrate the integration process with a practical example, consider a simple RESTful API exposed by Spring Data REST for managing Product entities.

```
@Entity
public class Product {

    @Id
    @GeneratedValue(strategy = GenerationType.IDENTITY)
    private Long id;

    private String name;
    private Double price;

    // Getters and Setters
}
```

```
@RepositoryRestResource
public interface ProductRepository extends JpaRepository<Product, Long> {
}
```

The RESTful endpoints provided by Spring Data REST for this repository would be available at '/products'.

For integration with an Angular client:

- Install Angular CLI:

```
$ npm install -g @angular/cli
```

- Create a new Angular application:

```
$ ng new product-management
```

- Create a service to interact with the RESTful API:

```
import { Injectable } from '@angular/core';
import { HttpClient } from '@angular/common/http';
import { Observable } from 'rxjs';
import { Product } from './product.model';

@Injectable({
  providedIn: 'root'
})
export class ProductService {

  private baseUrl = 'http://localhost:8080/products';

  constructor(private http: HttpClient) { }

  getProducts(): Observable<Product[]> {
    return this.http.get<Product[]>(`${this.baseUrl}`);
  }

  getProduct(id: number): Observable<Product> {
    return this.http.get<Product>(`${this.baseUrl}/${id}`);
  }

  createProduct(product: Product): Observable<Object> {
    return this.http.post(`${this.baseUrl}`, product);
  }

  updateProduct(id: number, product: Product): Observable<Object> {
    return this.http.put(`${this.baseUrl}/${id}`, product);
  }

  deleteProduct(id: number): Observable<any> {
    return this.http.delete(`${this.baseUrl}/${id}`);
  }
}
```

- Implement the product model:

```
export class Product {
    id: number;
    name: string;
    price: number;
}
```

- Integrate the service in a component to display the products:

```
import { Component, OnInit } from '@angular/core';
import { ProductService } from './product.service';
import { Product } from './product.model';

@Component({
  selector: 'app-product-list',
  templateUrl: './product-list.component.html',
  styleUrls: ['./product-list.component.css']
})
export class ProductListComponent implements OnInit {

  products: Product[];

  constructor(private productService: ProductService) { }

  ngOnInit(): void {
    this.productService.getProducts().subscribe(data => {
      this.products = data;
    });
  }
}
```

For integration with a React client:

- Install create-react-app:

```
$ npx create-react-app product-management
```

- Create a service to interact with the RESTful API:

```
import axios from 'axios';

const API_URL = 'http://localhost:8080/products';

class ProductService {

  getProducts() {
    return axios.get(API_URL);
  }

  getProduct(id) {
    return axios.get(`${API_URL}/${id}`);
  }

  createProduct(product) {
    return axios.post(API_URL, product);
  }

  updateProduct(id, product) {
    return axios.put(`${API_URL}/${id}`, product);
  }

  deleteProduct(id) {
    return axios.delete(`${API_URL}/${id}`);
```

```
  }
}

export default new ProductService();
```

- Implement the product component:

```
import React, { Component } from 'react';
import ProductService from './ProductService';

class ProductList extends Component {

  constructor(props) {
    super(props);
    this.state = {
      products: []
    };
  }

  componentDidMount() {
    ProductService.getProducts().then((res) => {
      this.setState({ products: res.data });
    });
  }

  render() {
    return (
      <div>
        <h2 className="text-center">Products List</h2>
        <div className="row">
          <table className="table table-striped table-bordered">
            <thead>
              <tr>
                <th> Product Name</th>
                <th> Product Price</th>
              </tr>
            </thead>
            <tbody>
              {
                this.state.products.map(
                  product =>
                    <tr key={product.id}>
                      <td> {product.name} </td>
                      <td> {product.price} </td>
                    </tr>
                )
              }
            </tbody>
          </table>
        </div>
      </div>
    );
  }
}

export default ProductList;
```

For integration with a Vue.js client:

- Install Vue CLI:

```
$ npm install -g @vue/cli
```

- Create a new Vue.js application:

```
$ vue create product-management
```

- Create a service to interact with the RESTful API:

```
import axios from 'axios';

const API_URL = 'http://localhost:8080/products';

class ProductService {

  getProducts() {
    return axios.get(API_URL);
  }

  getProduct(id) {
    return axios.get(`${API_URL}/${id}`);
  }

  createProduct(product) {
    return axios.post(API_URL, product);
  }

  updateProduct(id, product) {
    return axios.put(`${API_URL}/${id}`, product);
  }

  deleteProduct(id) {
    return axios.delete(`${API_URL}/${id}`);
  }
}

export default new ProductService();
```

- Implement the product component:

```
<template>
  <div>
    <h2 class="text-center">Products List</h2>
    <div class="row">
      <table class="table table-striped table-bordered">
        <thead>
          <tr>
            <th>Product Name</th>
            <th>Product Price</th>
          </tr>
        </thead>
        <tbody>
```

```
        <tr v-for="product in products" :key="product.id">
          <td>{{ product.name }}</td>
          <td>{{ product.price }}</td>
        </tr>
      </tbody>
    </table>
  </div>
</div>
</template>

<script>
import ProductService from './ProductService';

export default {
  data() {
    return {
      products: []
    };
  },
  created() {
    ProductService.getProducts().then((response) => {
      this.products = response.data;
    });
  }
};
</script>

<style scoped>
.table {
  width: 100%;
}
</style>
```

By following these steps, developers can effectively integrate RESTful APIs provided by Spring Data REST with popular front-end frameworks. This approach ensures a consistent and reliable communication pathway between the client-side and server-side components of the application.

8.10 Testing RESTful Web Services

Effective testing of RESTful web services is integral to ensuring their functionality, robustness, and reliability. Testing can be broadly categorized into unit testing, integration testing, and end-to-end testing, each serving a distinctive purpose. Spring Boot provides comprehensive support for testing web services, leveraging tools like JUnit, Mockito, and Spring's own testing framework.

Testing RESTful web services involves several components: 1. Testing Controllers: Ensuring the controller mappings, request handling, and response generation functions correctly. 2. Testing Services: Verifying the business logic within service classes works as intended. 3. Testing Repositories: Ensuring the data access layer correctly interacts with the database.

Let's delve into each of these testing components with practical examples.

Testing Controllers

Controller tests, also known as web layer tests, focus on testing the controller's request mappings and how they handle different types of requests. Spring Boot provides the '@WebMvcTest' annotation to configure this type of test. Consider a simple 'UserController' that exposes RESTful endpoints:

```
@RestController
@RequestMapping("/api/users")
public class UserController {

    @Autowired
    private UserService userService;

    @GetMapping("/{id}")
    public ResponseEntity<User> getUserById(@PathVariable Long id) {
        return new ResponseEntity<>(userService.getUserById(id), HttpStatus.OK);
    }

    @PostMapping
    public ResponseEntity<User> createUser(@RequestBody User user) {
        return new ResponseEntity<>(userService.createUser(user), HttpStatus.
              CREATED);
    }

    // Other CRUD methods
}
```

To test this controller, we can write a test class using '@WebMvcTest', 'MockMvc', and Mockito:

```
@RunWith(SpringRunner.class)
@WebMvcTest(UserController.class)
public class UserControllerTest {

    @Autowired
    private MockMvc mockMvc;

    @MockBean
    private UserService userService;

    @Test
    public void testGetUserById() throws Exception {
        User mockUser = new User(1L, "John Doe");
        Mockito.when(userService.getUserById(1L)).thenReturn(mockUser);

        mockMvc.perform(get("/api/users/1"))
              .andExpect(status().isOk())
              .andExpect(jsonPath("$.name").value("John Doe"));
```

```
    }

    @Test
    public void testCreateUser() throws Exception {
        User mockUser = new User(1L, "John Doe");
        Mockito.when(userService.createUser(Mockito.any(User.class))).thenReturn(
            mockUser);

        mockMvc.perform(post("/api/users")
                .contentType(MediaType.APPLICATION_JSON)
                .content("{\"name\": \"John Doe\"}"))
                .andExpect(status().isCreated())
                .andExpect(jsonPath("$.name").value("John Doe"));
    }

    // Other tests
}
```

Testing Services

Service layer tests are concerned with the core business logic. These tests typically use the '@SpringBootTest' or '@ExtendWith(SpringExtension.class)' annotations. Consider the following 'UserService':

```
@Service
public class UserService {

    @Autowired
    private UserRepository userRepository;

    public User getUserById(Long id) {
        return userRepository.findById(id).orElseThrow(() -> new
            ResourceNotFoundException("User not found"));
    }

    public User createUser(User user) {
        return userRepository.save(user);
    }

    // Other business methods
}
```

The test class for this service would look like:

```
@RunWith(SpringRunner.class)
@SpringBootTest
public class UserServiceTest {

    @Autowired
    private UserService userService;

    @MockBean
    private UserRepository userRepository;

    @Test
    public void testGetUserById() {
        User mockUser = new User(1L, "John Doe");
        Mockito.when(userRepository.findById(1L)).thenReturn(Optional.of(mockUser))
```

```
        ;
        User user = userService.getUserById(1L);
        assertEquals("John Doe", user.getName());
    }

    @Test
    public void testCreateUser() {
        User mockUser = new User(1L, "John Doe");
        Mockito.when(userRepository.save(Mockito.any(User.class))).thenReturn(
            mockUser);

        User user = userService.createUser(new User(null, "John Doe"));
        assertEquals("John Doe", user.getName());
    }

    // Other tests
}
```

Testing Repositories

Repositories form the data access layer, and their tests ensure that interactions with the database are correct. Spring Boot provides '@DataJpaTest' to test JPA repositories. An example 'UserRepository':

```
public interface UserRepository extends JpaRepository<User, Long> {
    Optional<User> findByName(String name);
}
```

To write tests for this repository, your class would look like:

```
@RunWith(SpringRunner.class)
@DataJpaTest
public class UserRepositoryTest {

    @Autowired
    private TestEntityManager entityManager;

    @Autowired
    private UserRepository userRepository;

    @Test
    public void testFindByName() {
        User user = new User(null, "John Doe");
        entityManager.persist(user);
        entityManager.flush();

        Optional<User> found = userRepository.findByName("John Doe");
        assertTrue(found.isPresent());
        assertEquals("John Doe", found.get().getName());
    }

    @Test
    public void testSaveUser() {
        User user = new User(null, "Jane Doe");
        User savedUser = userRepository.save(user);
        assertNotNull(savedUser.getId());
    }

    // Other tests
```

```
}
```

To test RESTful web services comprehensively, each layer of the application must be validated, from controllers to repositories. This guarantees that any issues are caught early and handled appropriately, ensuring the robustness and reliability of the services.

Chapter 9

Performance Tuning and Best Practices

This chapter addresses performance tuning and best practices in JPA. It starts with understanding the JPA caching mechanism and configuring the second-level cache. The chapter covers efficient fetching strategies, such as eager and lazy loading, optimizing database access with batch processing, and resolving N+1 query problems. It explores using query hints for performance enhancement and profiling and monitoring JPA performance. Best practices for entity design and mapping, as well as query optimization, are also discussed to ensure efficient and maintainable JPA applications.

9.1 Introduction to Performance Tuning in JPA

Performance tuning in Java Persistence API (JPA) involves various techniques and practices aimed at optimizing the speed and efficiency of database interactions. This process is critical for ensuring that JPA applications remain performant, scalable, and responsive under different load conditions. Tackling performance issues in JPA requires a deep understanding of the persistence context, caching mechanisms, fetching strategies, and the overall interaction between the application and the database layer.

One fundamental aspect of JPA performance tuning is the efficient management of the persistence context. The persistence context is a set of entity instances managed by JPA within a particular transactional scope. Properly handling the persistence context can prevent unnecessary database access and reduce memory consumption. Mismanagement can lead to performance bottlenecks such as high latency and memory leaks.

Caching plays a pivotal role in JPA performance. JPA uses two levels of caching: the first-level cache, which operates within the persistence context, and the second-level cache, which is shared across multiple contexts. Understanding the nuances and configurations of these caches is essential in minimizing database hits and improving data retrieval times.

Efficient fetching strategies also significantly impact JPA performance. Fetching strategies determine when and how entity relationships are loaded from the database. JPA supports both eager and lazy loading. Eager loading retrieves associated entities at the same time as the parent entity, whereas lazy loading delays the retrieval until explicitly accessed. Selecting the appropriate fetching strategy for given scenarios is crucial in optimizing the performance.

Batch processing and query optimization are techniques designed to enhance database access efficiency. Batch processing involves consolidating multiple database operations into a single unit, reducing the overhead associated with frequent database interactions. Query optimization, on the other hand, focuses on refining database queries to execute in an optimal manner, leveraging indexes and minimizing complex joins and subqueries.

Profiling and monitoring tools can help identify performance issues by providing detailed insights into database interactions and application behavior. These tools are essential for pinpointing problems such as N+1 query issues—a common performance pitfall where multiple queries are generated for each row in a result set.

Performance tuning extends to best practices for entity design and mapping. Proper entity modeling, avoiding unnecessary relationships, and leveraging lightweight entities can improve performance. Query design is equally critical; writing efficient JPQL (Java Persistence Query Language) queries, using native queries when necessary, and applying query hints can prevent performance degradation.

Below is an example of a JPA entity definition, demonstrating a basic configuration essential for further discussion on tuning strategies:

```
@Entity
@Table(name = "employees")
public class Employee {

    @Id
    @GeneratedValue(strategy = GenerationType.IDENTITY)
    private Long id;

    @Column(name = "first_name")
    private String firstName;

    @Column(name = "last_name")
    private String lastName;

    @ManyToOne(fetch = FetchType.LAZY)
    @JoinColumn(name = "department_id")
    private Department department;

    // Getters and setters omitted for brevity
}
```

In this example, note the use of lazy fetching for the 'department' relationship. This approach is a common practice to delay the loading of the associated 'Department' entity until it is explicitly accessed, conserving resources and reducing unnecessary database calls.

Understanding the default behaviors and options provided by JPA is the foundation for mastering performance tuning. As the chapter progresses, deeper insights into caching strategies, fetching configurations, and optimization techniques will be explored, providing a comprehensive toolset for developing high-performance JPA applications.

9.2 Understanding the JPA Caching Mechanism

Java Persistence API (JPA) caching mechanisms play a crucial role in enhancing the performance of an application by reducing the amount of database access required. JPA provides two levels of caching: First-Level Cache (shared at the entity manager level) and Second-Level Cache (shared across entity managers within the same persistence unit).

The First-Level Cache, also known as the Entity Manager Cache, is automatically active and managed by the JPA provider. This cache is scoped to the lifecycle of an EntityManager instance. When an application issues a query to retrieve an entity, the EntityManager first checks its First-Level Cache. If the entity is found, it skips the database access and returns the cached entity. If the entity is not found, a database query is issued, and the result is cached within the EntityManager for subsequent requests.

The Second-Level Cache, on the other hand, is more sophisticated and requires explicit configuration. It is shared among multiple EntityManager instances within the same persistence unit. The Second-Level Cache maintains a repository of entities that have been read from the database, minimizing database round-trips for subsequent requests across different EntityManager instances.

Cache Providers: The Second-Level Cache requires integration with a cache provider. Commonly used providers include EHCache, Hazelcast, and Infinispan. Each of these providers offers distinct features and optimizations, and their choice largely depends on the specific requirements and constraints of the application.

```
<persistence-unit name="exampleUnit">
    <provider>org.hibernate.jpa.HibernatePersistenceProvider</provider>
    <properties>
        <property name="hibernate.cache.use_second_level_cache" value="true"/>
        <property name="hibernate.cache.region.factory_class" value="org.hibernate.
            cache.ehcache.EhCacheRegionFactory"/>
        <property name="hibernate.cache.provider_class" value="net.sf.ehcache.
            hibernate.SingletonEhCacheRegionFactory"/>
    </properties>
</persistence-unit>
```

Cache Strategies: Different caching strategies can be employed depending on the specific use case. The most common strategies include:

- **Read-Only:** Suitable for entities that do not change often. Caching these entities can significantly improve performance as no write operations are performed.
- **Read-Write:** Allows read and write access to the cache while ensuring strong consistency using locks or other synchronization mechanisms.
- **Non-Strict Read-Write:** Provides a balance between performance and consistency. It allows concurrent access but might tolerate stale reads.
- **Transactional:** Integrates with the underlying JTA transaction

management, providing the highest level of consistency and isolation.

Configuring Caching at the Entity Level: Individual entities can be annotated to specify their caching strategy using the @Cacheable and @Cache annotations in JPA.

```
@Entity
@Cacheable
@org.hibernate.annotations.Cache(usage = CacheConcurrencyStrategy.READ_WRITE)

public class Product {
    // Entity attributes and methods
}
```

Cache Regions: Cache regions segregate different entities within the cache provider to allow fine-grained control over cache policies such as eviction and expiration. A region can be configured for each entity type or logically grouped entities.

```
@Entity
@Cacheable
@org.hibernate.annotations.Cache(region = "productCacheRegion", usage =
      CacheConcurrencyStrategy.READ_WRITE)
public class Product {
    // Entity attributes and methods
}
```

Eviction Policies: The management of cache size and eviction policies (like Least Recently Used - LRU, Least Frequently Used - LFU) ensures that the cache does not grow unbounded and that rarely accessed data is purged from the cache to make space for new data.

Expiration Policies: Setting expiration times helps in invalidating cache entries after a certain period, ensuring that the cached data reflects the most current state of the database without manual intervention.

```
<cache name="productCacheRegion"
       maxEntriesLocalHeap="1000"
       timeToLiveSeconds="600">
    <!-- Cache region-specific configuration -->
</cache>
```

Understanding these caching mechanisms and effectively configuring them is fundamental for achieving optimal application performance while maintaining data consistency. Proper usage of caching significantly reduces the load on the database by retrieving frequently accessed data from the cache, thereby enhancing the overall responsiveness of the application.

9.3 Configuring Second-Level Cache

In JPA, the second-level cache, also known as the shared cache, is designed to store entity data across multiple sessions or entity managers. This caching mechanism significantly reduces the number of database accesses, enhances performance, and decreases latency. Configuring the second-level cache in a JPA environment requires a thorough understanding of its architecture, proper configuration in persistence.xml, and a strategic approach to cache usage.

Second-level caching is distinct from the first-level (or session) cache. While the first-level cache is scoped to a single entity manager and automatically enabled by JPA, the second-level cache is scoped to the entire persistence context and must be explicitly configured.

1. Enabling Second-Level Cache

The second-level cache is often provided by third-party caching providers, such as Ehcache, Infinispan, or Hazelcast. Enabling the second-level cache typically consists of adding the appropriate provider dependencies and configuring cache-related properties in the persistence.xml file.

Consider an example setup using Ehcache as the cache provider:

```
<persistence xmlns="http://xmlns.jcp.org/xml/ns/persistence"
   xmlns:xsi="http://www.w3.org/2001/XMLSchema-instance"
   xsi:schemaLocation="http://xmlns.jcp.org/xml/ns/persistence
   http://xmlns.jcp.org/xml/ns/persistence/persistence_2_1.xsd"
   version="2.1">
   <persistence-unit name="examplePU" transaction-type="RESOURCE_LOCAL">
      <provider>org.hibernate.jpa.HibernatePersistenceProvider</provider>
      <properties>
         <property name="hibernate.dialect"
                  value="org.hibernate.dialect.H2Dialect"/>
         <property name="hibernate.cache.use_second_level_cache"
                  value="true"/>
         <property name="hibernate.cache.region.factory_class"
                  value="org.hibernate.cache.ehcache.EhCacheRegionFactory"/>
         <property name="net.sf.ehcache.configurationResourceName"
                  value="/ehcache.xml"/>
      </properties>
   </persistence-unit>
</persistence>
```

This configuration snippet demonstrates how to enable Hibernate's second-level cache and specify Ehcache as the caching provider by setting appropriate properties.

2. Configuring Ehcache

The Ehcache configuration file (ehcache.xml) defines cache-specific settings, including cache regions, expiration policies, and memory settings. An example configuration might look like this:

```
<ehcache xmlns:xsi="http://www.w3.org/2001/XMLSchema-instance"
    xsi:noNamespaceSchemaLocation="http://ehcache.org/ehcache.xsd">
    <cache name="com.example.MyEntity"
           maxEntriesLocalHeap="1000"
           timeToLiveSeconds="600"
           timeToIdleSeconds="300">
    </cache>
</ehcache>
```

This configuration specifies a cache named com.example.MyEntity with heap capacity for 1000 entities, a time-to-live (TTL) of 600 seconds, and a time-to-idle (TTI) of 300 seconds.

3. Annotation-Based Cache Configuration

Entities or collections can be marked for second-level caching using the \@Cacheable annotation. Additionally, the \@Cache annotation can define region-specific parameters:

```
import javax.persistence.Cacheable;
import org.hibernate.annotations.Cache;
import org.hibernate.annotations.CacheConcurrencyStrategy;

@Entity
@Cacheable
@Cache(usage = CacheConcurrencyStrategy.READ_WRITE, region = "entityCache")
public class MyEntity {
    // Entity fields, getters, setters...
}
```

CacheConcurrencyStrategy defines the cache's concurrency strategy, with options including READ_WRITE, NONSTRICT_READ_WRITE, READ_ONLY, and TRANSACTIONAL, outlining the interactions with the cache and the underlying database.

4. Validating Cache Configuration

Effective validation involves ensuring the cache behaves as expected. This includes confirming that entities are stored in the cache, monitoring cache hits and misses, and tuning cache parameters based on observed performance.

Example validation steps:

```
EntityManagerFactory emf = Persistence.createEntityManagerFactory("examplePU");
EntityManager em1 = emf.createEntityManager();
// Load entity for the first time, should result in a cache miss
MyEntity entity = em1.find(MyEntity.class, 1L);
em1.close();
```

```
EntityManager em2 = emf.createEntityManager();
// Load entity again, should result in a cache hit
MyEntity cachedEntity = em2.find(MyEntity.class, 1L);
em2.close();
```

For validation outputs, logging libraries like SLF4J can be configured to capture cache interactions:

```
INFO  Cache: Cache miss for entity with ID 1
INFO  Cache: Cache hit for entity with ID 1
```

5. Cache Tuning Considerations

Different application scenarios necessitate various cache configurations. Tuning the size of the heap, setting appropriate TTL and TTI values, careful selection of cache regions, and concurrency strategies play a crucial role in cache efficiency.

Key considerations include:

- **Heap Size:** Adequate heap size should be determined as per entity size and estimated simultaneous cache entries.
- **TTL and TTI:** Balancing between stale data and reduced database access by setting optimal TTL and TTI values.
- **Concurrency Strategy:** Selection based on transaction requirements and data consistency needs. READ_WRITE is commonly used for entities requiring consistent state between transactions, whereas READ_ONLY is suitable for rarely changing entities.

These configurations and principles lay the groundwork for proficiently leveraging second-level caching in JPA. By systematically enabling, fine-tuning, and validating the cache, substantial performance enhancements in database access and application responsiveness can be achieved.

9.4 Efficient Fetching Strategies: Eager vs Lazy

Fetching strategies play a crucial role in the performance of Java Persistence API (JPA) applications. Understanding when to use eager fetching versus lazy fetching can significantly impact both the efficiency of database interaction and the application's overall performance.

Eager fetching retrieves associated entities immediately upon querying the database. In contrast, **lazy fetching** retrieves associated entities only when they are accessed. Each of these strategies has its advantages and disadvantages, and selecting the appropriate strategy depends on the specific use case.

Eager Fetching

Eager fetching is employed when the related entities are expected to be used immediately along with the principal entity. This strategy minimizes the number of queries sent to the database, as all related entities are fetched in a single query, potentially loaded through a join operation.

In JPA, eager fetching is specified using the FetchType.EAGER attribute in the @OneToMany, @ManyToOne, @OneToOne, and @ManyToMany annotations. For instance:

```
@Entity
public class Author {

    @OneToMany(fetch = FetchType.EAGER, mappedBy = "author")
    private List<Book> books;

    // other fields, getters, and setters
}
```

In this example, when an Author entity is queried, all related Book entities are also fetched immediately.

However, eager fetching can lead to performance drawbacks, especially when dealing with large datasets or unnecessary data retrieval. For example:

```
@Entity
public class Employee {

    @OneToMany(fetch = FetchType.EAGER, mappedBy = "employee")
    private List<Project> projects;

    // other fields, getters, and setters
}
```

Querying an Employee entity would result in all associated Project entities being loaded into memory, which could be inefficient and resource-intensive if the number of projects is large and only a fraction of them are needed.

Lazy Fetching

Lazy fetching, defined by FetchType.LAZY, allows for deferred loading of associated entities until they are explicitly accessed. This can lead to significant performance gains by reducing the amount of data transferred and the memory footprint when only a subset of data is needed.

In JPA, lazy fetching is the default fetching type for @OneToMany and @ManyToMany relationships. It can be explicitly set using the fetch attribute:

```
@Entity
public class Author {

    @OneToMany(fetch = FetchType.LAZY, mappedBy = "author")
    private List<Book> books;

    // other fields, getters, and setters
}
```

When applying lazy fetching, associated entities are loaded on-demand during runtime. This lazy loading is typically achieved using proxy objects that delay the database hit until the associated entity's data is accessed. For example:

```
@Entity
public class Employee {

    @OneToMany(fetch = FetchType.LAZY, mappedBy = "employee")
    private List<Project> projects;

    // other fields, getters, and setters
}
```

Accessing the projects collection for an Employee entity will trigger a database query fetching the related projects if they had not already been loaded.

Choosing Between Eager and Lazy Fetching

The decision between eager and lazy fetching should consider the specific application context and use case scenarios. Here are practical aspects to consider:

- **Data Usage Patterns:** If related entities are frequently accessed along with the primary entity, eager fetching can be more beneficial. Conversely, if related data is often not needed, lazy fetching is preferable to minimize data transfer and memory usage.

- **Transaction Scope:** Lazy fetching requires the persistence context (e.g., the session or entity manager) to remain open until the entity is accessed. This can be a consideration for long-running transactions or detached entities.

- **Performance:** Both over-fetching and under-fetching can negatively impact performance. Eager fetching reduces the number of required queries but can lead to excessive data loading. Lazy fetching reduces initial data load but can lead to the N+1 query problem if used inappropriately.

Optimizing fetching strategies often involves fine-tuning based on profiling and monitoring results. Identifying frequently used entities and their access patterns will guide the choice between eager and lazy fetching, ensuring efficient database interactions tailored to the application's needs.

9.5 Optimizing Database Access with Batch Processing

Batch processing is a critical technique in optimizing database access, particularly in high-throughput applications. By reducing the overhead of multiple database interactions, it facilitates efficient data management and improves the overall performance of JPA-based applications. This section delves into the theory and practice of batch processing within JPA, ensuring readers can implement these techniques effectively.

Batch processing involves grouping multiple operations into a single unit of work. In JPA, this is particularly useful for improving the performance of bulk insert, update, and delete operations. To achieve optimal results, one must understand the configuration and the impact of various strategies on the persistence context and underlying database.

Configuring Batch Processing in JPA

JPA providers, such as Hibernate, offer built-in support for batch processing. Configuration of batch processing typically begins with setting the appropriate properties in the persistence.xml file or configuring them programmatically. For instance, to enable batch processing in Hibernate, the following properties can be set:

```
<property name="hibernate.jdbc.batch_size" value="50"/>
<property name="hibernate.order_inserts" value="true"/>
<property name="hibernate.order_updates" value="true"/>
```

The property hibernate_jdbc_batch_size specifies the number of SQL statements to be executed in a single batch. Setting this to an optimal number, such as 50, balances memory usage and performance gains.

The properties hibernate_order_inserts and hibernate_order_updates ensure that inserts and updates are executed in an ordered manner, which can significantly enhance batching efficiency by reducing the likelihood of deadlocks and improving row-level locking performance.

Batch Processing in Action

To illustrate batch processing, consider an example of inserting multiple Employee entities:

```
EntityManagerFactory emf = Persistence.createEntityManagerFactory("my-pu");
EntityManager em = emf.createEntityManager();
EntityTransaction transaction = null;

try {
    transaction = em.getTransaction();
    transaction.begin();

    for (int i = 0; i < 1000; i++) {
        Employee emp = new Employee("Employee" + i, "Department" + (i % 5));
        em.persist(emp);
        if (i % 50 == 0) { // flush and clear every 50 inserts to manage memory
            em.flush();
            em.clear();
        }
    }

    transaction.commit();
} catch (RuntimeException e) {
    if (transaction != null && transaction.isActive()) {
        transaction.rollback();
    }
    throw e;
} finally {
    em.close();
    emf.close();
}
```

In the above code snippet, the flush() and clear() methods are called every 50 inserts. flush() synchronizes the persistence context with the underlying database, executing the batched SQL insert statements. clear() detaches all entities from the persistence context, freeing up memory. This practice prevents memory overconsumption when dealing with large data sets.

Effectiveness of Batch Processing

The effectiveness of batch processing can be demonstrated by analyzing database logs and monitoring performance metrics. Batch processing reduces the number of round trips to the database, minimizing network latency and the overhead associated with multiple transaction commits.

```
DEBUG - Executing batch size: 50
DEBUG - Executing SQL: insert into Employee ...
DEBUG - Executing SQL: insert into Employee ...
// Repeated for each batch of 50 operations
```

Such logs confirm that batch processing groups multiple SQL statements into a single client-server interaction, validating its efficiency.

Considerations and Best Practices

While batch processing yields significant performance benefits, it necessitates careful consideration of transaction size and memory usage:

- **Optimal Batch Size**: The batch size should be tuned based on application behavior and database capacity. Excessively large batches can lead to memory issues, while too small batches may not fully leverage the performance benefits.
- **Transaction Management**: Proper handling of transactions is crucial. Maintaining a large persistence context can lead to memory overhead and potential transaction failures. Periodic flushing and clearing help mitigate these risks.
- **Resource Monitoring**: Continuous monitoring of database resources, such as connection pools and transaction logs, ensures smooth operation and early detection of bottlenecks.
- **Database-Specific Optimizations**: Different databases may provide specific configurations or limitations concerning batch processing. Tuning JDBC driver settings and SQL execution plans as per the database's recommendations ensures optimal performance.

Batch processing, when implemented correctly, significantly enhances the performance of JPA applications, particularly in scenarios involving bulk operations. Understanding and applying the appropriate configurations, coupled with prudent transaction management strategies, enable developers to exploit the full potential of batch processing in their applications.

9.6 Identifying and Resolving N+1 Query Problems

The N+1 query problem is a common performance issue in JPA (Java Persistence API) applications, arising when an entity and its related entities are fetched inefficiently. This results in executing multiple queries, causing substantial overhead. Understanding and addressing this problem is critical for optimizing database access and improving application performance.

The N+1 query problem typically occurs in two scenarios:

- Fetching a collection of entities.
- Accessing lazy-loaded relationships individually within a loop or similar construct.

Consider an example where a developer fetches a list of Author entities, each having a collection of Book entities. If improperly managed, fetching these authors and their respective books can generate an excessive number of SQL queries.

```
List<Author> authors = entityManager.createQuery("SELECT a FROM Author a",
    Author.class).getResultList();

for (Author author : authors) {
    System.out.println(author.getBooks().size());
}
```

In the above code, the initial query selects all authors. However, for each author, a separate query is executed to fetch the books, resulting in N+1 queries (one for authors and N for their books). This scenario is inefficient and can significantly degrade performance, especially with large datasets.

To identify an N+1 query problem, enable SQL logging in your persistence configuration. Observe the SQL output to verify if multiple similar SELECT statements are being executed.

```
SELECT * FROM Author;
SELECT * FROM Book WHERE author_id = ?;
SELECT * FROM Book WHERE author_id = ?;
...
```

A strategic approach should be taken to resolve the N+1 query problem, primarily focusing on batch fetching, eager fetching, and employing query joins.

Batch Fetching:

Batch fetching improves efficiency by retrieving entities in batches rather than one-by-one. Configuring JPA to fetch collections in batches reduces the total number of queries:

```
@BatchSize(size = 10)
class Author {
```

```
    @OneToMany(mappedBy = "author")
    private List<Book> books;
}
```

In the above example, the @BatchSize annotation specifies that books for up to 10 authors should be fetched in each SQL query, significantly minimizing the total number of queries.

Eager Fetching:

Eager fetching can pre-fetch relationships, preventing multiple queries, though it should be used selectively to avoid loading unnecessary data. There are two ways to achieve eager fetching:

- *Using* FetchType.EAGER *in Entity Mapping:*

```
class Author {
    @OneToMany(fetch = FetchType.EAGER, mappedBy = "author")
    private List<Book> books;
}
```

This approach alters the fetch type at the attribute level, ensuring books are fetched with their parent author.

- *Using* JPQL *Fetch Joins:*

```
List<Author> authors = entityManager.createQuery(
    "SELECT a FROM Author a LEFT JOIN FETCH a.books", Author.class).
        getResultList();
```

Fetch joins instruct the persistence context to fetch both authors and their related books in a single query, substantially reducing database interactions.

Using Entity Graphs:

Entity graphs provide a more flexible way to specify attribute nodes and fetch plans. They allow overriding the default fetch type, suitable during runtime:

```
@Entity
@NamedEntityGraph(name = "author-books-graph",
    attributeNodes = @NamedAttributeNode("books"))
class Author {
    @OneToMany(mappedBy = "author")
    private List<Book> books;
}
```

Execute the query with the entity graph:

```
EntityGraph<?> graph = entityManager.getEntityGraph("author-books-graph");
List<Author> authors = entityManager.createQuery("SELECT a FROM Author a",
      Author.class)
    .setHint("javax.persistence.loadgraph", graph)
    .getResultList();
```

Entity graphs allow nuanced control over the fetch strategy, balancing eager and lazy loading efficiently based on context.

Careful analysis and the application of these techniques ensure that the performance is effectively optimized, reducing the overhead caused by the N+1 query problem.

9.7 Using Query Hints for Performance

Query hints are directives provided to the JPA provider that can influence the way a query is executed, enabling various optimizations. They do not alter the logic or output of the query, but they can fine-tune aspects such as caching, locking, and fetching strategies. Query hints are an advanced feature that can significantly impact the performance of your JPA application, and they need to be used judiciously based on a thorough understanding of the underlying database and application requirements.

To use query hints in JPA, you typically utilize the Query or TypedQuery interfaces and apply the setHint method. This allows you to pass specific hints for query execution.

```
TypedQuery<Employee> query = em.createQuery("SELECT e FROM Employee e
      WHERE e.department = :dept", Employee.class);
query.setParameter("dept", "Sales");

// Apply a query hint
query.setHint("javax.persistence.cache.retrieveMode", CacheRetrieveMode.BYPASS);
List<Employee> results = query.getResultList();
```

In this example, the javax.persistence.cache.retrieveMode hint is used to bypass the cache during the execution of the query, ensuring the query retrieves fresh data directly from the database.

Commonly Used Query Hints

1. **Caching Hints**

Caching hints control whether the query should interact with the cache. This influences whether the results are retrieved from the cache or bypass it.

- - CacheRetrieveMode.USE: Indicates that the cache should be consulted for query results.
- - CacheRetrieveMode.BYPASS: Forces the query to bypass the cache and retrieve results directly from the database.
- - CacheStoreMode.USE: Suggests that the results of the query should be stored in the cache.
- - CacheStoreMode.REFRESH: Forces the query results to refresh the cache with the latest data.

Example:

```
query.setHint("javax.persistence.cache.retrieveMode", CacheRetrieveMode.BYPASS);
query.setHint("javax.persistence.cache.storeMode", CacheStoreMode.REFRESH);
```

2. **Read-Only Queries**

The javax.persistence.lock.timeout hint specifies the maximum time the query should wait to acquire a lock.

Example:

```
query.setHint("javax.persistence.lock.timeout", 3000);
```

3. **Fetch Size**

The fetch size hint sets the number of rows to fetch from the database when more rows are needed.

Example:

```
query.setHint("eclipselink.jdbc.fetch-size", 100);
```

This hint is particularly useful for optimizing memory consumption and improving performance during bulk data retrieval.

4. **Query Timeout**

The javax.persistence.query.timeout hint specifies the maximum time in milliseconds the query should run.

Example:

```
query.setHint("javax.persistence.query.timeout", 5000);
```

Setting this hint can avoid long-running queries that could potentially degrade system performance.

5. **SQL Execution Hints**

Providers like Hibernate offer additional proprietary hints to optimize query execution, such as setting the comment for a query or controlling the fetch mode.

Example:

```
query.setHint("org.hibernate.comment", "Fetch all employees in Sales department");
query.setHint("org.hibernate.fetchSize", "100");
```

Best Practices for Using Query Hints

When using query hints, consider the following best practices:

- - **Understand the Database**: Different databases have varied levels of support and optimization for query hints. Ensure compatibility and test for performance gains.
- - **Test and Measure**: Before applying hints in a production environment, thoroughly test their impact on performance using a profiling tool. Performance can vary based on dataset size, database load, and network latency.
- - **Use Sparingly and Strategically**: Overuse of hints can complicate query tuning and maintenance. Use them strategically where significant performance gains are realizable.
- - **Document Usage**: Clearly document the purpose and intent of each applied hint within the codebase to assist future developers in understanding the optimizations in place.

By carefully selecting and applying query hints, one can fine-tune JPA query execution, leading to substantial performance improvements in specific scenarios. This advanced mechanism, when properly understood and judiciously employed, can elevate the efficiency of your JPA-based application.

9.8 Profiling and Monitoring JPA Performance

To thoroughly understand and enhance the performance of JPA-based applications, profiling and monitoring are indispensable activities. Profiling involves detailed analysis of application performance, identifying bottlenecks, and understanding the runtime behavior. Monitoring, on the other hand, is about continuously observing the application over time to ensure that performance remains within acceptable parameters. This section dives into both practices, providing practical techniques and tools useful for developers.

Profiling tools enable analysis of various aspects of a JPA-based application. Some of the critical areas include query performance, transaction time, cache usage, and memory consumption. Various tools are available, such as VisualVM, JProfiler, and YourKit, each offering unique features tailored to Java applications.

```
// Add the following JVM argument to enable JMX for VisualVM
-Dcom.sun.management.jmxremote
-Dcom.sun.management.jmxremote.port=9010
-Dcom.sun.management.jmxremote.ssl=false
-Dcom.sun.management.jmxremote.authenticate=false
```

Once the application is configured, VisualVM can connect to the JVM process. By navigating through the 'Monitor' and 'Sampler' tabs, developers can examine CPU and memory usage, monitor heap dumps, and analyze thread activities. These features are essential for identifying memory leaks, inefficient resource usage, and performance bottlenecks.

JProfiler and YourKit provide more advanced profiling capabilities, such as detailed SQL query analysis and transaction monitoring. JProfiler, for instance, offers an 'SQL Timings' view, showing various executed SQL statements, along with their execution time and frequency:

```
SQL Timings:
---------------------------------------------
SELECT * FROM User WHERE id = ? [1.2 ms] [12 invocations]
INSERT INTO Orders (user_id, product_id) VALUES (?, ?) [0.8 ms] [6 invocations]
...
```

This detailed output allows pinpointing slow queries and understanding their impact on the overall performance.

Monitoring tools such as New Relic, AppDynamics, and Dynatrace offer continuous insights into application performance. These tools typically integrate with JPA applications via agents, providing real-time dashboards displaying various metrics like response times, throughput, error rates, and specific JPA-related metrics.

For example, integrating New Relic with a Spring Boot application involves adding the New Relic agent:

```
java -javaagent:/path/to/newrelic/newrelic.jar -jar myapp.jar
```

After deployment, New Relic's dashboard offers insights into transaction times, database call durations, and potential slowdowns. One of the critical features of such tools is their ability to alert developers when performance degrades beyond a defined threshold.

Enabling SQL logging in JPA is another crucial approach to monitoring:

```
spring.jpa.show-sql=true
spring.jpa.properties.hibernate.format_sql=true
```

While SQL logging is beneficial for development and troubleshooting, high log verbosity may impact performance in production environments. Therefore, it should be used judiciously.

JPA provides built-in support for monitoring via JMX (Java Management Extensions). By configuring JPA entities and persistence units with appropriate properties, developers can expose various metrics:

```
hibernate.jmx.enabled=true
hibernate.jmx.statistics=true
hibernate.generate_statistics=true
```

With JMX enabled, various runtime metrics, such as entity load counts, cache hit/miss ratios, and query execution times, become accessible through JMX clients like JConsole or Java Mission Control.

```
Hibernate Statistics:
---------------------------------------------
Entity fetch count: 128
Second-level cache hit count: 57
Query cache put count: 14
...
```

The integration of these monitoring techniques helps continuously evaluate the performance, ensuring that the application adheres to expected SLAs (Service Level Agreements).

Moreover, Application Performance Management (APM) tools provide deeper integration by capturing end-to-end transaction traces. By correlating these traces with underlying JPA operations, they help in identifying performance bottlenecks not only within the JPA layer but across the entire application stack.

To summarize, profiling and monitoring are vital practices in performance tuning for JPA applications. They provide insights necessary to make informed decisions about optimizing code, refining queries, and ensuring the overall robustness and efficiency of the application. Properly configured tools and methodologies enable developers to detect, diagnose, and rectify performance issues proactively, maintaining smooth and efficient application operation.

9.9 Best Practices for Entity Design and Mapping

When designing and mapping entities in Java Persistence API (JPA), adhering to best practices is essential for creating efficient, maintainable, and high-performance applications. This section delves into several critical aspects, such as employing appropriate data types, ensuring proper indexing, managing relationships, and leveraging inheritance strategies.

Choosing Appropriate Data Types

Selecting the right data types for entity attributes is foundational. Primitive data types in Java (e.g., int, float) should be used for required fields to avoid nullability. For optional fields, wrapper classes (e.g., Integer, Float) are preferable. Careful attention to the choice of data types can significantly affect both the application's performance and portability across different databases.

Defining Primary Keys

Primary keys must be defined carefully. Utilize the @Id annotation for primary keys and prefer generating values with the @GeneratedValue annotation using strategies like GenerationType.AUTO, GenerationType.IDENTITY, GenerationType.SEQUENCE, or GenerationType.TABLE. For high performance and portability, GenerationType.SEQUENCE and database sequences are often optimal.

```
@Entity
public class Employee {
    @Id
    @GeneratedValue(strategy = GenerationType.SEQUENCE, generator = "
        employee_seq")
    @SequenceGenerator(name = "employee_seq", sequenceName = "
        employee_sequence")
    private Long id;
    // other attributes and getters/setters
}
```

Managing Relationships

Properly managing entity relationships (one-to-one, one-to-many, many-to-one, many-to-many) influences both the maintainability and performance of the database schema. Utilize appropriate JPA annotations such as @OneToOne, @OneToMany, @ManyToOne, and @ManyToMany.

For example, in a @OneToMany relationship, the mappedBy attribute is crucial to define the owner of the relationship. Lazy fetching should be the default strategy to prevent unnecessary data loading, while eager fetching can be specified for essential relationships:

```
@Entity
public class Department {
    @Id
    @GeneratedValue(strategy = GenerationType.IDENTITY)
    private Long id;

    @OneToMany(mappedBy = "department", fetch = FetchType.LAZY)
    private List<Employee> employees;
    // other attributes and getters/setters
}

@Entity
public class Employee {
    @Id
    @GeneratedValue(strategy = GenerationType.IDENTITY)
    private Long id;

    @ManyToOne(fetch = FetchType.LAZY)
    @JoinColumn(name = "department_id")
    private Department department;
    // other attributes and getters/setters
}
```

Utilizing Inheritance Strategies

When dealing with entity inheritance, choosing the right inheritance strategy is key. JPA supports SINGLE_TABLE, JOINED, and TABLE_PER_CLASS strategies. Each has its advantages depending on the use case.

- SINGLE_TABLE: All entities are stored in a single table. This strategy can reduce the number of joins required but may lead to sparse tables.
- JOINED: Each class has its table, and tables are joined to fetch complete entities. This is normalized and space-efficient but can introduce complexity in join operations.
- TABLE_PER_CLASS: Each class/table holds its persistent fields, which can lead to redundant columns across tables.

```
@Entity
@Inheritance(strategy = InheritanceType.JOINED)
public abstract class User {
    @Id
    @GeneratedValue(strategy = GenerationType.IDENTITY)
    private Long id;
    private String username;
```

```
    // other attributes and getters/setters
}

@Entity
public class AdminUser extends User {
    private String adminKey;
    // other attributes and getters/setters
}

@Entity
public class RegularUser extends User {
    private String subscriptionType;
    // other attributes and getters/setters
}
```

Optimizing Index Usage

Indexes can dramatically speed up query performance. Using the @Index annotation on columns accessed frequently by queries is a best practice. This ensures the database can locate data swiftly, optimizing search operations.

```
@Entity
@Table(name = "employee", indexes = {
    @Index(name = "idx_employee_email", columnList = "email")
})
public class Employee {
    @Id
    @GeneratedValue(strategy = GenerationType.IDENTITY)
    private Long id;

    @Column(nullable = false, unique = true)
    private String email;
    // other attributes and getters/setters
}
```

Avoiding Bi-Directional Relationships Unless Necessary

While bi-directional relationships can be useful for navigation and encapsulating data integrity rules, they introduce additional complexity and potential performance pitfalls. Whenever possible, use unidirectional relationships to simplify the design and avoid issues like infinite recursion during serialization.

Leveraging JPQL and Native Queries Wisely

Leverage JPQL (Java Persistence Query Language) for portability and maintainability. Native SQL queries should be used sparingly and primarily for performance-critical operations that JPQL can't handle efficiently.

```
String jpql = "SELECT e FROM Employee e WHERE e.department.id = :deptId";
TypedQuery<Employee> query = entityManager.createQuery(jpql, Employee.class);
query.setParameter("deptId", departmentId);
List<Employee> results = query.getResultList();
```

Adhering to these best practices in entity design and mapping ensures that your JPA-based applications are robust, maintainable, and perform efficiently. Through careful consideration of data types, relationships, inheritance strategies, and appropriate indexing, you can significantly enhance database interactions and overall system performance.

9.10 Best Practices for Query Optimization

Efficient query optimization is crucial for the performance and scalability of JPA applications. This section delves into best practices that can significantly enhance query performance, ensuring efficient data retrieval and processing.

1. Use of Indexes: One of the fundamental techniques for query optimization is the strategic use of indexes. Indexes can dramatically improve the speed of data retrieval operations. In JPA, indexes can be established using annotations such as @Index and @Column. Here's an example of creating an index on a field:

```
@Entity
@Table(name = "employee", indexes = {
   @Index(name = "idx_employee_email", columnList = "email")
})
public class Employee {

   @Id
   @GeneratedValue(strategy = GenerationType.IDENTITY)
   private Long id;

   @Column(nullable = false, unique = true)
   private String email;

   // ... other fields, getters, setters
}
```

2. Using Criteria API and Querydsl: For dynamic and type-safe queries, using the Criteria API or Querydsl is recommended. They provide a programmatic way to create queries, ensuring compile-time checking and reducing the risk of runtime errors. Below is an example of using the Criteria API:

```
CriteriaBuilder cb = entityManager.getCriteriaBuilder();
CriteriaQuery<Employee> cq = cb.createQuery(Employee.class);
Root<Employee> employee = cq.from(Employee.class);
cq.select(employee).where(cb.equal(employee.get("email"), "someone@example.com"));
TypedQuery<Employee> query = entityManager.createQuery(cq);

List<Employee> results = query.getResultList();
```

3. Proper Use of Fetch Type: When defining associations, selecting the proper fetch type (eager or lazy) is crucial. Incorrect fetching strategies can result in performance bottlenecks. Eager fetching retrieves associated entities immediately, while lazy fetching defers the retrieval until explicitly accessed. For instance:

```
@Entity
public class Department {

    @OneToMany(fetch = FetchType.LAZY, mappedBy = "department")
    private List<Employee> employees;

    // ... other fields, getters, setters
}
```

Lazy fetching is recommended for associations that are not always needed, reducing unnecessary data loading and enhancing performance.

4. Pagination: For queries that return large datasets, using pagination minimizes memory consumption and speeds up response times. JPA supports pagination through the setFirstResult and setMaxResults methods. Here's an example:

```
TypedQuery<Employee> query = entityManager.createQuery("SELECT e FROM
      Employee e", Employee.class);
query.setFirstResult(50); // Offset
query.setMaxResults(20); // Limit

List<Employee> employees = query.getResultList();
```

This approach limits the amount of data retrieved at once, making the application more responsive and efficient.

5. Avoiding N+1 Select Problem: The N+1 select problem occurs when a query retrieves a list of entities and then individually fetches their associations, resulting in numerous queries. This issue can be mitigated using FETCH JOIN clauses or the @EntityGraph annotation. Below is an example using a fetch join:

```
String queryStr = "SELECT d FROM Department d JOIN FETCH d.employees";
TypedQuery<Department> query = entityManager.createQuery(queryStr, Department.
      class);

List<Department> departments = query.getResultList();
```

This approach ensures that the associated entities are loaded in a single query, significantly improving performance.

6. Batch Fetching: JPA's batch fetching optimizes the loading of collections and associated entities by batching select statements. Configurable through the ORM provider's settings, batch fetching reduces the number of queries and enhances performance. Example using Hibernate:

```
@Entity
public class Department {

    @OneToMany(fetch = FetchType.LAZY, mappedBy = "department")
    @BatchSize(size = 10)
    private List<Employee> employees;

    // ... other fields, getters, setters
}
```

7. Leveraging Database-Specific Features: Utilizing database-specific features such as stored procedures, native queries, and custom SQL functions can provide performance benefits. While JPA abstracts database interactions, in certain scenarios, invoking native queries or stored procedures can be optimized. For example:

```
@NamedNativeQuery(
    name = "Employee.findByEmail",
    query = "SELECT * FROM employee WHERE email = ?",
    resultClass = Employee.class
)
public class Employee {
    // Fields, getters, setters
}

// Using the named native query
TypedQuery<Employee> query = entityManager.createNamedQuery("Employee.
    findByEmail", Employee.class);
query.setParameter(1, "someone@example.com");
List<Employee> results = query.getResultList();
```

8. Caching: Effective use of first-level and second-level caches in JPA can improve performance by reducing database access. First-level cache (session cache) is enabled by default, storing entities within a transaction. Second-level cache can be configured using EHCache, Infinispan, etc., and annotations like @Cacheable can be used to specify cacheable entities:

```
@Entity
@Cacheable
@org.hibernate.annotations.Cache(usage = CacheConcurrencyStrategy.READ_WRITE)

public class Employee {

    @Id
    @GeneratedValue(strategy = GenerationType.IDENTITY)
    private Long id;

    private String name;

    // ... other fields, getters, setters
```

```
}
```

9. Analyzing and Tuning JPQL and Criteria Queries: Profiling tools and query analysis can identify inefficient queries. Tools like Hibernate's statistics, or JPA providers' query plans aid in understanding query performance. Optimize such queries by refining join conditions, projection fields, and leveraging database indexes.

10. Utilizing Query Hints: Query hints provide additional instructions to the JPA provider for optimizing SQL generation and execution. Examples include:

```
Query hintQuery = entityManager.createQuery("SELECT e FROM Employee e
    WHERE e.email = :email")
                                .setHint("javax.persistence.query.timeout", 5000);
hintQuery.setParameter("email", "someone@example.com");

List<Employee> employees = hintQuery.getResultList();
```

Implementing these practices will enhance query performance, ensuring efficient and scalable JPA applications.

Chapter 10

Testing and Debugging JPA Applications

This chapter covers the essential aspects of testing and debugging JPA applications. It begins with setting up a test environment and explains how to conduct unit testing for JPA repositories using JUnit. The chapter delves into integration testing with Spring and JPA, as well as mocking JPA dependencies. It discusses leveraging in-memory databases for testing purposes and provides guidance on writing effective test cases. Additionally, it covers techniques for debugging JPA applications, resolving common issues, and outlines best practices for ensuring reliable and maintainable code.

10.1 Introduction to Testing JPA Applications

Testing Java Persistence API (JPA) applications effectively is crucial for ensuring the reliability and maintainability of the software systems that depend on them. A well-structured and robust testing strategy not only helps identify defects early in the development lifecycle but also facilitates the smooth evolution of the codebase over time.

JPA abstracts the interactions between Java applications and relational databases, offering a standardized approach to data persistence.

While this abstraction simplifies development, it also introduces unique challenges in testing. To address these challenges comprehensively, a multi-faceted approach to testing that includes unit tests, integration tests, and end-to-end tests is essential.

Unit testing focuses on individual components of the application in isolation, primarily targeting the business logic contained within JPA entities and repositories. The goal is to verify the correctness of each component by testing the smallest possible units of functionality. This type of testing often involves mocking dependencies to isolate the component under test.

For instance, a typical JPA repository method might be tested as follows:

```
@RunWith(SpringRunner.class)
@DataJpaTest
public class UserRepositoryTest {

    @Autowired
    private TestEntityManager entityManager;

    @Autowired
    private UserRepository userRepository;

    @Test
    public void whenFindByName_thenReturnUser() {
        User user = new User("JohnDoe");
        entityManager.persistAndFlush(user);

        User found = userRepository.findByName(user.getName());
        assertThat(found.getName()).isEqualTo(user.getName());
    }
}
```

In this example, 'TestEntityManager' is used to manage test entities, and 'DataJpaTest' sets up an in-memory database automatically with configuration suitable for JPA tests. The test case verifies that the 'findByName' repository method correctly retrieves a 'User' entity based on the name.

Integration testing, on the other hand, aims to verify the correct interaction between various components of the application and the actual database. This type of testing usually involves a more realistic environment with a real or in-memory database, allowing the tester to validate the proper functioning of the persistence layer, transaction management, and other infrastructure concerns.

Consider the following integration test for a JPA service:

```
@RunWith(SpringRunner.class)
@SpringBootTest
```

```
public class UserServiceIntegrationTest {

    @Autowired
    private UserService userService;

    @Autowired
    private UserRepository userRepository;

    @Before
    public void setUp() {
        userRepository.deleteAll();
    }

    @Test
    public void whenValidUser_thenUserShouldBeSaved() {
        User user = new User("JaneDoe");
        User savedUser = userService.saveUser(user);

        assertThat(savedUser.getId()).isNotNull();
        assertThat(savedUser.getName()).isEqualTo(user.getName());
    }
}
```

In this integration test, Spring Boot's '@SpringBootTest' annotation loads the full application context. The test ensures that a 'User' entity is correctly saved and can be fetched from the database, validating the integration between 'UserService' and 'UserRepository'.

Moreover, leveraging in-memory databases such as H2 or HSQLDB for testing purposes can improve the efficiency and speed of the test execution. This practice is valuable in both unit and integration tests. For example, configuring an in-memory database in the test environment can be accomplished through the following properties in an application's configuration file (usually 'application.yml' or 'application.properties'):

```
spring.datasource.url=jdbc:h2:mem:testdb
spring.datasource.driverClassName=org.h2.Driver
spring.datasource.username=sa
spring.datasource.password=password
spring.jpa.database-platform=org.hibernate.dialect.H2Dialect
```

This configuration sets up an H2 database running entirely in memory, allowing for fast and isolated test execution. The chosen database dialect, in this case, 'H2Dialect', ensures that Hibernate correctly generates the appropriate SQL queries for the H2 database.

Furthermore, mocking is an invaluable technique in unit testing JPA repositories as it allows for the isolation of the unit of work being tested. Mocking frameworks, such as Mockito, facilitate the creation of mock objects to simulate the behavior of dependencies without the need for actual implementations or database interactions.

Here, an example demonstrates how to mock a JPA repository:

```
@RunWith(MockitoJUnitRunner.class)
public class UserServiceTest {

    @Mock
    private UserRepository userRepository;

    @InjectMocks
    private UserService userService;

    @Test
    public void whenSaveUser_thenUserShouldBeSaved() {
        User user = new User("TomDoe");
        when(userRepository.save(any(User.class))).thenReturn(user);

        User savedUser = userService.saveUser(user);

        assertThat(savedUser.getName()).isEqualTo(user.getName());
        verify(userRepository, times(1)).save(user);
    }
}
```

In this test, the 'UserRepository' dependency is mocked using Mockito. The 'when' clause specifies that when the 'save' method is called, it should return the provided 'User' object. This setup isolates the 'UserService' and allows the test to focus solely on the business logic.

Overall, understanding the nuances of testing JPA applications is fundamental for developers to build resilient and maintainable systems. Effective testing encompasses a range of strategies from isolated unit tests to comprehensive integration tests, leveraging various tools and frameworks to minimize the risk of defects and ensure reliable application behavior.

10.2 Setting Up Test Environment for JPA

Warmer's intricate settings and configurations lay the groundwork for effective and efficient testing of JPA applications. Establishing an appropriate test environment involves configuring multiple components, such as database configurations, ensuring consistency with production settings, and synchronizing dependencies.

Firstly, we need to set up a dedicated database configuration for testing purposes. Using an in-memory database like H2 can simplify this process since it requires minimal configuration and speeds up test execution. To illustrate the basic setup, consider the following application properties:

```
spring.datasource.url=jdbc:h2:mem:testdb
spring.datasource.driverClassName=org.h2.Driver
```

```
spring.datasource.username=sa
spring.datasource.password=password
spring.jpa.database-platform=org.hibernate.dialect.H2Dialect
spring.h2.console.enabled=true
```

In the Java configuration file, we create a DataSource bean that references these properties. The DataSource bean can be defined using the Spring framework as follows:

```
import org.springframework.context.annotation.Bean;
import org.springframework.context.annotation.Configuration;
import org.springframework.beans.factory.annotation.Value;
import javax.sql.DataSource;
import org.springframework.boot.jdbc.DataSourceBuilder;

@Configuration
public class DataSourceConfig {

    @Value("${spring.datasource.url}")
    private String url;

    @Value("${spring.datasource.username}")
    private String username;

    @Value("${spring.datasource.password}")
    private String password;

    @Value("${spring.datasource.driverClassName}")
    private String driverClassName;

    @Bean
    public DataSource dataSource() {
        return DataSourceBuilder.create()
            .url(url)
            .username(username)
            .password(password)
            .driverClassName(driverClassName)
            .build();
    }
}
```

Next, it is essential to ensure that our JPA entity manager and transaction manager are configured correctly. Spring Boot typically auto-configures these components, but they can also be explicitly defined for greater control. The entityManagerFactory and transactionManager beans can be explicitly defined as follows:

```
import javax.persistence.EntityManagerFactory;
import org.springframework.orm.jpa.JpaTransactionManager;
import org.springframework.orm.jpa.LocalContainerEntityManagerFactoryBean;
import org.springframework.context.annotation.Bean;
import org.springframework.orm.jpa.vendor.HibernateJpaVendorAdapter;

@Configuration
public class JpaConfig {

    @Bean
    public LocalContainerEntityManagerFactoryBean entityManagerFactory(
```

```
            DataSource dataSource) {
        LocalContainerEntityManagerFactoryBean emf = new
            LocalContainerEntityManagerFactoryBean();
        emf.setDataSource(dataSource);
        emf.setPackagesToScan("com.example.demo.model");
        emf.setJpaVendorAdapter(new HibernateJpaVendorAdapter());
        return emf;
    }

    @Bean
    public JpaTransactionManager transactionManager(EntityManagerFactory emf) {
        return new JpaTransactionManager(emf);
    }
}
```

With the database and entity manager configured, we can proceed to set up our test framework. Using JUnit and Spring's testing support, we can create a test class annotated with @SpringBootTest to bootstrap the Spring application context. Consider the following test class:

```
import org.junit.jupiter.api.Test;
import org.springframework.beans.factory.annotation.Autowired;
import org.springframework.boot.test.context.SpringBootTest;
import javax.persistence.EntityManager;
import static org.assertj.core.api.Assertions.assertThat;

@SpringBootTest
public class JpaApplicationTests {

    @Autowired
    private EntityManager entityManager;

    @Test
    public void contextLoads() {
        assertThat(entityManager).isNotNull();
    }
}
```

The @SpringBootTest annotation ensures that the entire Spring context is loaded, including the JPA components we previously configured. The @Autowired annotation is used to inject the EntityManager bean, which is then validated within the test method using assertThat from the AssertJ library.

Additionally, when dealing with test-specific configurations, we can segregate them using profiles. A profile-specific application configuration file, such as application-test.properties, allows for the isolation of test-related settings. For example, an application-test.properties file might include properties specific to the test environment:

```
spring.jpa.hibernate.ddl-auto=create-drop
spring.jpa.show-sql=true
```

To activate the test profile, set the spring.profiles.active property in the test class or use the system property during the build:

```
@SpringBootTest(properties = {"spring.profiles.active=test"})
public class JpaApplicationTests { ... }
```

Using these techniques, we can establish a robust, isolated environment for thoroughly testing our JPA components. The combination of an in-memory database, precise configuration of JPA components, and the Spring test framework offers a powerful setup for ensuring the integrity and performance of our persistence layer.

10.3 Unit Testing JPA Repositories with JUnit

Unit testing is a fundamental practice in software development that involves testing individual components in isolation to ensure they function as intended. In the context of Java Persistence API (JPA), unit testing repositories verifies that the data access layer works correctly and handles transactions properly. This segment elucidates the methodologies for unit testing JPA repositories using JUnit.

To begin with, we need to set up the dependencies and configurations required for conducting JPA tests. Maven is typically used for handling dependencies in Java projects. Add the following dependencies to your pom.xml file for JUnit, Spring, and an in-memory database like H2:

```
<dependencies>
  <dependency>
    <groupId>org.springframework.boot</groupId>
    <artifactId>spring-boot-starter-data-jpa</artifactId>
  </dependency>
  <dependency>
    <groupId>org.springframework.boot</groupId>
    <artifactId>spring-boot-starter-test</artifactId>
    <scope>test</scope>
  </dependency>
  <dependency>
    <groupId>com.h2database</groupId>
    <artifactId>h2</artifactId>
    <scope>test</scope>
  </dependency>
</dependencies>
```

Following the integration of dependencies, configure the persistence context. Spring Boot simplifies this process through its auto-configuration feature. Nevertheless, ensure the application properties are designated appropriately for the test profile:

```
spring.datasource.url=jdbc:h2:mem:testdb
spring.datasource.driverClassName=org.h2.Driver
spring.datasource.username=sa
spring.datasource.password=password
spring.jpa.database-platform=org.hibernate.dialect.H2Dialect
```

Create an entity class to be tested. For instance, consider a simple User entity:

```
import javax.persistence.Entity;
import javax.persistence.GeneratedValue;
import javax.persistence.GenerationType;
import javax.persistence.Id;

@Entity
public class User {
    @Id
    @GeneratedValue(strategy = GenerationType.IDENTITY)
    private Long id;

    private String name;
    private String email;

    // getters and setters ...
}
```

Now, define a repository interface extending JpaRepository. For example:

```
import org.springframework.data.jpa.repository.JpaRepository;

public interface UserRepository extends JpaRepository<User, Long> {
    User findByName(String name);
}
```

Proceed to write a unit test for the UserRepository utilizing JUnit. The test class should be annotated with @RunWith(SpringRunner.class) and @DataJpaTest to leverage Spring's testing support:

```
import org.junit.jupiter.api.Test;
import org.springframework.beans.factory.annotation.Autowired;
import org.springframework.boot.test.autoconfigure.orm.jpa.DataJpaTest;
import org.springframework.boot.test.autoconfigure.jdbc.AutoConfigureTestDatabase;
import org.springframework.test.context.junit4.SpringRunner;
import static org.assertj.core.api.Assertions.assertThat;

@DataJpaTest
@AutoConfigureTestDatabase(replace = AutoConfigureTestDatabase.Replace.NONE)
public class UserRepositoryTests {

    @Autowired
    private UserRepository userRepository;

    @Test
    public void testSaveAndFindUser() {
        User user = new User();
        user.setName("John Doe");
```

```
        user.setEmail("johndoe@example.com");

        userRepository.save(user);

        User foundUser = userRepository.findByName("John Doe");
        assertThat(foundUser).isNotNull();
        assertThat(foundUser.getName()).isEqualTo("John Doe");
    }
}
```

In the above JUnit test, the UserRepositoryTests class is annotated with @DataJpaTest, which configures an in-memory database, scans for @Entity classes, and configures Spring Data JPA repositories. The @AutoConfigureTestDatabase(replace = AutoConfigureTestDatabase.Replace.NONE) annotation ensures the use of the specified database configuration rather than replacing it with the default in-memory database configuration.

The test method testSaveAndFindUser() demonstrates the process of saving a User entity to the repository and subsequently retrieving it by name to assert its persistence. The assertThat statements from the AssertJ library are used to verify the correctness of the operation.

Further, it is essential to handle more complex queries and boundary conditions. Consider scenarios where no results are found or multiple results match a query. Extending the UserRepositoryTests class, additional test cases may look as follows:

```
@Test
public void testFindByName_NoResult() {
    User foundUser = userRepository.findByName("Non Existent");
    assertThat(foundUser).isNull();
}

@Test
public void testSaveAndFindMultipleUsers() {
    User user1 = new User();
    user1.setName("Alice");
    user1.setEmail("alice@example.com");
    userRepository.save(user1);

    User user2 = new User();
    user2.setName("Alice");
    user2.setEmail("alice2@example.com");
    userRepository.save(user2);

    List<User> foundUsers = userRepository.findByName("Alice");
    assertThat(foundUsers.size()).isEqualTo(2);
}
```

In this extended implementation, the testFindByName_NoResult() test case assures that querying for a non-existent user returns null. The testSaveAndFindMultipleUsers() test case validates saving multiple users with the same name and subsequently retrieving them.

Complete and effective unit tests not only test the repository methods but also ensure that transactions are managed correctly and data integrity is maintained. Utilizing an in-memory database like H2 for these tests facilitates rapid feedback and ease of setup, fostering a robust and agile development workflow.

10.4 Integration Testing with Spring and JPA

Integration testing is crucial to ensure that different application components work together as expected. Specifically, when working with Spring and Java Persistence API (JPA), it is essential to verify that the interactions between your repositories, services, and database are functioning correctly. Integration tests differ from unit tests as they cover interactions between multiple units rather than isolated components. Here's a detailed exploration of how to set up and perform integration testing with Spring and JPA.

To begin, integration tests in a Spring application typically involve the Spring TestContext Framework, which provides support for loading an application context and integrating with JUnit. The primary advantage is the ability to manage the bean lifecycle, transaction management, and dependency injection within your test setup. The process includes configuring an application context that closely resembles your production configuration but uses a test-specific database and other resources.

To create an integration test for a JPA repository, follow these steps:

1. **Include Required Dependencies** Ensure your 'pom.xml' or 'build.gradle' includes the necessary dependencies for Spring Testing, JPA, and a test database such as H2 or HSQLDB. Below are the Maven dependencies:

```
<dependency>
    <groupId>org.springframework.boot</groupId>
    <artifactId>spring-boot-starter-data-jpa</artifactId>
</dependency>
<dependency>
    <groupId>org.springframework.boot</groupId>
    <artifactId>spring-boot-starter-test</artifactId>
    <scope>test</scope>
</dependency>
<dependency>
    <groupId>com.h2database</groupId>
    <artifactId>h2</artifactId>
```

```
    <scope>test</scope>
</dependency>
```

2. **Configure Test Application Context** Create a configuration class for your integration test to set up the test database and other beans.

```
@Configuration
@EnableJpaRepositories(basePackages = "com.example.repository")
@EntityScan(basePackages = "com.example.entity")
public class TestConfig {

    @Bean
    public DataSource dataSource() {
        return new EmbeddedDatabaseBuilder()
                .setType(EmbeddedDatabaseType.H2)
                .build();
    }

    @Bean
    public LocalContainerEntityManagerFactoryBean
     entityManagerFactory(DataSource dataSource,
                                EntityManagerFactoryBuilder builder) {
        return builder
                .dataSource(dataSource)
                .packages("com.example.entity")
                .persistenceUnit("test")
                .build();
    }

    @Bean
    public PlatformTransactionManager transactionManager(EntityManagerFactory
        entityManagerFactory) {
        return new JpaTransactionManager(entityManagerFactory);
    }
}
```

3. **Write the Integration Test** Annotate your test class with '@SpringBootTest' and '@RunWith(SpringRunner.class)', and use '@Test' methods to perform testing.

```
@RunWith(SpringRunner.class)
@SpringBootTest(classes = TestConfig.class)
@Transactional
public class UserRepositoryIntegrationTest {

    @Autowired
    private UserRepository userRepository;

    @Test
    public void whenSave_thenFindsByName() {
        User user = new User();
        user.setName("John");
        userRepository.save(user);

        User found = userRepository.findByName("John");
        assertNotNull(found);
        assertEquals("John", found.getName());
    }
}
```

4. **Execute and Validate** Once the test is set up, running it within your IDE or through the command line will trigger the Spring TestContext Framework. The framework will load the context defined in 'TestConfig', inject dependencies, manage transactions, and execute the test methods. Verify that the expected outcomes match the actual results using assertions.

5. **Transaction Management** By default, tests annotated with '@Transactional' will roll back the transaction upon completion, ensuring a clean state for each test. This behavior prevents side effects from interfering with subsequent tests.

6. **Profiling and Conditional Configurations** Utilize profiles and conditional testing configurations to separate integration test settings from other environments. Modify application properties for testing:

```
spring.datasource.url=jdbc:h2:mem:testdb;DB_CLOSE_DELAY=-1
spring.datasource.driverClassName=org.h2.Driver
spring.datasource.username=sa
spring.datasource.password=password
spring.jpa.database-platform=org.hibernate.dialect.H2Dialect
```

Implementing these practices cultivates a reliable integration testing strategy. The illustrated setup ensures that the components in your Spring and JPA application interact correctly within controlled test conditions, bolstering confidence in your application's overall stability and correctness.

10.5 Mocking JPA Dependencies in Tests

Mocking JPA dependencies is a fundamental technique used in unit testing to isolate the components under test and ensure that the tests are fast and reliable. When working with Java Persistence API (JPA), it becomes crucial to mock the dependencies to avoid the overhead of interacting with the actual database during unit tests. This section details the nuances of mocking JPA dependencies, focusing on the use of Mockito, a popular mocking framework, to create and manage these mocks effectively.

Mocking is desirable in tests primarily to:

- Isolate unit tests from the database layer.
- Improve test performance by eliminating the need for database operations.

- Facilitate the simulation of various scenarios, including edge cases and error conditions.
- Make tests more deterministic and less flaky.

Integration with Mockito

Mockito provides a rich API for creating mock objects in Java. It allows developers to create, configure, and verify interactions with mocks. In a typical JPA repository test, we will mock the EntityManager, Query, and other JPA-related classes to ensure our repository methods can be tested in isolation.

To illustrate, consider the following repository class:

```
public class BookRepository {
    @PersistenceContext
    private EntityManager entityManager;

    public Book findBookById(Long id) {
        return entityManager.find(Book.class, id);
    }

    public List<Book> findBooksByTitle(String title) {
        TypedQuery<Book> query = entityManager.createQuery(
            "SELECT b FROM Book b WHERE b.title = :title", Book.class);
        query.setParameter("title", title);
        return query.getResultList();
    }
}
```

To unit test the BookRepository class, we need to mock the EntityManager and the TypedQuery. Start by configuring Mockito in the test class:

```
@RunWith(MockitoJUnitRunner.class)
public class BookRepositoryTest {
    @InjectMocks
    private BookRepository bookRepository;

    @Mock
    private EntityManager entityManager;

    @Mock
    private TypedQuery<Book> query;

    @Test
    public void testFindBookById() {
        Book book = new Book();
        book.setId(1L);

        Mockito.when(entityManager.find(Book.class, 1L)).thenReturn(book);

        Book result = bookRepository.findBookById(1L);

        assertEquals(book, result);
        Mockito.verify(entityManager).find(Book.class, 1L);
    }
```

```
}
```

In this example, Mockito annotations @InjectMocks and @Mock are used to auto-wire the BookRepository and mock the EntityManager, respectively. The Mockito.when() method is used to define the behavior of entityManager.find() to return a dummy Book object when invoked.

Mocking Queries

For methods involving queries, such as findBooksByTitle, mocking requires additional steps to replicate query creation and result retrieval:

```
@Test
public void testFindBooksByTitle() {
    List<Book> books = Arrays.asList(new Book(), new Book());

    Mockito.when(entityManager.createQuery(
        Mockito.anyString(), Mockito.eq(Book.class))).thenReturn(query);
    Mockito.when(query.setParameter(Mockito.anyString(), Mockito.any()))
          .thenReturn(query);
    Mockito.when(query.getResultList()).thenReturn(books);

    List<Book> result = bookRepository.findBooksByTitle("Effective Java");

    assertEquals(books, result);
    Mockito.verify(entityManager).createQuery(Mockito.anyString(), Mockito.eq(Book.
          class));
    Mockito.verify(query).setParameter("title", "Effective Java");
    Mockito.verify(query).getResultList();
}
```

This example demonstrates the process of setting up mocks for methods invoked on TypedQuery. Here:

- The entityManager.createQuery() method is stubbed to return the mock TypedQuery object.
- query.setParameter() is stubbed to return the query itself, enabling method chaining.
- query.getResultList() is stubbed to return the predefined list of books.

Validation and Verification

Mocks need to be verified to ensure the correct methods were invoked during the test execution. Mockito provides the verify method for this purpose. For instance, verifying interaction with mocks in the previous example is done by calling:

```
Mockito.verify(entityManager).createQuery(Mockito.anyString(), Mockito.eq(Book.class));
Mockito.verify(query).setParameter("title", "Effective Java");
Mockito.verify(query).getResultList();
```

Benefits of Using Mockito

Using Mockito for mocking JPA dependencies provides several benefits:

- Simplifies the process of creating and manipulating mocks.
- Supports annotations for injecting and managing mocks seamlessly.
- Facilitates behavior-driven development (BDD) through methods like when() and thenReturn().
- Offers extensive verification capabilities to ensure accurate interaction with mocks.

Effective mocking of JPA dependencies with Mockito ensures that unit tests are both isolated from the database layer and indicative of the intended functionality of the repository classes. This results in higher test confidence and faster feedback during the development process.

10.6 Using In-Memory Databases for Testing

In-memory databases are essential tools for testing JPA applications. These databases offer several advantages, including speed and isolation from production data. Among the popular choices are H2 Database, HSQLDB, and Apache Derby, each serving well for different testing scenarios.

For JPA testing, the H2 Database is frequently preferred due to its robust feature set and ease of configuration. The following subsections elaborate on how to set up and utilize H2 for your JPA testing needs, configuring it with Spring Boot for streamlined integration.

To start with H2, you need to include the dependency in your pom.xml file. For Maven users, this is done as follows:

```
<dependency>
    <groupId>com.h2database</groupId>
    <artifactId>h2</artifactId>
    <scope>test</scope>
</dependency>
```

Including the dependency within the test scope ensures that H2 is only utilized during testing and does not interfere with production environments.

Next, configure the application properties to use H2. This configuration will be part of your application-test.properties or similar custom properties file dedicated to testing:

```
spring.datasource.url=jdbc:h2:mem:testdb
spring.datasource.driverClassName=org.h2.Driver
spring.datasource.username=sa
spring.datasource.password=password
spring.datasource.platform=h2
spring.jpa.database-platform=org.hibernate.dialect.H2Dialect
```

The URL jdbc:h2:mem:testdb signifies an in-memory database that resides in the memory and is lost when the JVM is terminated. The configuration sets H2 as the database platform and specifies Hibernate's H2 dialect to ensure compatibility.

For advanced use cases where you may need schema or data initialization scripts executed on startup, create schema.sql and data.sql files within the resources directory. Spring Boot, by default, scans and executes these scripts upon context initialization.

Consider a scenario where you have an entity UserEntity and a corresponding repository UserRepository. To write integration tests that leverage the in-memory H2 database, use the following setup:

```
@RunWith(SpringRunner.class)
@SpringBootTest
public class UserRepositoryIntegrationTest {

    @Autowired
    private UserRepository userRepository;

    @Test
    public void whenSavingUser_thenUserShouldBeFound() {
        // given
        UserEntity user = new UserEntity();
        user.setName("John Doe");
        user.setEmail("john.doe@example.com");
        userRepository.save(user);

        // when
        UserEntity foundUser = userRepository.findByName("John Doe");

        // then
        assertNotNull(foundUser);
        assertEquals("john.doe@example.com", foundUser.getEmail());
    }
}
```

This integration test uses the in-memory H2 database to save and retrieve a UserEntity, ensuring the repository functionality works as expected.

Switching between the production and test database configurations dynamically is facilitated by Spring Profiles. Ensure that the testing profile (e.g., test) is activated during test execution by annotating your test class with:

```
@ActiveProfiles("test")
```

Managing persistence and transactional contexts in testing is crucial to avoid unwanted side effects. Spring's @Transactional annotation ensures that each test method runs in a transaction, which is rolled back after the test method completes, maintaining a clean state for subsequent tests.

Here is an example:

```
@RunWith(SpringRunner.class)
@SpringBootTest
@Transactional
@ActiveProfiles("test")
public class UserServiceIntegrationTest {

    @Autowired
    private UserRepository userRepository;

    @Test
    public void givenUser_whenSave_thenEntityIsPersisted() {
        // given
        UserEntity user = new UserEntity();
        user.setName("Alice Johnson");
        user.setEmail("alice.johnson@example.com");
        userRepository.save(user);

        // when
        UserEntity retrievedUser = userRepository.findByName("Alice Johnson");

        // then
        assertNotNull(retrievedUser);
        assertEquals("alice.johnson@example.com", retrievedUser.getEmail());
    }
}
```

Leveraging in-memory databases such as H2 for JPA testing enhances test performance and reliability. It allows for isolating tests from external data influences and ensures a consistent testing environment.

10.7 Writing Effective Test Cases for JPA Components

Writing effective test cases for JPA (Java Persistence API) components is crucial for ensuring the accuracy, reliability, and maintainability of your application. This section will highlight key practices that should be observed to develop comprehensive test cases, enhance test coverage, and facilitate early detection of potential issues.

1. Defining the Scope of Test Cases

The first step in writing effective test cases is to determine the scope of your tests. This includes identifying the specific JPA components to be tested, such as entities, repositories, and services. Each test should have a clear objective, focusing on a single aspect or functionality of the component under test.

2. Setting Up Test Data

Effective testing requires representative and meaningful test data. Test data should cover a wide range of scenarios, including typical cases, edge cases, and exceptional conditions. In JPA applications, this often involves setting up database records that reflect various states and relationships.

```
@BeforeEach
public void setUp() {
    // Initialize the database with test data
    EntityTransaction transaction = entityManager.getTransaction();
    transaction.begin();

    Customer customer = new Customer();
    customer.setName("Test Customer");
    customer.setEmail("customer@example.com");
    entityManager.persist(customer);

    Order order = new Order();
    order.setAmount(BigDecimal.valueOf(100.00));
    order.setCustomer(customer);
    entityManager.persist(order);

    transaction.commit();
}
```

3. Isolating Tests

To ensure that tests are independent and do not interfere with one another, use transaction rollbacks and in-memory databases. Transaction rollbacks ensure that data modifications do not persist across tests, maintaining a clean state.

```
@Test
@Transactional
public void testCreateCustomer() {
    Customer customer = new Customer();
    customer.setName("John Doe");
    customer.setEmail("john.doe@example.com");

    customerRepository.save(customer);
    Customer found = customerRepository.findByName("John Doe");
```

```
    assertEquals("john.doe@example.com", found.getEmail());
}
```

4. Utilizing Assertions

Leverage a variety of assertions to verify expected outcomes. Utilize assertions for basic properties, complex conditions, database states, and relationship validations.

```
@Test
public void testFindOrderByCustomer() {
    List<Order> orders = orderRepository.findByCustomerEmail("
        customer@example.com");
    assertNotNull(orders);
    assertFalse(orders.isEmpty());

    Order order = orders.get(0);
    assertEquals("Test Customer", order.getCustomer().getName());
    assertEquals(BigDecimal.valueOf(100.00), order.getAmount());
}
```

5. Mocking Dependencies

For unit testing services that have dependencies on repositories or external systems, employ mocking frameworks like Mockito. Mocking ensures that the unit tests are focused on the logic of the service under test, not on its dependencies.

```
@ExtendWith(MockitoExtension.class)
public class CustomerServiceTest {

    @Mock
    private CustomerRepository customerRepository;

    @InjectMocks
    private CustomerService customerService;

    @Test
    public void testFindCustomerByEmail() {
        Customer customer = new Customer();
        customer.setEmail("test@example.com");
        Mockito.when(customerRepository.findByEmail("test@example.com")).
            thenReturn(customer);

        Customer found = customerService.findCustomerByEmail("test@example.
            com");
        assertEquals("test@example.com", found.getEmail());
    }
}
```

6. Verifying Database States

In addition to verifying in-memory data structures, ensure that the database's state aligns with expectations, particularly for operations involving persistence, updates, and deletions.

```
@Test
public void testDeleteCustomer() {
    Customer customer = customerRepository.findByEmail("test@example.com");
    assertNotNull(customer);

    customerRepository.delete(customer);
    Customer deletedCustomer = customerRepository.findByEmail("test@example.
        com");
    assertNull(deletedCustomer);
}
```

7. Parameterized Tests

Utilize parameterized tests to run the same test logic with different inputs, enhancing test coverage. This is particularly useful for testing various input combinations and edge cases in a systematic manner.

```
@ParameterizedTest
@ValueSource(strings = {"first@example.com", "second@example.com"})
public void testFindCustomerByEmails(String email) {
    Customer customer = customerRepository.findByEmail(email);
    assertNotNull(customer);
    assertEquals(email, customer.getEmail());
}
```

8. Exception Handling

Test and validate exception handling logic to ensure that your application gracefully handles unexpected scenarios. Verify that appropriate exceptions are thrown and handled as expected.

```
@Test
public void testFindNonexistentCustomer() {
    assertThrows(EntityNotFoundException.class, () -> {
        customerRepository.findById(-1L).orElseThrow(EntityNotFoundException::
            new);
    });
}
```

9. Coverage Analysis

Leverage test coverage analysis tools to identify untested code paths. Aim for comprehensive coverage of all persistence-related operations, entity relationships, and business logic.

By following these practices when writing test cases for JPA components, you ensure that your tests are robust, maintainable, and effectively validate the application's behavior, leading to higher quality and confidence in the application.

10.8 Debugging JPA Applications

Debugging JPA (Java Persistence API) applications requires a thorough understanding of both JPA internals and the mechanisms provided by the Java programming language. Unlike traditional Java applications, JPA applications are inherently more complex due to ORM (Object-Relational Mapping) and interactions with the database layer. In this section, we will explore various strategies and tools to diagnose and fix issues in JPA applications, focusing on logging configurations, analyzing SQL statements, inspecting entity states, and utilizing advanced debugging techniques.

The first step in debugging a JPA application is configuring logging to capture relevant information. JPA implementations such as Hibernate provide extensive logging options that can be configured to show SQL statements, parameter values, and internal operations. Here's an example of configuring logging for Hibernate using the log4j framework:

```
log4j.rootLogger=WARN, stdout
log4j.logger.org.hibernate=DEBUG

log4j.appender.stdout=org.apache.log4j.ConsoleAppender
log4j.appender.stdout.Target=System.out
log4j.appender.stdout.layout=org.apache.log4j.PatternLayout
log4j.appender.stdout.layout.ConversionPattern=%d{HH:mm:ss} %-5p %c{1} - %m%n
```

With this configuration, Hibernate's internal operations and generated SQL statements will be logged to the console. This enables the developer to inspect the SQL being executed, which is crucial for identifying issues related to incorrect SQL generation or unexpected queries.

Once logging is configured, the next step involves examining the SQL statements generated by Hibernate (or any JPA provider you are using). Ensuring that the SQL matches expected queries is important in diagnosing issues such as N+1 select problems, which occur when the application generates a separate query for each associated entity. For example:

```
10:00:01 DEBUG SQL - select course0_.id as id1_0_, course0_.name as name2_0_
from Course course0_
10:00:01 DEBUG SQL - select students1_.course_id as course_i1_1_0_,
students1_.name as name1_1_0_ from Student students1_
where students1_.course_id=?
```

If such behavior is observed, it can often be mitigated by appropriately using join fetching strategies such as FETCH JOIN. For instance, consider the following JPQL query:

```
String jpql = "SELECT c FROM Course c JOIN FETCH c.students";
```

```
TypedQuery<Course> query = entityManager.createQuery(jpql, Course.class);
List<Course> courses = query.getResultList();
```

Using JOIN FETCH instructs the persistence provider to fetch related entities in a single query, thus avoiding multiple SQL executions.

Analyzing and understanding entity state transitions can also provide insights into potential issues. JPA entities have different states: New, Managed, Detached, and Removed. It's crucial to track these states to comprehend why certain operations may not work as intended. For example, entities may become detached if they are no longer managed by the entity manager, leading to issues where changes are not persisted.

To inspect entity states, leverage the EntityManager's methods:

```
EntityManager em = entityManagerFactory.createEntityManager();
em.getTransaction().begin();

Course course = em.find(Course.class, courseId);
System.out.println(em.contains(course)); // true

em.detach(course);
System.out.println(em.contains(course)); // false

em.getTransaction().commit();
em.close();
```

In cases where deeper inspection of JPA operations is necessary, using breakpoints and stepping through code in an Integrated Development Environment (IDE) can be beneficial. IDEs like IntelliJ IDEA and Eclipse provide powerful debugging tools that allow developers to step through JPA operations, inspect variable values, and understand control flow.

Moreover, dealing with LazyInitializationException, a common issue in JPA, involves ensuring that lazy-loaded associations are initialized before the persistence context is closed. One strategy is to use the Open Session in View pattern, but this should be applied judiciously to avoid performance overhead and maintain transactional integrity.

Another advanced debugging approach is to use JPA provider-specific tools. Hibernate provides a tool called Hibernate ORM's statistics module, which offers detailed insights into second-level cache usage, entity load counts, and query execution metrics. This can be enabled in the Hibernate configuration file via:

```
hibernate.generate_statistics=true
```

Hibernate statistics can then be accessed programmatically:

```
Statistics stats = sessionFactory.getStatistics();
System.out.println("Entity load count: " + stats.getEntityLoadCount());
```

Understanding the output of Hibernate statistics can help in identifying performance bottlenecks and inefficiencies.

Debugging JPA applications entails a multi-faceted approach involving adequate logging, SQL analysis, understanding entity state transitions, judicious use of lazy loading, and employing provider-specific debugging tools. These efforts collectively contribute to identifying and resolving issues efficiently, leading to more robust and performant JPA applications.

10.9 Common JPA Issues and How to Resolve Them

In this section, we address the common issues encountered when working with Java Persistence API (JPA) and provide practical solutions. Understanding these issues and their resolutions is essential for developing robust and efficient JPA applications.

One of the frequent challenges developers face is the 'LazyInitializationException'. This occurs when an entity with a lazily-initialized association is accessed outside a transaction context. The issue usually manifests after a certain part of the application attempts to access a lazily-initialized collection or association that has not been loaded.

```
@Entity
public class Author {
    @Id
    @GeneratedValue(strategy = GenerationType.AUTO)
    private Long id;

    @OneToMany(mappedBy = "author", fetch = FetchType.LAZY)
    private Set<Book> books;

    // getters and setters
}
```

Attempting to access the 'books' collection outside the transactional context results in:

```
javax.persistence.LazyInitializationException: failed to lazily initialize a collection of role: Author.books, could not initialize proxy - no Session
```

To resolve 'LazyInitializationException', consider the following strategies:

- **Ensure Entity Access Within Transaction Context**: Ensure that entity associations are accessed within the bounds of a transaction. Utilize the '@Transactional' annotation to maintain a transaction scope.

```
@Service
public class AuthorService {
    @PersistenceContext
    private EntityManager entityManager;

    @Transactional
    public void fetchAuthorBooks(Long authorId) {
        Author author = entityManager.find(Author.class, authorId);
        author.getBooks().size(); // Accessing within transaction
    }
}
```

- **FetchType.EAGER**: Change the fetch type of associations to 'FetchType.EAGER'. This forces JPA to load the association eagerly, thus avoiding lazy loading issues.

```
@Entity
public class Author {
    @Id
    @GeneratedValue(strategy = GenerationType.AUTO)
    private Long id;

    @OneToMany(mappedBy = "author", fetch = FetchType.EAGER)
    private Set<Book> books;
}
```

- **Join Fetch**: Use JPQL or Criteria API to join fetch the associations, ensuring they are loaded with the parent entity.

```
public List<Author> findAuthorsWithBooks() {
    String query = "SELECT a FROM Author a JOIN FETCH a.books";
    return entityManager.createQuery(query, Author.class).getResultList();
}
```

Another common issue is the 'OptimisticLockException', which occurs when two transactions attempt to update the same entity concurrently. This is handled using '@Version' fields in JPA entities.

```
@Entity
public class Article {
    @Id
    @GeneratedValue(strategy = GenerationType.AUTO)
    private Long id;

    @Version
    private int version;

    private String content;

    // getters and setters
```

```
}
```

When an 'OptimisticLockException' happens:

```
javax.persistence.OptimisticLockException: Row was updated or deleted by another transaction
```

To resolve 'OptimisticLockException':

- **Ensure Proper Handling in Application Logic**: Catch and handle the exception properly in code, possibly triggering a retry mechanism.

```
public void updateArticleContent(Long articleId, String newContent) {
    try {
        Article article = entityManager.find(Article.class, articleId);
        article.setContent(newContent);
        entityManager.merge(article);
    } catch (OptimisticLockException e) {
        // Handle transaction retry or user notification
    }
}
```

- **User Notification**: Inform users about the concurrent update conflict, providing them options to retry or to merge changes.

One more frequent issue is performance degradation due to N+1 Select problems. This typically arises when lazy loading collections within nested loops. Each loop iteration triggers a new SQL query, leading to performance inefficiencies.

Consider an example where fetching authors with their books:

```
public List<Author> findAuthors() {
    List<Author> authors = entityManager.createQuery("SELECT a FROM Author a"
        , Author.class).getResultList();
    for (Author author : authors) {
        System.out.println(author.getBooks().size());
    }
    return authors;
}
```

In the example above, if there are 10 authors, this results in 1 query for authors and 10 additional queries for books.

To resolve the N+1 Select problem:

- **Join Fetching**: As illustrated, use join fetch in JPQL or Criteria API to load associations eagerly in a single query.

```
public List<Author> findAuthorsWithBooks() {
    String query = "SELECT a FROM Author a JOIN FETCH a.books";
    return entityManager.createQuery(query, Author.class).getResultList();
}
```

- **Batch Fetching**: Configure batch fetching in the JPA provider to efficiently load collections.

```
<property name="hibernate.default_batch_fetch_size" value="10"/>
```

Addressing caching issues is another common challenge. L2 cache misconfiguration can lead to stale data being returned. Proper configuration and understanding of cache eviction policies are crucial.

```
<property name="hibernate.cache.use_second_level_cache" value="true"/>
<property name="hibernate.cache.region.factory_class" value="org.hibernate.cache.
    ehcache.EhCacheRegionFactory"/>
<property name="hibernate.cache.provider_configuration_file_resource_path" value=
    "ehcache.xml"/>
```

Make sure the cache is invalidated or updated during write operations to maintain data consistency.

10.10 Best Practices for Testing and Debugging JPA Applications

Ensuring the robustness and reliability of Java Persistence API (JPA) applications requires the implementation of systematic and well-defined testing and debugging practices. This section elucidates several best practices designed to foster effective testing and debugging of JPA applications.

Isolate Test Environment: It is crucial to isolate the test environment from the production environment to avoid test data contamination and system performance issues. Utilize dedicated test configurations and databases. For instance:

application-test.properties

Configure application properties specifically for testing, ensuring they do not interfere with the production settings.

```
spring.datasource.url=jdbc:h2:mem:testdb
spring.datasource.driverClassName=org.h2.Driver
spring.datasource.username=sa
spring.datasource.password=password
spring.jpa.hibernate.ddl-auto=create-drop
spring.jpa.show-sql=true
```

Embrace In-Memory Databases: Using in-memory databases for testing, such as H2 or HSQLDB, facilitates faster test execution and ease of setup. An in-memory database allows automatic setup and teardown for each test, ensuring a clean slate for test execution.

Layered Testing Approach: Adopt a layered testing approach, encompassing unit tests, integration tests, and end-to-end tests.

- **Unit Tests:** Focus on testing the individual JPA entities and repository methods. These tests should be quick to execute.
- **Integration Tests:** Validate the interactions between multiple components. Utilize Spring Test framework to set up the application context.
- **End-to-End Tests:** Ensure the entire application workflow functions correctly, integrating all layers of the application stack.

Automate Test Execution: Integrate continuous integration tools such as Jenkins or GitHub Actions to automate test execution. This helps in early identification of issues and ensures the code base remains in a deployable state.

Use Assertions Effectively: Leverage assertions in your test cases. Assertions validate the expected behavior of the code, ensuring the output meets the test criteria.

```
@Test
public void whenFindByUsername_thenReturnUser() {
    User found = userRepository.findByUsername("john_doe");
    assertEquals(found.getUsername(), "john_doe");
}
```

Mock JPA Dependencies: Using mocking frameworks such as Mockito helps in isolating the component under test by mocking JPA dependencies. This practice is indispensable for unit tests.

```
@Mock
private UserRepository userRepository;

@BeforeEach
void setUp() {
    MockitoAnnotations.openMocks(this);
}
```

Transaction Management in Tests: Ensure transactions are correctly managed within tests. Spring provides @Transactional annotation, which can be used in test cases to roll back transactions after test execution.

```
@Test
```

```
@Transactional
public void whenSave_thenRollbackAfterTest() {
    User user = new User("john_doe");
    userRepository.save(user);
    // Assertion can be performed here
}
```

Analyze SQL Queries: JPA's show-sql configuration helps in viewing the SQL generated by Hibernate. Analyzing these queries helps in debugging and performance optimization.

```
spring.jpa.show-sql=true
spring.jpa.properties.hibernate.format_sql=true
```

Handle Common Issues: Familiarize yourself with common JPA issues, such as the N+1 select problem, lazy loading exceptions, and manage them using best practices like fetching strategies, DTO projections, and appropriate query optimizations.

Test Data Management: Maintain separate datasets for different test scenarios. Use fixtures or builders to create test data dynamically. This practice ensures that tests are not interdependent and repeatable.

Examine Logs: Implement logging at various levels, including DEBUG and INFO, to capture crucial information during test execution. This information aids in diagnosing and troubleshooting issues.

```
logging.level.org.springframework=WARN
logging.level.com.yourapp=DEBUG
```

Assert JPA State Transitions: Verify the state transitions of JPA entities, particularly in complex transaction scenarios. Use JPA entity listeners to track and log state changes.

Verification of Lazy Loading Behavior: Write test cases to assert lazy loading behavior. Use tools like Hibernate's EnableLazyInitialization and Hibernate.initialize() method to manually initialize proxies.

```
@Test
public void whenLazyLoading_thenVerifyInitialization() {
    Order order = orderRepository.findById(1L).get();
    assertFalse(Hibernate.isInitialized(order.getItems()));
    Hibernate.initialize(order.getItems());
    assertTrue(Hibernate.isInitialized(order.getItems()));
}
```

These best practices serve as guidelines to improve the reliability, maintainability, and performance of JPA applications through rigorous and systematic testing and debugging processes.

Made in the USA
Monee, IL
05 November 2026

67911530R00177